SOCIAL WORK AND THE COURTS

Social Work and the Courts

Edited by
Howard Parker

Edward Arnold

Printed and bound in Great Britain at
The Camelot Press Ltd, Southampton

Contents

Note on Contributors

Paul Burgess spent ten years in engineering before taking a degree in Economics and Politics. Since 1972 he has worked as a welfare rights officer and is currently the Senior Welfare Rights Officer with Manchester Social Services.

Pat Carlen has carried out research into the workings of magistrates' courts. She has two degrees and is currently a lecturer in criminology at the University of Keele.

Eric Cooper spent some years as a customs officer before undertaking professional training as a probation officer. He has experience in general probation fieldwork, residential work with children and team management. He is an Open University graduate and is at present Student Unit Supervisor with the Merseyside Probation and Aftercare Service.

Donald Dickie graduated in Social Anthropology before studying criminology at Cambridge and Columbia University. He has been a Reporter to the Children's Panel in Aberdeen and is a qualified social worker at present working in Edinburgh.

Henri Giller is carrying out research, as a doctoral student at the Cambridge Institute of Criminology. He is focusing upon the workings of Community Homes with education on the premises. He has written extensively, with Allison Morris, about the Children and Young Persons Act 1969.

Pauline Hardiker has worked as a medical secretary and community worker. She has two social science degrees and is a lecturer at the School of Social Work, Leicester University. She has carried out research into probation officers' social enquiry reports and written about 'practice theories' in social work.

Greg Kelly has worked as a probation officer and senior social worker on Merseyside. A graduate and qualified social worker, he is now a lecturer in Applied Social Studies at Queen's University, Belfast.

Allison Morris has extensive teaching and research experience and is currently Assistant Director of Research at the Cambridge Institute of Criminology. She has special interest in juvenile justice in both Scotland and England and is herself a JP.

Elwyn Owens has extensive social work experience as a probation officer and child care officer. He was a district officer in Liverpool Social Services for five years. A graduate and qualified social worker, he has recently become a lecturer in social work at Liverpool University's Institute of Extension Studies.

Howard Parker spent a brief period in industry before becoming a youth worker. He has made studies into various aspects of adolescence and delinquency as a research worker. He has two degrees and is now a lecturer with the social work course in the Department of Sociology at Liverpool University.

Phyllida Parsloe has a background in probation and psychiatric social work. She taught in an American law school before taking up the Chair of Social Work at Aberdeen. A member of the Parole Board for Scotland and regular contributor to social work journals, she is now Professor of Social Work at Bristol University.

Margaret Powell is a graduate of Warwick and Brunel Universities. She has worked as a probation officer in Inner London and is chairperson of the National Association of Probation Officers there.

Introduction

We know that the public are unclear about who social workers are and what they do. What is more frightening is that social workers themselves, in terms of their overall occupation, all too often don't know who they are and what they do. Recent attempts to define the social work task (BASW 1977a) are thus to be welcomed as a useful beginning. There have been so many changes in the past decade with the welter of new statutory responsibilities, the reorganization of local authority social work, the changing role of the probation service, the introduction of 'generic' training. These are both a reflection of the rapid social changes going on in British society and a source of confusion for social workers operating in such a paranoid social climate.

This confusion and tension has made social work very defensive of late. It has also produced an atmosphere of self-torture in which internal dissent and distrust have been rampant: between social service worker and the probation service, community-based workers and residential staff, field workers and trainers, front-line and management, or between BASW and NALGO, NUSW and NUPE. Much worse, these skirmishes have all too often been anecdotal and parochial.

This volume attempts to transcend the letter columns of the social work journals. It consists of a set of eleven specially commissioned essays in which social workers, probation officers, educationists and researchers have turned their experience towards achieving a set of clear aims and objectives. One major aim of this volume is to provide a comprehensive overview of the content and nature of social work practice in and around the courts. Each of the component chapters, whilst it can stand alone as a succinct contribution, builds into the whole. The provision of such an overview involves recourse to the law, to agency function and to that more subtle area of 'coping' theory – the rules for everyday survival.

The second aim of this volume is to provide a contribution to the 'social work task' debate. Explicit in the chapters is a set of definitions of the present social worker-probation officer court function. Implicit in the chapters is a critique of this present function, of practice as it stands. Criticism is not always focused upon the individual worker but upon other 'professionals', the legislation or the actual ideology underpinning the legislation. This critique highlights areas of dilemma, confusion and contradiction, identifying points where modification, redefinition or actual withdrawal from practice might be considered in the long term and where extreme caution should be exercised in present social worker action in the courts.

Allison Morris and Henri Giller (chapter 1) provide an overview of the juvenile justice debate which has continued to rage so intensely in the UK over the past decade. Their paper provides a highly instructive backcloth against which to place present statutory social work with juveniles and against which to consider how social work as a 'profession' should conduct itself in the policy debate. For those still in any doubt about the political nature of contemporary social work or the ideological nature of social policy renovation, chapter 1 must itself be mandatory. Although the various competing factions within the debate disagree on several fundamental issues the goal which they all appear to share is that of effective social control of youthful deviance, or in some cases parental malpractice. Social work, for many reasons, now finds itself championing its professional skills – the welfare or treatment approach – as a more *effective* approach to delinquency control than punitive and incarcerating measures. Morris and Giller provide some potentially useful information for this manifesto. However, they show that the social work strategy in this debate has been both confused and defensive and they have some strong final remarks about social work's tactics in the juvenile justice debate.

Although fully conscious of the problematic nature of contemporary statutory arrangements for the care and control of children and young persons, Elwyn Owens (chapter 2) provides a 'here and now' analysis of both the range of responsibilities of the local authority (social worker) and some hints about how the worker can marry these mandatory tasks with 'essence' social work principles as he sees them. Whilst never glossing over the dilemmas and ambiguities inherent in present legislative arrangements, Owens is often able to define quite clearly the social workers' tasks in and around juvenile courts. Nevertheless, as an 'English' social worker it is obvious that he occasionally casts an envious eye north of the Border where social workers do not have such a hybrid system to work in.

Donald Dickie (chapter 3) analyses the social worker role in Scottish Panels – the alternative outcome of the 'sixties debate involving the abolition of juvenile courts in Scotland. The Scottish system of juvenile justice is certainly more workable and more comprehensible than its English counterpart, although as yet not demonstrably more 'effective'. It is of course 'early days' for this innovatory system but certainly already the Panels appear to have become institutionalized, that is, broadly accepted by all influential parties. Ideological debates will of course continue, sporadically fanned by media-aroused moral panics, but it now seems more likely that the Scottish system will be influential in changing the English/Welsh and Northern Ireland systems (see chapter 10) rather than being itself repealed. The Scottish system also provides us with valuable material for defining the fundamentals of the social work task, for as Dickie shows, there is an available comprehension for both worker and client within the Hearings system which is not sabotaged and booby-trapped by the numerous inherent contradictions so evident in the English juvenile court. Worker self-confidence and the inclination to be concerned for clients' needs and rights are strengths which Dickie presents as clearly achievable.

In chapter 4 Elwyn Owens and Eric Cooper provide a sophisticated overview of the implications of the Children Act 1975 which, whilst interwoven with aspects of the 1969 Children and Young Persons Act, in general etches out a new and comprehensive area of statutory local authority and probation service responsibilities. As with the juvenile justice scenario of the past decade the 1975 Act also illustrates the ever-changing attitudes in society towards what are, for instance, the best interests of a child with family 'problems', the rights of natural as opposed to substitute parents, and what constitutes the State's definition of satisfactory child-rearing. The authors agree that the 1975 Act is concerned more than any previous legislation with the rights and wishes of children in need of a substitute 'growing' environment. They demonstrate the importance of the social work role in the operation of these new statutory arrangements: in adoption proceedings, acting as guardian *ad litem* or advocate for the child, and in advising the courts and involved parties in custodianship proceedings. Here especially is a new range of social worker/ probation officer duties in which we can readily identify a positive relationship between enabling legislation and necessarily skilful social work practice. The elusive social work task and given social worker functions may well prove to be in unison in this area of practice.

Chapter 5 concludes our analysis of court work with children and families. In this shorter paper on domestic proceedings Eric Cooper untangles what for most of us is an endless jungle of duties, responsibilities, court appearances and diverse report-writing. Again, for Cooper at least, there is a clearly recognizable 'professional' social work task amidst the complexity of domestic court proceedings (with the exception of the objectives of some related supervision orders). What this piece does question, however, is whether the probation service, increasingly involved in work with adult offenders (chapter 9) is sufficiently geared up and committed to marital and child-care work. Cooper feels that this issue is one which should be taken up by the Probation Service at national level and clearly it is yet another facet of the social work task discourse.

Chapters 6 and 7 should themselves be married and without disharmony for they provide the very best examples of how sociological research can inform social work – in this case in providing a penetrating analysis of the courtroom professionals and the stage upon which social workers and probation officers manage their identities and ply their trades. These two chapters and my own which follows are, if I dare say it, abrasively impartial. They go into the everyday workings of the prosecution and sentencing process and watch, listen and question. The subsequent analysis provides a *demystification* of the court process and in so doing probably makes a definition of *social work* in the courts more, rather than less, problematic.

Pat Carlen and Margaret Powell translate the professional cum political rivalries we noted in earlier chapters into the microcosm of the courtroom where they become much more subtle and softer and increasingly concerned with the efficient flow of everyday work. In exposing, as they do, the underbelly of the magistrate's court, the authors implicitly outline a further set of skills that the beginning social worker and probation officer probably know little of until they are themselves 'stabbed in the back' or 'put on the spot'.

Pauline Hardiker in similar mood demonstrates how 'experienced' probation officers immersed in the wheelings and dealings of criminal justice develop and apply their own strategic blueprint particularly in the preparation of social enquiry reports.

The preparation and presentation of reports as Hardiker demonstrates is a process dialectically related to the courtroom forum already analysed. The creation of the social enquiry report for most probation officers, most of the time, is not apart from but fundamental to their overall social work performance in criminal courts. In particular, Hardiker's 'reverse tariff' hypothesis is a stimulating example of how focused sociological research can inform social work practice and help develop what Hardiker (1978) herself calls 'practice theory'. The identification of aspects of 'practice theory' is, I hope, one of the strengths of this book – the analysis of the way social workers theorize about day to day practice, a description of what they actually do, how they cope, how they rationalize their practices. This knowledge is as vital to the debate as any edict by policy makers in committees, or social work teachers cloistered from the slippery surface, identifying what social workers *should* be doing.

In chapter 8 I set myself the difficult task of giving the client-defendant-offender a voice. The client-defendant whilst certainly 'lost' in the system is not quite the dummy that Carlen found the court professionals assumed. As this book clearly illustrates, defining the social work task is highly problematic. Yet if social work is mainly about 'helping' other people then we should ask repeatedly if the court social worker provides this service in the client's terms. The little we do know about the feelings of those on the receiving end of criminal and juvenile justice is, as I demonstrate, not very encouraging in this regard. Chapter 8 provides a negative learning experience for social work by documenting the impact of the gradual enlargement and redefinition of the social work role with offenders. Whilst I do, I hope, provide some general ground rules about how the social worker-probation officer can maximise the positive aspects of this decreed relationship with defendant-offender in the here and now, the fundamental issue is surely again our initial dilemma. Is the social worker function, as defined by law, court rules and everyday practice, compatible with our ideas about an essence social work function yet to be adequately defined? When some probation officers say they are *not* social workers have they got a point?

The supervision of offenders in the community, mainly as a direct outcome of a court decision, is surveyed by Phyllida Parsloe in chapter 9. There has not been sufficient room in this volume to consider in detail the supervisory tasks of the social worker and probation officer. Nevertheless, the comprehensive overview

which we are aiming at would be incomplete without a consideration of after-court and in particular after-custody supervision.

Earlier chapters have already identified the 'supervision' of
clients as a grey area lacking in clarity and reciprocity. Parsloe
develops this theme fully in her contribution. Using an historical
analysis she traces the institutionalization of the various weaknesses in penal practice which affect social workers and their
charges. The nature of parole licensing well illustrates Parsloe's
thesis. Parole supervision and the criteria for parolee recall are
areas of worker-offender exchange patently suffering from
ambiguity. Thus whilst voluntary after-care by its very nature has
the obvious potential of leading to agreed objectives, statutory
after-care is in practice still an area of contact where the social work
function is unclear and ever arbitrary. Parsloe seeks the
development of mutually agreed and comprehensible after-care
worker-client *contracts* and not restricted to a social casework
approach. The parole system also fails to provide an openness
about its procedures, particularly over the reasons for refusing
parole. In common with many other compulsory 'treatment'
measures, the system clearly lacks a concise set of safeguards and
rights for prisoner-parolees. The probation officer (social worker
in Scotland)-client relationship, acted out amidst such complexity
and confusion, is thus in general predisposed to difficulty. That so
many after-custody relationships between worker and client are
'successful' should not divert us from this conclusion. The
identification of structural weaknesses in the after-care social work
function, at an operational level, is a further key piece in our
construction and we should note that these weaknesses occur yet
again on the frontier where care meets control.

The role of social workers and probation officers in Northern
Ireland's courts is more restricted than on the mainland. In
chapter 10 Greg Kelly traces the development of Ulster's distinctive system. Here probation officers have responsibility for
work with juveniles but not with adult offenders, politically
motivated or otherwise. Indeed adult offenders are not released
through a parole system or given any statutory after-custody
supervision. Kelly emphasizes three features in explaining the
stunted growth of a social work service in and around the courts of
Northern Ireland. First and most obviously, the nature of the
political and religious conflicts in Ulster is directly relevant.
Secondly, a piecemeal 'step by step' policy of attempts to keep
Northern Ireland social policy broadly in line with the rest of
Britain has tended to leave gaps, and thirdly, Kelly emphasizes the

significance of a fully professional resident magistracy in Ulster's lower courts. To state that the nature of officially sanctioned and sponsored social work is dependent upon the socio-political climate and development of that social system is not a verbose ideological cliché. Moreover, a comprehension of the significance of this social fact is a prerequisite to any discussion of the nature of the contemporary social work and social worker task in Britain. The State-employed social worker can exercise neither care nor control in a socio-political vacuum. The Northern Ireland situation exemplifies this fact.

In the final chapter (11) Paul Burgess makes the provocative but logical progression into social work representation in county courts and appeal tribunals. For some readers this extension may seem unnecessary but the reasoning is, I think, consistent with the volume's aims. First, Burgess is able to demonstrate how the representation and advocacy role of social workers in 'familiar' courts (e.g. as guardian *ad litem*) can be extended into other legal proceedings. Secondly, he shows how the needs of 'typical' Social Services Department clients *require* resort to, for instance, Supplementary Benefit Appeal Tribunals, National Insurance Local Tribunals and for the chronically sick and disabled in particular, Medical Appeal Tribunals. In the absence of alternative representatives and/or advocates should the social worker take on such a role? This is, of course, no giveaway line but the crux of a massive dilemma for social workers. This final chapter then illustrates the breadth and complexity of the nature of the potential social work task in and around courts and their close neighbours, appeal tribunals.

Whilst each of these eleven essays can be treated separately as a provider of technical and practical knowledge or as a succinct argument, each is also clearly a part of a larger whole which makes up a panorama of the contemporary social worker/probation officer function in and around British courts. The mere provision of this picture is, almost unbelievably, a large step forward. The juxtaposition of this overview with a critique of practice, with a discussion of what may lead to a clearer definition of the as yet ill-defined social work task, is we hope the major contribution of this volume.

Chapter 1

Juvenile Justice and Social Work in Britain

Allison Morris and Henri Giller

Articles often refer to the 'juvenile justice system' as if agreement and cooperation existed with respect to its aims and methods. We hope to show that although there may be a sharing of certain broad objectives each unit within that system has its own specific purposes and methods of operation and that often these work in *opposition* to the aims and methods of other units. There exists clear evidence of both latent and manifest disjunctions between different parts of the system, and interactions may have more to do with power politics than with cooperation. What is really going on in current debates? Is it anything more than a power struggle among the various interest groups to get *their* values reflected in current policy? Bearing in mind the lack of *real* change, why has the Children and Young Persons Act 1969 been the focus of so much criticism? In an attempt to answer these questions we trace in this paper the path towards the 1969 Act. We will argue that conflict among participants creates and becomes exacerbated by ambivalence in the juvenile court. Juvenile courts have always performed a variety of functions. This means that they are constantly confronted with contradictions in their ideology, structure and operation. These contradictions then become magnified because different groups (social workers, schools, police, etc.) expect the court to meet *their* expectations. These pressures create competitions between conflicting demands.

From conduct to status

Juvenile delinquency has not always been seen as a distinct social problem. Until the middle of the nineteenth century both adults and juveniles (from the age of seven) were subjected to the same laws and penalties – imprisonment, hanging and flogging. However, beliefs that prisons were breeding grounds for criminality and that juvenile offenders could be reformed if the right processes were applied early enough led gradually to the development of separate establishments for juveniles. Early investigations into the aetiology of juvenile delinquency, such as the Report of the Committee into Crime in the Metropolis (1816), identified as causes of delinquency squalid living conditions, the poor moral climate in which children were brought up, and the rigorous application of harsh laws. Reducing these penalties and improving living conditions were unpalatable remedies. But the moral degeneracy of offenders suggested a form of intervention which was thought to be as effective yet left untouched the foundations of the existing socio-political structure: the industrial and reformatory schools. Reformation by segregation was seen as the panacea for crime by the pioneers of the reformatory movement (Platt 1969, 46–74).

These developments were matched by changes in the legal processes for dealing with children. Attempts to reduce the stigma of full criminal process and, thereby, to reduce the child's affiliation to a life of crime were constantly rejected during the first part of the nineteenth century, but by the 1850s summary trial for juvenile offenders who had committed minor thefts was possible (Pinchbeck and Hewitt 1973, 431–95). This procedure, however, remained the exception rather than the rule. It was not until the Children Act 1908 that a distinct tribunal for children was established. The tribunal created was a *court*. As such, its primary purpose was to discover whether or not the child was responsible for his conduct and to sentence him for it. The prevailing idea was that the child was a wrong-doer and the old procedures for dealing with adult offenders were not thought to be inappropriate in most respects. Although there were minor modifications and simplifications in the procedure to facilitate the child's understanding of what was happening, the mode of trial was similar to that for adults.

But these new juvenile courts had an additional responsibility. Herbert Samuel, introducing the Children Bill into the House of Commons, said that the courts should be agencies for the rescue as well as the punishment of the child. The juvenile offender was also seen as the victim of circumstances which had moulded his criminality. These two contradictory notions collided within the framework of the first juvenile courts.

The juvenile courts also had jurisdiction over children who were suffering from cruelty and neglect (either malicious or circumstantial) and here the courts gave primacy to the welfare of the child. Likewise, society was compelled to 'do something', but the vital difference between these two groups was that intervention in the life of the delinquent was based upon his *conduct* – a matter over which he was assumed to have responsibility; intervention in the life of the neglected child was based on his *status* – a matter over which he was assumed to have no responsibility.

This conceptual distinction, however, gradually became blurred, partly as a result of the work in the new juvenile courts. In 1927, a Departmental Committee on the Treatment of Young Offenders stated quite forcibly that 'there is little difference between the neglected and the delinquent child. . . . Neglect leads to delinquency and delinquency is often the direct outcome of neglect' (Molony Committee Report 1927, 71).

The Children and Young Persons Act 1933 carried this emphasis further: the appointment of justices with a special interest in children, restrictions on the reporting of cases, the abolition of the terms 'conviction' and 'sentence' and the direction that justices should have regard to the welfare of the child.

But this homogeneity had only limited application. At the adjudicative stage the delinquent act was viewed as an act of conscious defiance. It was only after the act was proved or admitted to that it was viewed as a product of personal or external forces and that dispositions were reached with these forces in mind. The dual image of the delinquent child was perpetuated.

This dualism is clearly illustrated during periods when the pattern of juvenile delinquency (as officially recorded) increased. The post-war increase in juvenile crime, for example, led to the establishment of detention and attendance centres in the Criminal Justice Act of 1948. The philosophy underlying these measures was that children are responsible for their criminal acts and are able to respond to and be deterred by short, sharp, shocks or by deprivation of their spare time. (For a further discussion see Land, 1975, 311–70.) In the same year, however, the major recommendations of the Curtis Committee (1946) were implemented in the Children Act. This report had a major impact on the organization of services for children suffering from family breakdown, and led to the establishment of a centrally coordinated child-care service. Its function was 'to see that all deprived children have an upbringing likely to make them sound and happy citizens and that they have all the chances, educational and vocational, of making a good start in life that are open to children from normal homes' (para. 435). The Committee felt that at least some delinquent children fell within this category.[1]

The blurring of the distinction between the 'deprived' and the 'depraved' accelerated over the next decade. There seem to be two reasons for this. First, there was a fairly rapid expansion in influential empirical studies into the aetiology of juvenile delinquency. Previously such work had been sporadic and statements made by committees like the Morton Committee (1927) were often based on similarities between *institutionalized* neglected and delinquent children rather than on analyses of the characteristics of all children coming before the courts. Increasingly, however, studies of a more scientific nature were being undertaken. In 1942, for example, Carr-Saunders, Mannheim and Rhodes reviewed nineteen pieces of research into the aetiology of juvenile delinquency ranging over the previous hundred years, and concluded that 'there exists, generally speaking, unanimity with regard to the predominant significance of family conditions, work and unemployment, urban as contrasted with rural life' (Carr-Saunders *et al.*, 42). Their own study of 1,000 children dealt with by a London juvenile court found a 'well-marked degree of association between delinquency and families of abnormal structure' (Carr-Saunders *et al.*, 149). Dramatic confirmation of one of these family abnormalities – maternal deprivation – came with the work of Dr John Bowlby (1946, 1952). The remedy for this defect – the bolstering of existing family structures – provides the second reason for the blurring of this distinction.

The essence of the new child-care service was the provision of good *substitute* care. The Curtis Committee clearly disliked existing residential facilities for children and preferred the use of foster care. Not surprising, therefore, the initial efforts of the new child-care officers were directed towards the *product* of family dysfunction, the child, rather than to the *unit* of dysfunction, the family. Gradually, however, involvement with delinquents[2] and, more generally, the recurring pressure put on the service to deal with family problems, caused attention to shift to the prevention of family breakdown (Packman 1975). Moreover, such a strategy appealed not only to economic good sense (residential facilities were expensive) but also to 'scientific' good sense (given the impact of the work of Bowlby and others).[3] Indeed, so persuasive was the promise of prevention that in 1956 the Ingleby Committee was appointed not only to review the operation of the juvenile court but also to consider whether local authorities should be given 'new powers and duties to prevent or forestall the suffering of children through neglect *in their own homes*' (our italics) (1960, ii).

The evidence presented to the Ingleby Committee stretched

along a continuum which, at the extremes, viewed the child as either 'non-responsible'[4] or responsible for his conduct. The conception of the delinquent as 'non-responsible' for his conduct (as a social casualty in need of social assistance) meant that there was no need for adjudication, punishment or deterrence. Proponents of this view[5] argued that the age of criminal responsibility should be raised to fifteen and that below this age juveniles should be subject to care and protection proceedings. Indeed, there was no need for a juvenile court other than to enable social service action to take place where it was resisted (in this case the *parent* was *irresponsible*) or where the facts were disputed.

For those who viewed the child as a responsible person these proposals were anathema. The proponents of this view[6] argued that a court was 'necessary for the proper protection of those who are the subject of proceedings . . . and that the power to interfere with personal liberty should be entrusted only to a court' (op. cit., 1960, para. 70). They also emphasized the deterrent value of an appearance before a court. The welfare of the child was not disregarded; rather it was confined to intervention *before* the offence was committed (preventive work with the family and the child on a voluntary basis) or *after* the offence had been adjudicated upon (if other kinds of responses – the need to deter the offender or to protect the public – were not appropriate).

The Ingleby Committee, though recommending the retention of the juvenile court, attempted a compromise. It suggested that the age of criminal responsibility should be raised from eight to twelve, but that a child below that age who committed an offence should be deemed in need of care. The thinking behind this proposal was that by removing the child offender from a jurisdiction based on criminal procedure, one would also remove the expectation that the sentence would be based on tariff principles.[7] The Committee felt that the older child offender should learn to stand on his own two feet and to accept greater responsibility for his actions. Criminal proceedings were accordingly to be retained for them and welfare considerations were to be minimized.

The Committee held a dual image of the delinquent child but it was an image determined by the age of the child. Children, it felt, came before the court because those responsible for their upbringing (parents, school, community) had failed to teach them how to behave in an acceptable manner. During childhood, therefore, the responsibility for the child's actions should be shared between him and the parents. The Committee did not go to the extreme of denying the child *all* personal responsibility for his actions; it was enough that *some* of the responsibility was placed on the parents. As the child grew older, the Committee took the view that his own responsibility increased and that of others grew less.

Once the complaint was proved, whether in care and protection or criminal proceedings, the Committee recommended that the court should receive reports from the local authority children's department and probation department, that these reports should include any information which seemed relevant to the treatment of the child and that the offender should be given the treatment he required. The Committee, therefore, at least to some extent supported a social welfare approach towards both categories of children. But it came out strongly in favour of judicial rather than administrative discretion in the determination of dispositions.

The two main political parties received the Committee's recommendations differently. The reaction of the Conservative Party was cool: juvenile crime rates had continued to increase and the recent disturbances at Carlton Approved School (Home Office 1960) threw doubt on whether an extension of social work efforts were sufficient to check these rising crime rates. The Labour Party felt that the Committee's recommendations were not sufficiently far-reaching: insufficient weight had been given to keeping children out of the courts and there was no structure for the future development of a fully coordinated social service. Indeed the publication, during the subsequent debates on the Children and Young Persons Bill 1963, of a Scottish report on the prevention of the neglect of children, the McBoyle Report, which recommended the development of a comprehensive family welfare service, gave additional weight to Labour MPs' claims that the Ingleby Committee's recommendations were too narrow.

The period 1961 to 1963 provides a further graphic illustration of the schizophrenic nature of the response to juvenile offenders. The Ingleby Committee had also recommended that the transfer of children from approved schools to borstal should be made easier and this was given effect in the Criminal Justice Act 1961 which also reduced the age at which children could be sent to borstal and to attendance centres.[8] There were comments in Parliament at the time about the need to coordinate policies towards juvenile offenders but it was not until two years later that the other recommendations of the Ingleby Committee were debated and given effect, in part, in the Children and Young Persons Act 1963.

Subsequently, the Labour Party in 1964 set up a committee on criminal policy under the chairmanship of Lord Longford

(Labour Party Study Group 1964). The Report was fairly wide-ranging and a major proposal was the abolition of the juvenile courts. The Committee's starting point was that 'delinquents are to some extent a product of the society they live in and of the deficiencies in its provision for them', but felt that the machinery of the law was reserved for working-class children – children of other classes were dealt with by other means. Its proposals stemmed from the belief that 'no child in early adolescence should have to face criminal proceedings: these children should receive the kind of treatment they need, without any stigma'. Criminal proceedings were felt to be 'indefensible' where the offence was a trivial one and where it was serious this was 'in itself, evidence of the child's need for skilled help and guidance'. The causes of juvenile delinquency and child neglect were traced by the Committee to a primary source: inadequacy or breakdown in the family. 'It is a truism that a happy and secure family life is the foundation of a healthy society and the best safeguard against delinquency and anti-social behaviour.' Delinquency in a child was 'evidence of the lack of care, guidance and opportunities to which every child is entitled'. Accordingly, an alternative framework to the juvenile court was suggested: a 'family service' in which the child, family and social worker would discuss the treatment of the child. Only where agreement could not be reached or where the facts of the case were disputed would the case be referred to a new 'family court'.[9]

These proposals subsequently formed the basis of the Labour Government White Paper, *The Child, the Family and the Young Offender* (Home Office 1965), except that a 'family council' consisting of social workers and other persons selected for their understanding and experience of children replaced the 'family service'. There was considerable opposition to these proposals and the main criticisms centred on the inappropriateness of a social welfare approach towards children who offend. The probation service and the magistracy were both concerned with the protection of the legal rights of the child. They felt that there were too many possibilities for abuse in the proposed scheme and that it was undesirable that decisions which might affect the liberty of the young should be reached by social workers.

In 1968, in response to this opposition, the Government produced a second White Paper, *Children in Trouble* (Home Office 1968), which was the basis of the Children and Young Persons Act 1969.

The second White Paper was an attempt to retain the proposals of the earlier White Paper and, at the same time, to forestal further criticism. This was achieved by abandoning the controversial family council concept and retaining the juvenile court. The opposition was thereby deprived of much of its sting. The proposals of the new White Paper have often been described as less radical than its predecessor, but this is not so – what happened was that magistrates and others failed to realize 'how far the traditional functions and operating philosophy of the juvenile court were being eroded by the details of the new framework' (Bottoms 1974, 335). Magistrates, initially at least, considered the second White Paper to be a great improvement on the earlier one.

Basically both White Papers shared an emphasis on treatment or social welfare and on keeping children out of the reach of the criminal law.[10] *Children in Trouble* saw a child's behaviour as influenced by 'genetic, emotional and intellectual factors, his maturity, and his family, school, neighbourhood and wider social setting'. Although delinquency was seen in some situations to be an incident in the child's normal development, it was also seen as a response to 'unsatisfactory family or social circumstances, a result of boredom in and out of school, an indication of maladjustment or immaturity, or a symptom of a deviant, damaged or abnormal personality'. Consequently, the White Paper suggested that it was necessary to develop facilities for observation and assessment, and to increase the variety of facilities for continuing treatment.

Although the juvenile court was to be retained, the White Paper proposed that all children under the age of fourteen would cease to be tried for criminal offences. Further, in an attempt to narrow down the circumstances in which court proceedings would be possible, an offence in itself would cease to be a sufficient reason for a court appearance. 'Care and protection' proceedings would be possible for children between the ages of ten and fourteen who committed offences, but only where it could be established that the child was not receiving such care, protection and guidance as a good parent might reasonably be expected to give. Otherwise, such children would be dealt with on an informal and voluntary basis. Children between the ages of fourteen and seventeen, on the other hand, could be subject to criminal proceedings but only after mandatory consultation between police and social workers and after application to a magistrate for a warrant to prosecute. These would only be issued in exceptional circumstances; it was expected that such offenders would also, in the main, be dealt with under 'care and protection' proceedings or informally. The overall aims of the proposals were to reduce the number of cases heard in the juvenile courts and to reduce the number of cases in which the commission of an offence was a sufficient ground for intervention in itself.

Thus far the proposals seem little more than an extension of the approach suggested by the Ingleby Committee in 1960, but *Children in Trouble* envisaged also an enlarged and significant role for local authority social workers.[11] In addition to mandatory social work consultation prior to proceedings and to increased social work involvement with families and children on a voluntary basis, considerable power was also placed in the hands of social workers to vary and implement the disposition orders made by the courts. Commitment to the care of the local authority was to replace approved school and fit person orders; the implementation of the care order would be in the hands of the local authority social service department rather than with magistrates. Attendance centres and detention centres were to be replaced by a new form of treatment – intermediate treatment – and the form that this would take would also lie with the social services; approved schools were to be merged within the community home system and were to form part of a range of local authority facilities for all children in need. Magistrates were no longer to be involved in detailed decisions about the kind of treatment appropriate for the child. Social workers, within the limits of the particular order, were to determine this.

Compromise and contradictions

So far, we have outlined the attempt to amalgamate the categories of children with whom the juvenile court has to deal. The assumption underlying the White Papers of the late sixties is that offenders, like other children in trouble, are not responsible for the circumstances which bring them before the court. Because of this, the focus of the tribunal's attention moved, in theory, from the *conduct* of the juvenile to his *status*.

The next step is to explain this shift of emphasis. We feel that it is crystallized in two key issues which have recurred throughout debates on the reform of the juvenile court. The first is the appropriate age for criminal responsibility. The common law set the age at seven: thereafter, the child was held to be fully responsible for his actions. In the debates over the last sixty years, however, the question has not simply been one of deciding when the child should or should not be deemed responsible. It has also been about whether or not, by relieving the child of criminal responsibility, other, *more effective* measures of social control might be applied. Donninson and Stewart (1958), for example, in their evidence to the Ingleby Committee, argued in favour of raising the age of criminal responsibility and of extending the civil jurisdiction of the juvenile court because 'it would be no longer necessary to establish that a child knew what he was doing was wrong before dealing with him as a delinquent'. This would allow *more* children to be referred to the juvenile court. Viscount Ingleby, in commending to Parliament his Committee's recommendation to increase the age of criminal responsibility to twelve, used the same argument.[12] These views, and those later expressed by the Longford Committee, saw the apparatus of the criminal trial as both inept and inappropriate in the effective prevention of juvenile delinquency because the notion of the juvenile offender as a responsible person hindered the process by which he could be re-socialized.

The second theme in the debates rests on the question whether the focus of attention should be on the child as an unsocialized individual (Fry 1940) or as a calculating transgressor of the legal order. Policy statements stressing the child's lack of real responsibility and the need for extended social services have been consistently presented by socialist intellectuals and Labour party study groups. While presented as policies for dealing with juvenile delinquency, they contain, or are inexorably linked to, policies which seek to further the development of the socialist state. Legislation for dealing with juvenile delinquency was but a part of a legislative programme geared to develop a more socially just society in which the socialist values of equality of opportunity and equality of result would be achieved (George and Wilding 1976, 62–84). A feeling of community would be created within which each citizen owned rights and owed obligations. Key policies in the development of this social structure were the plans for comprehensive education, adequate housing and expansion of the economy. The Welfare State would meet the needs of those unable to participate in the social reconstruction because of some disability. 'Needs', however, within the post-war setting, were not limited to material needs. 'Secondary poverty' (Crosland 1963, 81–101) – family breakdown and delinquency – also prevented the full social participation of the individual and had to be met.[13] Delinquency was viewed as only one of many of the expressions of 'secondary poverty' and as a symptom of underlying social need. Intervention was justified only where the child's offence was due to 'causes for which the child has no personal responsibility';

'naughtiness' was to be tolerated by the community as a natural part of the child's growing up process (Crosland and Longford Report 1964, 14 and 21). The appropriate remedy for delinquency lay in the reconstruction of the family unit. By moving the debate away from the nature of the juvenile's *offence* to the nature of the juvenile *offender* the stage was set for the abolition of the juvenile court.

A very different conception of social order and of the appropriate response to juvenile offenders was offered by the Conservative party (George and Wilding 1976, 21–41). The stereotype of the delinquent was not the social casualty but the conscious perpetrator of social disruption. While juvenile delinquency was also viewed primarily as a personal problem, it was assumed to arise from personal iniquity rather than from social inequality. Moreover, this iniquity was exacerbated by the influence of socialist conceptions of social reconstruction generally and of the Welfare State in particular. The appropriate response to juvenile delinquency, therefore, was not the provision of social help but the correction of the offender by discipline and punishment. The basis of this conception is individual freedom in return for responsibility for that freedom. This produces equal opportunity but not equality of results. As Macleod put it, 'on our banners we will put "opportunity", an equal opportunity for men to make themselves unequal' (1958, 14). Within this framework, the State has only a minor role to play – that of ensuring individual freedom – and only where groups or individuals are considered to be 'non-responsible' should the State take paternalistic action (Friedman 1962, 22–36).[14] Difficulties in deciding where to draw the line of responsibility are recognized, especially with regard to children who offend. The Bow Group's response to the Longford Committee's proposals provide one example of an attempt to draw this line: 'It is easy to find excuses for children who have shown signs of anti-social behaviour, but we do feel that a child over the age of 10 is old enough to be responsible for his actions, or at least to appreciate the difference between right and wrong, and if not he should be corrected' (1964, 4).

Protagonists of this view, both those professionally interested (for example, many magistrates and police officers) and those politically interested (the Conservative party) have consistently reiterated the need for legalism in dealing with juvenile offenders; such departures as they have consented to (and which have occurred) have related only to inessential features.[15] This insistence on the retention of criminal procedures (and deterrent sanctions) ultimately rests on the belief that juvenile offenders, like adults, are responsible for their actions and must be subjected to the symbolic impact of courtroom procedures. These procedures are directed *primarily at others* who may act in a similar way and not at the offender himself; the effective treatment of the offender is a *secondary* aim. Many of the debates, therefore, centred on arrangements for this symbolic activity rather than on what should happen to individual offenders. Indeed such debates can deflect attention from changes in the balance of power which are occurring; this is essentially what happened during the passage of the 1969 Act.[16]

The 1969 Act, because it is a compromise, perpetuates both these conceptions of the juvenile offender: the full machinery of courtroom adjudication is retained for those who see him as responsible; an emphasis on social welfare exists for those who see him as the 'non-responsible' product of social circumstances. The spheres of influence of these conceptions are not, however, mutually exclusive and the people who operate the system are not isolated actors. This means that they collide at various stages: whether or not the child should be referred to court (and the nature of the proceedings), his adjudication, the determination of his disposal and its operation. The history of the 1969 Act is the history of the operation of these different conceptions in practice.

To a large extent, the social welfare philosophy endorsed by the Act has not been put into effect. Ideological differences between the political parties has meant that key sections have remained unimplemented.[17] The Act could, however, have been implemented *informally*; the fact that it was not suggests that the power to influence practice is more important than legislative policy. New systems may be set up but if those operating the system do not give primary allegiance to the values inherent in that system then its aims can be defeated. Many of the groups involved in the operation of the juvenile courts did not give primary allegiance to the social welfare values inherent in the Act.[18] What has happened since 1971 is that groups which found their roles in conflict with the new philosophy have continued to work within their traditional perspectives and have attempted to make other groups share them.

The lack of formal or informal implementation is revealed in Tables 1 : 1 and 1 : 2. First, although the proportion of males who admitted indictable offences and who were cautioned by the police increased from 1970 to 1977 by 108 per cent the number of males proceeded against in the juvenile courts increased by 28 per cent.

Table 1:1   1970 to 1977 percentage variations males under 14 (indictable crimes)

	%
Variation in numbers cautioned	93
Variation in numbers proceeded against	2
Variation in numbers found guilty	2
Variation in numbers on supervision	27
Variation in numbers on care	− 9
Variation in numbers on attendance centre orders	2
Variation in numbers fined	17

Table 1 : 2   1970 to 1977 percentage variations males 14–17 (indictable crimes)

		%
Variation in numbers cautioned	+	130
Variation in numbers proceeded against	+	42
Variation in numbers found guilty	+	43
Variation in numbers on supervision	−	1
Variation in numbers fined	+	48
Variation in numbers given attendance centre orders	+	100
Variation in numbers given care orders	−	25
Variation in numbers given S.28 remits in the Crown Court	+	97
Variation in numbers given detention centre orders	+	204

Source: Criminal statistics.

This could be explained in a variety of ways (e.g. by a vast increase in juvenile crime) but Ditchfield (1976) suggests that at least part of the reason is that the pool of officially labelled juvenile offenders increased as a direct result of changes in police practices since 1969. Secondly, although the use of care proceedings invoking the 'offence' condition as an alternative to criminal proceedings has been possible since 1971, they were used on eighty-one occasions in that year and the number has not appreciably increased. Supervision orders replaced probation orders in 1971, but in spite of the emphasis on treatment in the community 1,741 fewer supervision orders were made in 1977 than probation orders in 1970, a reduction of 11 per cent. Over the same period there has been an increase of 55 per cent in the number of boys given attendance centre orders and an increase of 204 per cent in the number of boys sent to detention centres. Although magistrates themselves cannot sentence young offenders to borstal training they can remit them to the Crown Court with a recommendation for borstal training. The number of boys in this category increased from 1970 to 1977 by 97 per cent.

The opposite to that intended by the Act has clearly occurred and the Act is blamed for this. But Figures 1 : 1 to 1 : 4 put these changes in perspective. Figures 1 : 1 and 1 : 2 show that the overall

Figure 1:1   Disposition patterns for males under 14 (indictable crimes) 1970 and 1977 (%)

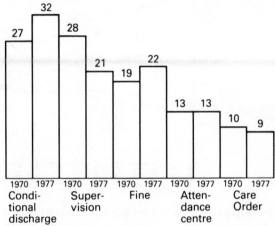

Figure 1:2   Disposition patterns for males 14–17 (indictable crimes) 1970 and 1977 (%)

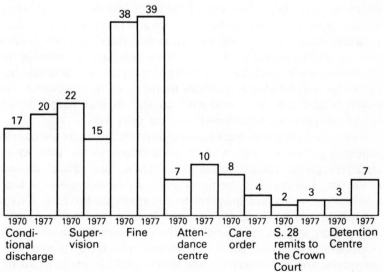

Source: Criminal Statistics

distribution of sentences in the magistrates' courts has radically changed since 1970. Figures 1 : 3 and 1 : 4, however, show the Act itself cannot be blamed for this.[19] The use of probation was *already decreasing* from at least 1964 onwards for under fourteens and it was

Figure 1:3   Disposition patterns for males under 14 (indictable crimes) 1964–77

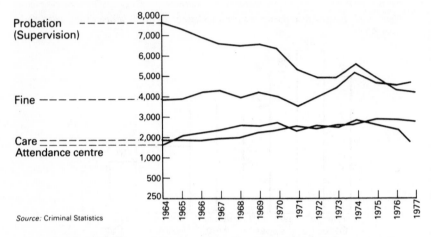

Probation
(Supervision)

Fine

Care
Attendance centre

Source: Criminal Statistics

used *more* frequently for the older group at various periods after 1971 than before. Figure 1:4 shows that the 'dramatic' increase in the use of detention centres, attendance centres and recommendations to the Crown Court for borstal is not what it seems at first sight. The use of these measures was increasing steadily throughout the period 1964–76 and in certain years before 1971 the rate of increase was as high as that since 1971. We are not seeking here to minimize the increases which have occurred in the absolute number of children in detention centres and borstals, but rather to suggest that alternative methods of interpretation are possible and are less conducive to the 'moral panic' which surrounds present discussions about the 1969 Act.

Basically there are two questions of interest: are there changes in sentencing trends? And, is there an increase in the number of children given certain measures? These are quite distinct questions; but many of the participants in the debates have used answers to the second question to comment on the first. This is inappropriate. It is not, however, without a reason. Magistrates and police, for example, point to the increased detention-centre population as evidence for the existence of a hard core of persistent offenders; social workers use the same figures as evidence of the failure of magistrates to work within the philosophy of the Act.

Figure 1:4 Disposition patterns for males 14–17 (indictable crimes) 1964–77

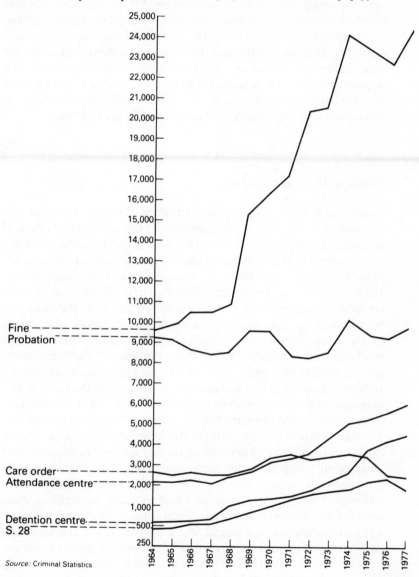

Fine
Probation

Care order
Attendance centre

Detention centre
S. 28

Source: Criminal Statistics

Magistrates respond by pointing to their lack of confidence in social workers as the reason for not placing children in the supervision or care of local authorities. But such a rationale has more to do with the power to determine the appropriate response to offenders and to delimit the sphere of influence of social workers. The *real* issue has become who should decide the appropriate placement for the child and, indirectly, the child's responsibility for his actions. By presenting juvenile delinquency as problematic, each group is able to criticize the existing machinery and to promote its own proposals for reform.

From status to conduct

There have been two themes running through most of the discussions surrounding the operation of the 1969 Act: the lack of resources and the existence of a hard core of troublesome children. It is assumed that additional resources would resolve many of the Act's difficulties. But there is no agreement (Giller and Morris 1976, 656–65) or knowledge (Brody 1976) about the kind of resources required and the issues are more complex than can be resolved by this simple solution.[20] The existence and extent of the hard core is also difficult to determine. There are no available statistics to confirm or deny its existence but impressions among magistrates and police are strong. This may or may not be accurate; more important, however, is the feeling that police and magistrates are *now* powerless to deal with such offenders and that, consequently, juveniles are being encouraged into further crime. The case against the Act rests on the belief that approved school orders were effective in preventing further immediate offences and absconding, and that care orders are ineffective – children are automatically sent home (or run away) and commit further offences. The little evidence which does exist contradicts these impressions. In surveys of twenty local authorities during 1972 and 1973 (unpublished) the Social Work Service of the DHSS found that it was comparatively rare for children subject to care orders to be returned home directly from court. And Zander's survey (1975) of a small sample of London children subject to care orders showed that while a high proportion of the children were returned home this was not inevitably associated with further offences. Those children placed in a community home in fact committed *more* offences subsequently than those placed at home. But whether these impressions are fact or fiction is probably irrelevant; beliefs have formed and affect the operation of the Act.

The establishment of a sub-committee of the House of Commons Expenditure Committee to review the operation of the Act provided a convenient source for the views of the various groups (1975). As we have written elsewhere (Morris and Giller, 1976), it seems to us that overall the evidence submitted to the sub-committee fell broadly into four categories: the radical view that the 1969 Act did not go far enough,[21] the crime control view that the Act was based on unsound principles,[22] the child care view which accepted the broad principles of the Act and called for full implementation,[23] and the crime control-child care view which suggests that children in trouble may be susceptible to child care but that some require penal measures regardless of their susceptibility to child care.[24]

The sub-committee's report is itself an interesting document for while reinforcing in some of its recommendations the philosophy underlying the Act it questions in others the basis of this philosophy. For example, it accepted that a social welfare approach was unlikely to reduce delinquency and instead presented two new guidelines: 'that of satisfying society's wish to punish an offender' and that of 'preventing him for a time from committing further offences at a reasonable cost and in the most humane way' (op. cit., 1975, Vol. 1, para. 13). The sub-committee was motivated less by an image of the child in need of care and more by an image of the responsible physically mature, often economically independent, adolescent who is a threat to established order. Thus, although the sub-committee suggested that the causes of crime lay in *social deprivation* (bad housing, poverty, broken families, etc.), it nevertheless felt that in addition to children 'who need care, welfare, better education and moral support', there are some who need '*strict control* and an *element of punishment*'. Also, while recognizing that many children grow out of delinquent behaviour, the sub-committee stated that some attempt must be made 'to hasten the process in the case of certain offenders, to *deter* others from embarking on criminal activities, *to contain* a hard core of persistent offenders and to *punish* some offenders'. The sub-committee wrote that 'there is a limit to the amount of delinquent behaviour which society is prepared to tolerate' and a major part of its recommendations seems to be a response to this. There is little emphasis on the needs of the child; concern is with the deeds of the child. The sub-committee recommended that when a care order is made agreement should be reached in court between the magistrates and social workers concerned on what should be done with the child; that when a juvenile already subject to a care order appears before a court, charged with an offence, the court should be able to impose a secure care order; and that attendance and detention centres should be retained. The sub-committee sought to restore the balance of power to those who have traditionally held the child responsible for his actions. Magistrates would determine not only the category into which a particular child would be placed but also the appropriate response to him.

The focus of much of the debate since the publication of the sub-committee's report has been the secure care order and the residential care order. The Magistrates' Association (1977), the Society of Conservative Lawyers (1976) and a Conservative party study group set up by William Whitelaw (Conservative Parliamentary House Affairs Committee 1976), have all pressed for these powers. The real issue, however, is often concealed and arguments are presented in terms of magistrates rather than social workers being the right group to make decisions which involve deprivation of liberty. The point ignored is that magistrates already have this power.

The Government, has, so far, resisted these pressures for a more detailed regulation of dispositions. An inter-departmental White Paper published in 1976 (Home Office, Welsh Office, DHSS and DES 1976) appears to endorse the social welfare philosophy underlying the 1969 Act but at the same time it supports the sub-committee's belief that there exists a group of children for whom the Act falls short. What is noteworthy is that these children are identifiable by the nature of *their behaviour* rather than by their needs. The unquestioning continuation of detention centres and the expansion of attendance centres also shows that the intention of the 1969 Act is long forgotten.

But there is one crucial area in which the White Paper did not go as far as the sub-committee's report. It explicitly accepts and reaffirms the different functions of juvenile court magistrates and social workers. Magistrates set the limits to an order (care or supervision); social workers decide the appropriate action within that framework. The White Paper, however, suggests giving magistrates a power to recommend what should be done with a child in those cases which cause them concern. Not surprisingly, the Magistrates' Association have rejected this attempted compromise and have continued to press for further powers.

An attempt was made in the recent Criminal Law Bill to add to various sections of the 1969 Act both a residential care order and a secure care order. The debates in the House of Commons rehearsed the familiar failings of the 1969 Act: lack of resources, lack of strong powers and lack of cooperation. The Act was blamed for 'the scandal of uncontrolled juvenile crime'. The new clause was, however, rejected. It is difficult to state the reasons for this because, as we have said already, impressions have taken the appearance of truths in this area. One reason – unstated – is a simple economic one. A total of £3½ million over a two-year period has already been allocated to local authorities for the provision of secure accommodation and it is unlikely that any government would, in the current financial climate, be willing to commit yet further resources. Other reasons emerge in the debates. The new powers (which included the power to fix a period of detention up to a maximum of two years) were far in excess of the powers which magistrates have in dealing with *adult* offenders; this is likely to have had weight with those who view juvenile offenders as responsible as adults, but not as more responsible. Some discussion also centred on the appropriate 'professional' to make decisions about the type of placement or the need for security: magistrates or social workers? The trump card was played by Edward Lyons. He pointed out that it did not really matter who made the decision because there were unlikely to be sufficient secure places anyway. Whatever the reasons for the rejection of the clause the 1969 Act limps on but for how long? The 'moral panic' about delinquent youth continues unabated.

By pressing for the introduction of secure care orders, the Right (magistrates/the police/the Conservative party) continues to present its stereotype of juvenile offenders across the *whole machinery* of the juvenile justice system. Its aim now seems to be to ensure that social service resources become more obviously mechanisms of social control. To achieve this the Right has created a bifurcated categorization of juvenile offenders: the 'majority' of children who are said to be satisfactorily accommodated by existing provisions and a 'minority' of hard core offenders characterized either by their commitment to crime or their psychiatrically abnormal features.[25] Both groups remain undefined but the 'professional' group is seen as needing punishment (in order to be deterred) and the 'abnormal' group as needing specialist help. To meet these 'needs' incarceration is required.

This does not mean that the Right is relinquishing its control of the majority of offenders to the social services. Magistrates can and do ultimately determine the proportion of offenders who will be allocated to the social services.[26] This battle has already been won. What is now happening is that social workers are being appealed to in their own terms and the aim of this is to force them to accept the logic of the Right as to the different categories of offenders which exist and their different levels of responsibility.

To a degree the Right has been successful in this strategy and, because of this, the social work response is confused. While rejecting the machinery by which magistrates would exercise their powers, social workers have not rejected the suggested categorization of offenders. One director of social services, for example, recently suggested that social work effort should be concentrated on the younger, less sophisticated delinquent, in the belief that this would increase the success of intervention (Community Care, 1976). But the Right are already willing to allow social services to control these children – their offences are minor and there is no need to protect society from them. The concomitant of this social service response, moreover, is that the 'hard core' is abandoned. This confirms the categorization of the Right that a social welfare approach for this group is inappropriate.

In an attempt to salvage a role for social workers with the 'minority' the British Association of Social Workers' recent guidelines (1977a) for social workers in making recommendations to the courts makes a gesture to the Right. This document suggests that social workers should not recommend detention centre sentences at all, or borstal training orders for fifteen-year-olds, and specifies the situations in which a care order should be recommended: where the child has certain vocational, medical or personal needs which can best be met in a residential institution or foster home; where the home circumstances of the child are such that more severe emotional damage or behavioural disorders would result if he or she was allowed to remain at home; and where the behaviour of the child is a positive danger to himself and/or the community. Social workers, therefore, have been forced to state that they can fulfil the social control function demanded by magistrates *in order that they can maintain their credibility*.[27] The import of the document is that social workers can control these children *as effectively* as detention centres and borstals. Resort to such tactics is a result of the weak position social workers occupy among juvenile justice 'professionals'. Their policy objectives have had to be reactions to and determined by the policy statements of others. The social work role outlined by BASW is not, therefore, the result of a compromise with the Right but of a dictate from it. It is a dictate which both delimits social workers' influence with the 'majority' of offenders and forces them to accept a greater degree of social control over the 'minority'. Even if this gesture is successful, there is no guarantee that magistrates will accept in the future that social workers can provide the necessary degree of social control. For the present, however, the result would be that disparate groups of children would become social work 'problems'. The anomalies of the policy in the present White Paper which promotes intermediate treatment with one breath and expands secure accommodation with the next can best be understood against this background.

Conclusion

What then does the social worker do when faced with a questioning of his role as an 'expert' and with an increasingly forceful lobby for punitive measures? Social work has traditionally been based on the belief that intervention in people's lives is both justified and beneficial. The Impact report, however, questions whether or not more intensive social work help improves results and there is support for the view that intensive intervention can make some offenders more likely to commit further offences (Folkard, Smith and Smith, 1976). Great expectations and hopes have been held of intermediate treatment. But it is doubtful whether thirty or ninety days can cancel out, for example, ten years of under-achievement at school or the fact that employment possibilities are limited. In pre-court diversionary schemes there lies the danger that inadequate treatment programmes are merely transferred to an earlier stage in the child's career. The fashionable device of making 'contracts' with offenders has the same defects – it assumes that the social worker can keep *his* end of the bargain. BASW, perhaps in an attempt to meet social work critics head on, recently defined the social work task as follows: 'Social work is the purposeful and ethical application of personal skills in interpersonal relationships directed towards enhancing the personal and social functioning of an individual, family, group or neighbourhood, which necessarily involves using evidence obtained from practice to help create a social environment conducive to the well-being of all' (1977, 11). But what does this mean? Is it more than an attempt to make social work *sound* professional (and, thereby, to cut the social worker off from his client to an even greater extent than currently)? And, more importantly, how is this achieved? The basic difficulty in the report is that it does not face up to the evidence: social work aid does not seem to help reduce recidivism and this is what the Right demands.[28]

Magistrates currently determine issues of responsibility; social workers determine questions of treatment. The difficulty here for the development of social work is that the latter is determined by the former. If social workers wish to develop their role in working with juvenile offenders and retain their social welfare emphasis they must be as involved in the issues of process as they are currently in issues of treatment. Until social workers enter *this* realm of the debate their role and influence must be subject to the power of others. Between conduct and status lies the politics of penal policy.

Recommended reading

BERLINS, M. and WANSELL, G. 1974: *Caught in the Act: Children, Society and the Law.* Harmondsworth: Penguin.

MORRIS, A. and McISAAC, M. 1978: *Juvenile Justice? The practice of social welfare.* London: Heinemann.

PARSLOE, P. 1978: *Juvenile Justice in Britain and the USA.* London: Routledge & Kegan Paul.

PRIESTLY, P., FEARS, D. and FULLER, R. 1977: *Justice for Juveniles: The 1969 Children and Young Persons Act – A case for reform?* London: Routledge & Kegan Paul.

Notes

1 The Committee did have some reservations. While recommending that some non-delinquents might be suitable for placement in approved school, these children were described as '*really* difficult or *very* unruly' and as children who had been exposed to '*very* depraved influences' (our italics).

2 The Children and Young Persons (Amendment) Act 1952 allowed delinquents under twelve to be remanded in local authority reception homes and gave the children's departments the power to act as after-care officers for children released from approved schools. Moreover, some individual local authorities, most notably Oxfordshire, expanded their work with delinquents on an experimental basis.

3 Notable among these was Dr Robert Andry (1960) whose work on the effects of paternal deprivation in the aetiology of delinquency rather

than contradicting Bowlby's gave support to a more broad-based parental deprivation thesis.

4 Rather than use the term 'irresponsible' which implies a degree of moral culpability for an act or omission, 'non-responsible' is used to denote a state of neutrality concerning blame.

5 For example, David Donninson and Mary Stewart writing for the Fabian Society, the Council for Children's Welfare and the Fisher Group.

6 For example, the Magistrates' Association, Justices' Clerks' Society and the Association of Social Workers.

7 Nevertheless, the Committee accepted that the ambiguity of any tribunal dealing with children in trouble was 'inherent in combining the requirement for proof as a specified event or condition with a general direction to have regard to the child's welfare'. See paras. 60 and 66.

8 The Criminal Justice Act 1961 S. 1 (1) reduced the minimum age for borstal to fifteen years and S. 10 (1) reduced the minimum age for attendance centres from twelve years to ten years.

9 The Kilbrandon Committee (1964) in Scotland reached a similar conclusion based on similar reasoning.

10 We have not considered in this article the validity of this approach and the sizeable volume of evidence against it. For a discussion of this see D. May (1971).

11 The Labour Party were also committed to a reorganization of the social services. A review was subsequently carried out by the Seebohm Committee (1968) and its recommendations were enacted in the Local Authority Social Services Act 1971.

12 Although both Ingleby and Donninson and Stewart emphasized the effective social control of delinquency, they differed radically in their methods. Ingleby felt that this would enable the law to be 'tougher'; Donninson and Stewart saw it as a way of meeting individual needs.

13 Crosland in using the term 'secondary poverty' goes on:

> If our present rate of economic growth continues, material want and poverty and deprivation of essential goods will cease to be a problem. We shall increasingly need to focus attention, not on universal categories, but on individual persons and families: not on economic causes of distress, but on the social and psychological causes.
>
> We shall want advice, not of the economist, but of psychiatrists, sociologists, and social psychologists. We shall rely less on broad sweeping measures of expenditure than on concentrated measures of aid to limited groups, based on patient, empirical social research into the real nature of the need. And the aid will often take the form, not of cash payments, nor even of material provision in kind, but of individual therapy, casework and preventive treatment (1963, 96).

14 According to Milton Friedman:
Freedom is a tenable object only for responsible individuals. We do not believe in freedom of madmen or children. The necessity of drawing a line between responsible individuals and others is inescapable, yet it means that there is an essential ambiguity in our ultimate objective of freedom. Paternalism is inescapable for those whom we designate not responsible (1962, 33).

15 For example, abolition of the terms 'conviction' and 'sentence', restrictions on reporting and physical separation from the adult court.

16 It is interesting that this did not happen during the debates on the Social Work (Scotland) Act 1968 which gave effect to the recommendation of the Kilbrandon Committee to abolish the juvenile courts and to replace them with welfare tribunals.

17 A Conservative Government replaced the Labour one in 1970.

18 See, for example, NAPO and the Children and Young Persons' Bill; *Justice of the Peace*, 1969, 133, 296–7; and The Children and Young Persons' Bill, *The Magistrate*, 1969, 35, 48–9.

19 Our conclusion must, of course, be tentative as a detailed statistical study of the impact of the Act would need to involve time series analysis controlling for changes in population structure, juvenile crime rates and other possible explanations for lack of change.

20 A similar conflict seems to be developing in the operation of the Social Work (Scotland) Act (May, D., 1977, 209–27).

21 The National Council for Civil Liberties, for example, felt that 'the roots of juvenile crime and thus measures to combat it are to be found in the social and physical environment. Handicaps such as bad housing; poor planning; schools; lack of opportunities for acceptable achievements; opportunity for crime against property; social institutions such as the welfare services, etc., require urgent attention.'

22 The Police Federation, for example, disagreed in principle with sections 4 and 5 and stated 'although we recognize there are sociological causes for crime and especially juvenile crime we are fundamentally concerned with the protection of the public, the prevention of crime, and the detection of offenders. Our concern in the treatment of offenders is therefore considered in the light of the above principles.'

23 The British Association of Social Workers suggested that the 'Act provides a legal structure for dealing with juvenile delinquency which is both enlightened and appropriate without substantial amendment'.

24 The Magistrates' Association, for example, stated that 'the Act sought broadly to substitute care and treatment for punishment of young offenders. For most of them this has worked quite well. For a minority of tough sophisticated young criminals (and some youths of fifteen and sixteen are strong young men) it has been disastrous. They prey on the community at will, even after courts have placed them in care.

They deride the powerlessness of the courts to do anything effective. They are encouraged to become criminals. The essential problem is therefore to provide the courts with greater powers and facilities where they are clearly needed for persistent young offenders.'

25 Such reasoning in relation to the 'minority' can be seen in appeals to the Court of Appeal against orders made under S. 53 of the Children and Young Persons Act 1933. In *R. v H*. (4418/B/76 21 October 1976) such an order was upheld because 'we think there is a real danger that he might become – in due time – a professional criminal'.

   In *R. v B*. (4673/R/73, 17 December 1973) a S. 53 order was upheld on the basis of his 'emotional instability, aggression and unpredictability' and made indefinite because 'none of the experts [gave] any sort of indication that a particular period of years can in this case be chosen to ensure that the public can be properly protected'.

26 Indeed in *R. v D*. (3894/B/76 20 October 1976) the Court of Appeal sanctioned the making of a borstal order instead of a care order (which was acknowledged to be a more suitable alternative) because '. . . it is not in the public interest that this youth should be roaming the streets just as he likes'. The case is notable for judicial criticisms of the administrative discretion and 'bureaucratic machinery' of local authorities dealing with delinquents subject to care orders.

27 Social workers are not the only group to have adopted this stance. A Howard League working party (1977) on secure accommodation unquestioningly accepted the need for such control strategies. A similar situation seems to be developing in relation to intermediate treatment. Spencer Millham is quoted in Community Care (1977) as advising social workers that 'control must be stressed and made visible in order "to sell" an intermediate treatment programme'.

28 One reaction to this has been the development of radical social work but, as Cohen (1975) shows, what this does for the here and now remains problematic.

Chapter 2

The Social Work Role in Juvenile Court Proceedings

Elwyn Owens

The history and role of the probation service are important in the consideration of the contribution of the local authority social worker to juvenile court proceedings. Since 1908 probation officers have been able to carve out for themselves a sense of identity and territory in respect of most courts. Their position has been reinforced repeatedly by legislation, by their own distinguished performance, and by their links with magistrates through local probation committees. In contrast, while local authority social workers have extensive responsibilities and access to various resources, their main connections with justices is when they provide a professional service to the court. The architects of the Children and Young Persons Act 1969 recognized quite properly that those working with offenders should have available a wide range of community and residential resources, and at the time it appeared that this could best be achieved through the facilities available in the then children's departments, spearheaded by child care officers. That children at risk of injury or neglect, children in care, and young offenders have basically the same social needs and should be provided for in similar ways was the cornerstone of the 1969 Act and it had several important implications. It reflected, in law at least, a shift of emphasis from the offence to the offender and gave to the local authority responsibilities in respect of the juvenile court which had belonged previously to the probation service. The tide of genericism in social services and a series of reorganizations within local government added to and confused the problems of the social worker as he began to undertake new roles in relation to the juvenile court and the children and young persons with whom it dealt.

Social services departments and their social workers have been criticized heavily for what is interpreted by some as their failure in dealing with young people in trouble, and there has been a significant decline in the number of court decisions which contain a social work element and an increase in those which have a punitive or custodial intention. These are also indicators of the formidable opposition to the spirit of the 1969 Act in the non-implementation of many important clauses and the failure of central government to provide financial help to ensure that local authorities have the proper means to care for and control young offenders. The raising of the age of criminal responsibility, first to twelve and then to fourteen, the phasing out of detention centres and attendance centres and lowering of the age of committal for borstal training and the introduction of more flexible methods of care and control are all provided for in law but not operating in practice. In addition, and probably the pivot of the whole package, are the compulsory consultation between police and local authorities before prosecution: and the emphasis on young offenders appearing before the court through care proceedings.

The social work contribution to juvenile court proceedings must be understood against this background and be seen as part of the whole of what the social worker and his department can offer in response to youngsters in trouble. It is also important to perceive social work in this field in a wider context. Those who appear before a juvenile court will generally belong to the lower streams of comprehensive schools and the income level of their families will normally be below the average industrial wage. Circumstances leading to court appearances are closely related to social and material factors as well as to emotional and family disturbance and sometimes what a social worker can provide can be an effective and helpful response. However, especially where serious economic and cultural factors are dominant, to expect change through social work intervention is to expect the impossible. What those who appear in juvenile courts have a right to expect and, within the spirit of the 1969 Act, what courts have a duty to provide, is a response which is pertinent to the personal needs and special circumstances of the offender or the juvenile in need of care or control. For the social worker and his client the court hearing may be a step on the way through a lengthy and potentially helpful relationship or sometimes it is just the focal point of a brief professional encounter.

The reduction of the complex dilemmas that exist for the social worker in the juvenile court to a straight conflict between 'welfare' and 'justice' is too simple because it does not, for instance, acknowledge how he can, and does, contribute to social control. His role in connection with delinquency contains elements of 'justice' which is linked to social rehabilitation; general 'welfare' provision, including family work and work with the community;

'treatment' occasionally requiring him to undertake therapy; and 'negotiation', putting the worker in the position of a broker or advocate on behalf of his client. Social work practice and the conceptual framework which underpins it should allow for the integration and legitimization of all these roles even though this is often made very difficult by the way in which juvenile courts are operated.

In Scotland (see chapter 3) the social work function seems to fit more easily into the 'panels' system of juvenile justice. The 'reporter' takes into account information he receives from the police authority, the social worker, and others if necessary, before deciding whether he should require a child to attend a hearing of the panel. Any dispute about 'guilt' is referred to the Sheriff's court for judicial decision, and the interest of the panel, to which the social worker contributes, is the decision about how to deal with a child or young person. Involvement with parents and other adults significant to the child is provided for, and in comparison the system in England and Wales, which can reduce children and parents to a state of apathy, seems anachronistic.

Throughout his work with juveniles the social worker has to combine within himself a sound knowledge of the law and court procedure, an appreciation of the role and function of his agency and its implications for his client, skills in applying these and the capacity to deal sensitively and knowledgeably with the responses and needs of those with whom he works. In addition he should have some theoretical understanding of both delinquency and of the court process.

He is a figure of authority and he must be clear about what is required of him. He must be competent to undertake the task and have come to terms with the ambivalence involved in the exercise of authority. He has to be able to act confidently both on his own behalf and often as a representative of his employing agency, and the extent to which he possesses personal strength and professional confidence will determine his ability to accept the various roles which are required of him. The social worker who is competent and unruffled in court is a support to his client. His professional presentation and performance 'on stage' are important, and what he has to offer in a court need not be modelled on any of the other professions within the legal system.

Most appearances in juvenile court are dealt with under the provisions of the Children and Young Persons Act 1969 and the Children Acts of 1948 and 1975. The legislation from 1933 to 1969 defines a child as a person under fourteen, and a young person as an individual aged fourteen who has not attained his seventeenth birthday, though there may be exceptions to this. The nature of the social work component and the role of the social worker are closely tied up with the function of the agency and the reason for the proceedings. Each worker brings to his role something which is personal and individual although he always acts as a representative of the local authority by whom is employed. As well as exhibiting a facet of the distinction between the terms of reference of a local authority social worker and of a probation officer, this highlights the social worker as part of a large organization to whose resources he has access, and which he sometimes represents in litigation. These roles are not new for the local authority social worker though some of them have to be seen in the juvenile court in a fresh perspective. For instance in respect of children up to the age of thirteen, and in some areas in respect of young persons up to seventeen, the primary roles as reporter and supervisor are being undertaken in the court by social workers whereas previously the work was done by probation officers. Social workers contribute to the court in a series of roles, and the court settings referred to in this chapter illustrate that in his work he can be 'litigant', 'reporter', or 'supervisor'. It is very apparent that these roles are interactive and although it is helpful to divide them for the purpose of description in practice they often run alongside each other.

The social worker as litigant

In name it is not the social worker who takes the legal action but in fact it is he who is usually most heavily involved in a departmental decision to do so. Legal proceedings (i.e. litigation) are initiated in the name of the director of social services and in most authorities there are specialist administrators and solicitors in this field on whose expertise social workers rely and through whom they work. It is interesting to consider whether this hierarchical organization affects a social worker's practice especially when he fulfils the roles of supervisor or reporter. Legislation specifies that reports should be prepared by, and supervision be undertaken by, a probation officer or by the 'local authority'.

Care proceedings and place of safety orders
Had the 1969 Act been fully implemented all children up to the age of fourteen who appear before a juvenile court would do so because they were in need of 'care or control'. This would mean

that there would only be proceedings if the person authorized to take them had clearly decided that there were no alternative ways of ensuring that the child or young person might receive care or control. This would have required the implementation of those sections of the Act which effectively raise the age of criminal responsibility and compel consultation between local authority social services department and police authorities before bringing a child or young person to court.

Care proceedings are started when voluntary means of helping a child and his family have failed or they are deemed quite impossible to achieve. They begin, sometimes, when a social worker decides to apply to a Justice of the Peace for a place of safety order which empowers the local authority to detain a child or young person in a place of safety for a period not exceeding twenty-eight days. The application may be made at any time though in some areas there are local guidelines which stipulate that the application should be made to the juvenile court, when it is in session, or to particular magistrates who may be approached out of office hours. An officer of the NSPCC has the right to apply for a similar twenty-eight-day order or a police constable may arrange for the detention of a child for a period of only eight days. In the case of detention by a police officer the case must be enquired into by an officer not below the rank of inspector. In all cases the law makes it clear that the parent or guardian must be informed of the detention and the reasons for it.

Place of safety orders are used usually in emergency situations and for that reason require special attention and skill. Children of all ages are bewildered by sudden change especially when it follows their removal by a stranger to an unfamiliar environment and their parents may well be overwhelmed by a sense of guilt and sometimes rage. The acknowledging and facing of the feelings of all these involved demand of the social worker a special kind of courage. He must be able to select the place of safety which will be most suitable to the needs of the child at the time, be it foster home, children's home or hospital. He has to share information with and respond to the feelings of the child and those who will assume his care. Of special importance is the return of the worker to the parents as soon as possible after the child is moved. There will be times when this may require bravery of physical proportions, but if theories of crisis intervention have any relevance then it is at such times that they are valid. Sometimes the company of a colleague or in some instances another member of the child's family who knows and accepts all that has happened, can be helpful.

Within twenty-eight days of the making of the place of safety order or the eight days in the case of a police order, a decision must be made by the local authority or the NSPCC on whether to proceed with care proceedings. The proper context for such a decision is within a case conference to which any professional agency to which the child or young person or his family is known is invited. Such conferences are now a matter of course following reports of non-accidental injury. It is at this point that particular attention is required to decide how help can best be offered to the child and his family and the court proceedings, if taken, should be seen as part of a strategy in achieving this end. The child, if he is old enough, and his parents should be told about any case conference and often it will be of considerable long-term value if they are allowed to attend, at least for part of the time.

Often, before the full hearing of the case, application is made to the juvenile court for an interim order because unless such an order is obtained the local authority cannot detain the child beyond twenty-eight days. Detailed presentation of evidence is not required for an interim care order, which may also extend for twenty-eight days, but the local authority should be able to show that there is a case to answer. The order requires the authority to bring the child or young person before the court on the expiration of the order or at such earlier time as the court may require. If the child is under five or evidence is produced that he is ill then the court need not require his attendance.

Care proceedings may also be instituted in circumstances where there has been no place of safety order. The local authority social services department institutes the proceedings and therefore a social worker should be acquainted with cases brought in this way. Children who appear before the juvenile court because of their failure to attend school do so after consultation between the education and social services departments of the local authority.

All care proceedings are brought to the court under the provisions of section 1 of the Children and Young Persons Act 1969 and the requirement in all instances is to show that two conditions apply. Before applying for a place of safety order the social worker, whose name will be on the order, must have reasonable grounds for believing that the same two conditions apply. They are:

1 *The primary condition* The court must be satisfied that
   (i) the child's development is being avoidably prevented or

neglected; his health is being avoidably impaired or
neglected, or he is being ill-treated;

(ii) that similar conditions to those indicated above have been
proved in respect of another child in the same household;

(iii) he is exposed to moral danger;

(iv) he is beyond the control of his parent or guardian;

(v) he is truanting when of compulsory school age;

(vi) he is guilty of an offence in law, excluding homicide.

These are a summary of section 1 (2) (a)–(f) of the Act and their
precise wording is important.

2 *The care or control condition*   The court must be satisfied that the
child or young person is in need of care or control which he is
unlikely to receive unless the court makes an order. Evidence
may be heard from several sources, although it is no longer
normal practice to make parents give evidence against their own
children. The Children and Young Persons Act 1963 sought to
prevent this happening and evidence about the behaviour of a
child or young person is frequently given by the social worker. It
will be helpful practice for the social worker to prepare two
documents for such a hearing, one which is a summary of his
notes and the basis of his evidence, and the other the social
enquiry report which assists the court in its decision about
disposal, after the two conditions have been applied and the case
proved. The social enquiry report is not admissible as evidence
for the care or control test. At this stage in care proceedings the
social worker assumes the role of 'reporter' and provides a
written report to assist the court in its decision. The court has the
power to make a care order, a supervision order, an order that
requires the parents to enter into recognizance to take proper
care and control of their child or it may also make orders under
the Mental Health Act 1959 or the Guardianship Act 1973.

Variation and discharge of supervision orders

The variation and discharge of a supervision order is a course of
action which is always open for a social worker to consider
(section 15, Children and Young Persons Act 1969). After the
implementation of the Criminal Law Act 1977 (section 37) the
litigation procedure will be different in those cases where a
supervision order was made following care proceedings from

those which follow a court appearance for an offence. In respect of supervision orders made after care proceedings the social worker must provide evidence to the court that the application for a change in the original order 'is appropriate' and the court may then:

1 Cancel any particular requirements included in the order;
2 Insert a particular requirement, e.g. a condition of residence;
3 Extend the order beyond the subject's eighteenth birthday;
4 Make a care order and discharge of supervision order;
5 Discharge the supervision order.

A department which brings these proceedings should send a notice to the Clerk of the court. Also it should send copies of the notice, including the date, the place, the time and the purpose, to the 'relevant infant' unless because of his age and understanding this appears to be inappropriate, to the parent or guardian, and to the local authority and the probation service where appropriate, to secure their attendance. Magistrates have the power, on the application of the supervising officer, to issue a summons to secure the attendance of the supervised person and if he fails to attend a warrant for his arrest. The proceedings are initiated by the local authority, and the social worker's tasks, having made the decision to take legal action, are to provide his professional colleagues, solicitors or administrators with all the relevant information, and to inform the child or young person of his intentions.

The effect such notices have on the people involved and their response to the court proceedings will vary and to a large extent will be determined by the way in which the matter is dealt with by the social worker. It should be handled in a way which allows the supervised person and his family to talk about feelings to do with authority, which can pose problems for people who appear in court. It will require sensitive skill to face a client or group of clients so that they can perceive in the social worker both the firmness of an authority figure and the warmth of someone who is concerned. A notice or summons should never come to the client as a bolt out of the blue, and should always be preceded by careful and thorough explanation of all the reasons for the particular course of action.

The Criminal Law Act 1977 will considerably strengthen the terms of supervision orders made in respect of offenders and will affect social work practice. (Section 37 amends section 12 of the Children and Young Persons Act 1969.) Stipulations about the behaviour and the authority of the supervisor will sharpen the focus for social work intervention. They will provide an opportunity, which has actually been available but not used, for workers to set clear goals in their work with delinquents, one of which may be the early discharge of the order. The change brings supervision orders for offenders more or less into line with probation orders for adults, and as well as making possible clearer contracts between workers and clients, it may be that magistrates will have more confidence in social workers who have the responsibility of supervising within the terms of the stronger conditions.

Application for the variation or discharge of a care order

The implications and problems which social workers may face as a result of applying for a variation of a care order were dealt with thoroughly by the report into the care and supervision of Maria Colwell. Some changes, particularly in respect of a child's right to individual representation in a court, have occurred as a result of that report. These are incorporated in the Children Act 1975 and they are dealt with in detail in chapter 4. A care order gives, most crucially, to a local authority the right to decide where a child or young person should reside, and this includes the right to allow that child or young person to live with his own family or with relatives if this is thought to be in his best interests. What becomes the issue is the basic philosophy of a social services department and its workers, and the balance between the rescuing and protection of children at risk on the one hand, and the promotion of family life particularly by supporting vulnerable families on the other. Decisions to return home children who are the subject of care orders should not be taken lightly nor by individual social workers. Most departments have established administrative procedures whereby decisions to return a child or young person who is the subject of a care order 'home on trial' can only be made by a case conference and thereby become a departmental decision. Sometimes the delicacy of the issues involved shows up bureaucratic and legal processes in a very mechanistic light. All children need individual respect and care from competent adults, an environment conducive to their emotional, physical, social and intellectual development, and individual attention which shows respect for unique identity. Any decision that a child in care should be returned to natural parents should be made in the light of a constellation of such factors many of which may change in shade or degree each day. In cases where the care order was made following an appearance in court for an offence this should also be taken into consideration. A crucial element in the decision is the ability of the social worker in the community and the residential setting, to perceive sensitively and evaluate the significance of each one of the issues involved. The likelihood is that, as in the case of Maria Colwell, applications from the local authorities for the revocation of a care order will only be made after a period of 'home trial'.

The procedure is basically similar to the one used in the variation of the discharge of supervision orders. It is another occasion when the social worker will be acting in the court both as 'litigant' and as 'reporter' and it will be helpful to make this distinction in practice. It is the worker's task to produce for the court grounds for the variation or discharge of the order, and then, after the grounds have been established, to produce a written report to help the court to make a decision. The court may discharge the order, or, providing the child or young person has not attained the age of eighteen, make a supervision order. This returns fundamental rights to the natural parents, though the supervision order would retain for the social worker the right to maintain contact with the family.

Appeal against the assumption of parental rights

A power vested in local authorities involves them in assuming the parental rights of one or more parent in respect of their children, providing the children are already in care under a voluntary agreement. In England, and Wales, but not in Northern Ireland, this profound step can be taken without reference to court. A hearing only takes place if either parent appeals within a month of receiving the notice of the resolution of the local authority committee. It may well be an important part of the social worker's task to see that parents are enabled to take the case to court. If such an appeal is lodged then it is the local authority which, as the litigant, institutes the proceedings within fourteen days. There is no need for the children to appear before the court in these hearings and the law governing such cases is now contained in section 57 of the Children Act 1975 which incorporates and supersedes Sections 2 of the Children Act 1948.

Broadly the grounds relate to factors concerning the parents, and in this way they contrast with care proceedings which in general require evidence about the child or young person. In summary the grounds for assuming parental rights are:

1 The death of parents, guardian or custodian.
2 The abandonment of the child.
3 The suffering by the parent or guardian of a permanent disability rendering him incapable of caring for the child.
4 The suffering by the parent or guardian from a mental disorder within the meaning of the Mental Health Act 1959 which renders him incapable of caring for the child.
5 The parents being of such habits and mode of life as to be unfit to have the care of the child.
6 The parent having so failed, without reasonable cause, to discharge the obligations of a parent as to be unfit to have care of the child.
7 A parental rights order may be obtained where a resolution was already in force in relation to one parent of the child who is likely to become a member of the household comprising the child and his other parent.
8 That through the three years preceding the passing of the resolution the child has been in the care of the local authority or a voluntary agency.

These last two grounds are new and contained within the 1975 Children Act which further breaks new ground by providing for voluntary agencies to apply for the parental rights in respect of children in their care.

If any of these conditions apply in respect of children in its care the local authority may serve a notice on the natural parents of the children involved, assuming the parental rights of the children. The decision is a profound one with far reaching implications. Although it is one in which the social worker has particular responsibilities, especially in involving the child and the parents in what is taking place, the responsibility for the decision rests with the local authority or the agency. This usually means a case conference involving all who know the child and his family and then a formal resolution by the relevant committee. It is notice of this resolution which is sent to the parents, who have the right of appeal as long as their intention to appeal is lodged within twenty-eight days with the authority which passed the resolution. Once the intention to appeal is received it is for the local authority or voluntary agency to institute the hearing before the juvenile court. The proceedings in the court can be very distressing. Cast in the role of litigant and 'witness for the prosecution' many social workers find it hard to reconcile their attempts to work with parents with taking a course of action which sometimes seems to condemn the people they are trying to help. Nonetheless, such a course of action is important because of the protection it affords to some children for whose care the local authority has the responsibility. Providing the social worker is secure within himself and in his own role, the experience is one which can be used constructively for the parents as well as for the child. The social worker must explain to the parents their rights of appeal and to legal aid. Sometimes the occasion provides an opportunity to review with parents their own relationship with their child and for exploring with a child his feelings about his natural parents. It is a time for making plans which include all those involved, and which are sufficiently flexible to respond to any significant changes which may arise in the future.

Application for removal into the penal system
Fundamental to the thinking behind much welfare legislation is the principle that the community should accept the responsibility and find ways of coping with its deviants. It therefore strikes at the root of the sound intention of the 1969 Act for social workers to have to implement one of the two clauses, 23 (2) and 31, which allow application to be made to a juvenile court to remove a young person from local authority care into a remand centre, prison or borstal. Apart from the dangerous 'thin end of the wedge' type implication which goes with these clauses the issue is occasionally one of insufficient resources, in which the social worker, and, more unfortunately, his client, are reduced to being pawns in an argument between local and central government. At issue too may be the adequacy of the regard accorded by local authorities to residential staff in their care of young people who are extremely difficult to look after in any setting. It is propounding the obvious that there should be sufficient skilled and well-supported staff at those points in residential care where they are most needed.

Within this context a social worker, on behalf of his local authority, may be involved in a juvenile court in an application for one of the following orders:

1 An order for a young person to be remanded, pending trial for an offence, to a remand centre, or, if the court has not been notified that a remand centre is available, to a prison. For such an order to be granted, evidence must be provided for the court that the young person is of 'so unruly a character

that he cannot safely be committed to the care of the local authority' on remand. A decision to apply for such an order cannot be taken by an individual social worker but must be the corporate responsibility of a department.

2 Section 31 of the 1969 Act allows a local authority, with the consent of the Secretary of State, to apply to a juvenile court for the removal to borstal of a young person of fifteen or over. Before making such an order the court will require evidence of the consent of the Secretary of State and evidence that the young person's behaviour is such that it will be 'detrimental to other persons in any community home' for him to be accommodated there.

It usually falls to the social worker to be in court with the child or young person on such occasions and to prepare him and his family for what is happening and to be the link between all those involved.

The social worker as reporter

Before disposing of a case magistrates in the juvenile court must take into consideration such information about the child or young person's 'general conduct, home surroundings, school record and medical history'. Though he lacks the probation officer's traditional links with the judiciary the social worker is aware of the provisions, particularly within the local authority, available for delinquents. He assumes this role at some stage in almost every case which appears before a juvenile court, and in criminal proceedings it is often his only contribution.

Social workers in criminal proceedings
Many more children and young persons than was intended by the Children and Young Persons Act 1969 appear before the court for offences. The intention of the Act was that social work intervention diverting offenders from the courts would occur at an early stage, so that prosecutions would take place only after there had been consultation between police authorities and local authority social services departments. As it is, however, while most police authorities have juvenile liaison schemes, there is very little evidence of social workers being involved with offenders as early as was intended by the Act.

Juvenile courts, although they operate within the rules laid out by the Magistrates' Courts (Children and Young Offenders) Rules 1970, are a model of what was intended for the adult offender. Hearings in respect of offences are two-sided affairs consisting of the prosecution and the defence. The proceedings could not be designed more effectively to inhibit the ability of children and young persons and their families to participate and to restrict social work participation to that of an afterthought.

As 'reporter', the social worker must provide information for the magistrates to help them decide about the disposal of the case, and this requires interviews with the child or young person and the family before the hearing. On his first contact with the family he should offer general assistance, ascertain the 'plea intention' and only prepare a report if there is a clear intention to plead guilty. In all instances, despite being distinct from the probation service, the social worker is identified with the judicial system and is in fact one of the servants of the court and his report part of the judicial proceedings. The report may contain a recommendation which should follow logically from the description of the offender, his domestic circumstances and personal history, and it should also take account of the offence or offences which have been committed and the attitudes towards the offence. The range of options which magistrates have available in their decisions about offenders are much more extensive than those in care proceedings. Broadly they are:

1 A binding-over of the parents, with their consent.
2 The binding-over of the offender, with his consent.
3 Absolute or conditional discharge.
4 Hospital or guardianship order where the provisions of the Mental Health Act 1959 apply.
5 Fine, compensation up to £400, or the restitution of property. Fines and compensation may be payable by the parent or guardian (though in fact fines levied on children and young persons are very difficult to enforce as there is at present no effective sanction in the event of non-payment).
6 Attendance centre order. It may be made for twenty-four or thirty-six hours, requiring a child or young person to attend a centre on Saturday afternoons, thus depriving him of his liberty for two hours a week. Such centres are run by the police authority and the child is usually required to involve himself in a range of activities requiring manual effort and physical skill. Such centres should not be more than ten

miles or forty-five minutes travelling time from the home of the young offender.

7 Detention centre order. The minimum age is fourteen and attendance centre and detention centre orders may only be used when the offence is punishable with imprisonment. Both are part of the penal system and not administered by the local authority. The intention of the 1969 Act was that they should both be phased out and replaced by supervision orders in which were inserted specific conditions which, used imaginatively, would contribute to the diversion of the offender from crime. A juvenile court can only commit to detention centre when there is a vacancy and consequently there are occasions when young persons are recommended for borstal sentence or given other sentences 'by default' and not as the first choice of the justices. Detention centre orders are for three or six months and there is a twelve-month period of after care which is usually undertaken by the probation service. If the young person is the subject of a care order and providing he is under eighteen when he is discharged from detention centre local authorities may undertake after care instead. Before a detention centre order is made a court must ensure that a young offender has legal aid or that he has the opportunity to have it.

8 Borstal training. Juvenile courts can commit to the Crown Court with the recommendation for borstal training. The minimum age is still fifteen years as Section 7 (1) of the 1969 Act is not in force. Again the court must ensure that the offender has legal aid or the opportunity of having it.

9 Deferment of sentence. Under the Criminal Justice Act 1972 (section 22) a juvenile court may defer sentence for a period of up to six months without making a remand order.

10 Deprivation of property. The Criminal Justice Act 1972 (section 23) enables the court to deprive an offender of property which has been used or was intended to be used for criminal purposes.

11 A supervision order. The order is made for a specific period of up to three years and in criminal proceedings the period may extend beyond the eighteenth birthday. The responsibility for supervision is undertaken by the local authority where the child or young person resides in all cases for children up to the age of thirteen. Where there is local agreement with the probation service some local authorities supervise young persons up to the age of seventeen. The

duties of the supervisor are to advise, assist and befriend the supervised person (section 14, 1969 Act). Probation officers are subject to the Probation Rules 1965 which specify the records to be kept, the need to explain the order, the frequency of visiting, enquiry as to progress at school, the use of voluntary and other facilities and reference to the case committee and to the court. No such provisions bind local authority social workers though some authorities have produced their own guidelines. The purpose of the order is not stated in the Act, nor in its guide, but the implication is that it should create an opportunity for a relationship with the supervised person in which the supervision may 'bring to bear influences which are not punitive but will discourage further offences'. Reference has already been made to the Criminal Law Act 1977 (S37) which amends the provisions of the 1969 Act in respect of supervision orders. Offenders who are the subject of such orders are required to be 'of good behaviour' and comply with such conditions as the court may lay down 'for the purpose of preventing the commission of further offences' and supervisors are provided with grounds for bringing their clients back before the magistrates on the evidence of their behaviour and not just their needs.

12 A supervision order which includes specific requirements (section 12 of the 1969 Act). These requirements may be:
    (i) a condition to live with a specified person, providing the specified person agrees;
    (ii) a condition to comply with certain directions of the supervisor:
        (a) To live at a specified place for not more than ninety days within the first year.
        (b) To present himself at a certain place as and when specified by the supervisor.
        (c) To take part in activities as and when specified by the supervisor.

Each of these requirements refers of course to 'intermediate treatment', a term which does not itself appear within the Act, but the arrangements must be approved by the Regional Planning Committee of the Department of Health and Social Security. The local authority bears the cost and the periods of residence may not exceed ninety days. It was the intention of the 1969 Act that supervision orders within these conditions

should replace detention centre and attendance centre
orders.

(iii) Medical treatment, providing, on medical evidence, the
court deems it necessary. The consent of a person over
fourteen is required.

13 A care order. Such an order can only be made in criminal
proceedings if the offence is punishable in the case of an
adult by imprisonment. The effect of these orders is to
convey to the local authority such powers as the parent or
guardian would otherwise have. There are limits to these
powers. The child or young person cannot be brought up in
a religious creed other than that in which he would have
been brought up apart from the order. The local authority
cannot consent to adoption, marriage or emigration. The
local authority can restrict the freedom of the child and
decide where and with whom he should reside.

14 Remand to the care of the local authority. Courts may make
an order for up to twenty-eight days which gives local
authorities in effect the same rights that they have through a
care order. Such an order requires the local authority to
produce the child either in a juvenile court or a higher court
for sentence. The order presupposes that the court has not
yet reached a finding of guilt or decided on disposal.
Sometimes the period, providing guilt has been established,
may be used to obtain medical reports or to enable social
workers to make particular enquiries which will be of
assistance to the court.

Despite the arguments to the contrary, the powers of the juvenile
court in respect of young offenders are extensive and varied. They
are an inconsistent mixture of 'punitive' and 'therapeutic'
measures reflecting an ambivalent rather than a consistent
underlying philosophy.

The social worker as supervisor

Social work supervision is not confined to a relationship within the
terms of a supervision order made following care or criminal
proceedings. It includes supervision within the framework of a
care order and any voluntary intervention which takes place
without recourse to legal process. It is the most influential of the
social worker's roles and possibly the most important. It is cer-

tainly the role in which he has been most vulnerable to criticism. What is at stake is the precise nature of social work supervision provided by local authority and its credibility in the courts. The House of Commons Expenditure Committee (Cmnd. 6494) commented that 'at least at present, the probation service is better experienced and better equipped to deal with delinquency than local authority social workers.' (para. 35). So far social workers have not been able to demonstrate convincingly how the supervision they can offer can, when undertaken imaginatively and backed by adequate resources through the local authority, be effective for young delinquents. The same committee endorsed the need for some specialized response and the development of intermediate treatment schemes within social service departments and in so doing it expressed its support for the future development of supervision of delinquents being undertaken by social workers. A doubt that some people appear to have is that supervision offered by social workers does not contain an adequate element of social control, and experience of local authority workers being seen to be effective in this respect will be the best way of meeting such a challenge.

The social worker on the defensive

The two most notable occasions when the social worker is on the defensive in juvenile court are:

1 When there is an application for the revocation of a care order (1969 Act S21 (2)). A parent or guardian does not have the right to apply for a revocation but does so on behalf of the child who is technically the litigant. In some cases the provisions of S64 of the Children Act 1975 may apply and these are dealt with in chapter 4.

2 When a parent applies for the rescission of a parental rights resolution (Children Act 1948 S4). This applies in instances where parents failed to lodge their intention to appeal within the statutory twenty-eight days of receiving the notice. Parents are the litigants and have the right to legal aid.

That a social worker should be required in a juvenile court to justify the stand that he and his department take, and that he should be forced on to the defensive before a court, is proper. In fact the social worker should take pains to ensure that those with whom he is involved and particularly those over whom he or his authority has power should know their right of appeal. For some adults, and for children, to have a social worker who can maintain links and a relationship while going through such proceedings will be an important and sometimes helpful experience.

Defensiveness of a different kind seems to be at present the most distinctive characteristic of the local authority social worker in juvenile court proceedings and it is most explicable and apparent in criminal proceedings. To a great extent it seems to stem from the attitudes of other professionals in the arena and their failure to be convinced of the value of the social work contribution. The 1969 Act heralded the potential of this contribution but owing to political compromise, social ambivalence and an economic recession, social workers have not been able to demonstrate adequately, especially to magistrates, either the effectiveness of their skills or the value of having access to a range of resources which can be used flexibly. Social workers can respond to those who appear in court individually, and where necessary with authority and firmness. The House of Commons Expenditure Committee and policy statements and guidelines from BASW show a firm commitment to the retention of the present legal system and of the opportunities for social workers in this field to be creative. The Personal Social Service Council and the National Children's Bureau in their publications confirm the potential for social work with troubled teenagers. It is to be hoped that a revival of the nineteen sixties debate about children, families, young offenders and courts, will see and perhaps precipitate a reaffirmation of faith in social work as a means of intervention in this field and an improvement and sharpening of focus in its practice. To achieve this social workers and the local authorities which employ them need to be enabled and allowed to move from their defensive position to one in which their practice proves their worth in the juvenile court setting.

Chapter 3

The Social Work Role in Scottish Juvenile Justice

Donald Dickie

This chapter on the Scottish children's hearing system is intended
to serve as an introduction for social workers and social work
students. In discussion of the social work role in the system it will
be argued that effective social work with children who may never
appear at hearings is as vital to the success of the system as work
with those who do. It is also the writer's intention to highlight
some of the dilemmas, challenges and areas of conflict which
confront the social worker in Scotland who is concerned with
children in trouble.

Before the structure and operation of the system are described,
reference is made to its historical roots and to some of the more
controversial aspects of its underlying principles.

Historical perspectives

Examination of the changes in approach to children in trouble
during this century suggests that the children's hearing system is
not revolutionary but rather a bold development of ideas which
have had currency for a long time.

The Children Act of 1908 applied to Scotland as well as England
and provided for the setting up of a juvenile court system directed
primarily towards education and reform rather than the
punishment of children. However, the Morton Committee of 1928
noted that the Scottish Sheriff and Burgh Courts were still the
venue for most proceedings against children. Within a few years
Scottish legislation of the 1930s made possible the setting up of
specially constituted juvenile courts to be presided over by Justices
of the Peace. But when the Kilbrandon Committee reported in
1964 only four of these special courts had come into operation.[1]
Most children still appeared in any one of the other three types of
Scottish court and there was no uniformity of approach.

Several conclusions emerged from the Committee's deliberations. First, that deprived and delinquent children had similar needs and should be treated on that basis. Secondly, that courts were equipped to adjudicate upon disputed facts but not to determine the most appropriate treatment for children. It followed that 'all juveniles under sixteen should in principle be removed from the jurisdiction of criminal courts; instead, juvenile panels should have powers . . . to order special measures of education and training according to the needs of the juvenile concerned'. The Sheriff Court would retain only its functions of deciding in appeals and in matters of disputed fact. It was estimated that facts would be disputed in only 5 per cent of cases. All referrals to the panel would be at the instance of a single independent official, 'the reporter', and the panel's executive arm would be a new 'social education department'.

A Government White Paper of 1966[2] accepted Kilbrandon's panel recommendations but advocated a new integrated 'social work department' as the matching professional field organization. Another new element in the White Paper was the concept of community involvement. Whereas Kilbrandon's criteria for panel membership had been couched in terms of personal suitability, the White Paper sought the recruitment of members 'from a wide variety of occupations, neighbourhood, age groups and income groups' who would have 'a personal knowledge of the community to which the child belongs'.

Most of the principal recommendations of the Kilbrandon Committee as modified by the White Paper were embodied in Part III of the Social Work (Scotland) Act 1968. This Act also established integrated local authority social work departments which encompassed the functions of the former child care, probation, health and welfare service departments. The new departments' duties in relation to the children's hearing system were therefore but one part of their overall responsibility for the promotion of social welfare. They became operational from 1969 but Part III of the Act was not implemented until 15 April 1971.

Philosophical and theoretical issues

The Kilbrandon approach to juvenile justice relied heavily on a medical model in which delinquency and deprivation were seen as pathological problems to be tackled by a diagnostic-treatment agency responding to individual needs. This was reflected in the Social Work (Scotland) Act 1968 which requires that decisions be taken 'in the best interests of the child' who is 'in need of compulsory measures of care' (Section 43). The lack of explicit reference to the control of delinquency may be interpreted as a commitment to a 'welfare' rather than a 'social control' ideology. It has been suggested, however, that this commitment is in rhetoric rather than in reality in that offences, and therefore social control, are still central to referral and hearing decisions (May 1977).

Critics of the welfare approach that characterizes the Scottish system point to the dangers of abandoning notions of due process and natural justice. Fox (1974), for example, sees individualization of treatment, indeterminate disposals and extensive use of discretion as abuses of children's rights. Morris (1973) has also suggested that the inevitable consequences of the treatment approach include excessive intervention in family life and scant regard for legal safeguards which might be seen as restricting the availability of treatment. Furthermore, she has pointed to the lack of evidence that treatment is effective. Fox (op. cit.) criticizes welfare ideology for 'excluding children's rights to punishment' – the child expects, and is entitled to expect, to be dealt with on the basis of his behaviour, and denial of this right opens the way for the 'abuses of treatment'.

The Kilbrandon Report and subsequent social policy has been accused of failing to take account of the complex aetiology of delinquency. Primary focus on child and family pathology is said to result in insufficient attention being paid to other schools of criminological thought which attempt to understand the problem in terms of opportunity, cultural deviance, 'drift' and 'labelling' theories.[3]

Another live issue is community involvement. What is the role of lay participation in the hearing system? Smith (1977) has pointed to possible ambiguities. For example, should the lay members be representative of the community they serve or should they receive sophisticated training for a diagnostic-treatment task? His and other research (Parsloe 1976) suggests that there are three ideologies inherent in the Scottish system. The welfare, social control and community involvement sets of values are all present and they may well conflict with one another.

The main parties

Who are the main parties or groups involved in the Scottish system? Which children come within the compass of the system, who is the reporter, what are the panel and the hearing and what part must the social work department play? The principal statutory requirements and provisions described in the following pages are to be found in Sections 30 to 58 of the Social Work (Scotland) Act 1968.

The children

For the purposes of the hearing system a child is defined as any person between birth and the age of sixteen years but this limit is extended to eighteen for those children already subject to supervision before their sixteenth birthday.

Although the juvenile courts have been abolished, children may still be prosecuted in the Sheriff and High Courts on the instructions of the Lord Advocate. He has instructed his procurators-fiscal only to proceed against children who have committed grave offences, or have been accused together with an adult so that a joint prosecution is essential or in certain other special circumstances. Prosecution of children less than thirteen years old requires specific authorization in each instance. Before sentencing a child who has been prosecuted, the court may ask the advice of a children's hearing and consequently remit the case for disposal and, indeed, *must* ask for advice if the child is already subject to a hearing's supervision requirement. Around 3,000 children's cases are prosecuted in the Sheriff Courts each year, one fifth of the number of cases that are heard by children's hearings and about one tenth of all cases referred to the reporter.[4]

Any person may refer a child to the reporter but it appears that few private individuals choose to do so. In 1976 around 71 per cent of reports came from the police, 10 per cent from education authorities and 3 per cent from social work departments. Procurators-fiscal who decided not to take children to court accounted for around 15 per cent. Of about 30,000 reports referred to the reporter in 1976, 84 per cent concerned offences, 10 per cent involved truancy, and cases of alleged inadequacies of parental care accounted for the remaining 6 per cent.[5] It is offending, then, that brings most children into the system. It should also be noted that many first offenders are not referred to the reporter by the police who issue a formal warning instead. Murray (1976) has observed that in 1974 nearly 11,000 such warnings were given, usually for minor offences. Several police forces also operate juvenile liaison schemes in conjunction with the warnings. The police, then, exercise considerable discretion and divert many children from the hearings system.

The reporter

This official is often described as the 'gatekeeper' of the system since it is his role to decide which children may be in need of compulsory measures of care and therefore require referral to children's hearings. There is a reporter in each local authority area but he is not accountable for his decisions to the local authority, nor indeed to any other authority. He must investigate each report he receives (unless he considers it trivial or malicious) and decide upon one of three courses of action. Having made one decision about a referral he cannot, at a later date, make another on the basis of the same facts.

One option is to take 'no further action'. In practice, this is rarely interpreted literally as the reporter will write to the child and his parents, discuss the matter with them or refer the child to the police who may issue a warning. This decision is most often taken when the reporter considers that the substance of the report does not warrant intervention or that the child does not require any care additional to that he is already receiving. The reporter deals with around 42 per cent of referrals in this way.[6]

The reporter's second option is to refer the child to the social work department for 'advice, guidance and assistance'. Reporters take this decision in approximately 5 per cent of cases.

The third alternative is to refer the child to a children's hearing. To do this he must have evidence to support his claim that the child is in need of compulsory measures of care. The legislation requires that at least one of several conditions must be satisfied.[7] These include: (1) that the child is beyond the control of his parent; (2) that he is falling into bad associations or is exposed to moral danger; (3) that he has committed an offence; (4) that lack of parental care is likely to cause the child unnecessary suffering or seriously to impair his health or development; (5) that he has been the victim of a sex or cruelty offence; (6) that he is a member of a household in which there is, or is likely to be, the perpetrator of such an offence. Around 53 per cent of all referrals to the reporter reach a hearing.

When the reporter has decided to refer a child to a hearing, he makes the necessary administrative arrangements for its sitting which include obtaining reports for it as well as giving the family due notice and securing their attendance. The reporter also has a role in the Sheriff Court. If the grounds for referral are disputed, the reporter must attempt to prove them if the hearing so instructs him and he must also appear when appeals against hearing decisions are heard by the Sheriff.

The reporter, therefore, has much discretionary power in relation to referrals and can divert children from any formal proceedings.

The panel

There is a panel in each regional authority area and in 1976 there were approximately 1650 panel members.[8] The panel is the body of people from which three members are drawn for each hearing. Its members are appointed for three-year periods of office by the Secretary of State for Scotland on the advice of regional children's panel advisory committees which also oversee their training. Recruitment is usually by open advertisement and there are few restrictive qualifications. A review of the extensive research of the selection process suggests that although a broad cross-section of the community is represented, people who could be fairly described as 'middle class' predominate (Curran 1977). Their training is usually intended to familiarize members with the system, the professions participating in it, children's needs and the types of resources available.

The hearing

A children's hearing is 'a sitting of members of the children's panel' and consists of a chairman and two other members. There must be both a man and a woman among the members of the hearing, which must not be held in premises associated with the police or courts. Because of the emphasis on informality, the chairman has a duty to keep the number of persons present to the minimum necessary for the proper consideration of the case, although he cannot exclude certain persons, e.g. any representative of the child or his parents, and members of the Press. The latter may not identify the child when reporting the case. Parents have a right to be present at all stages of the hearing and also have a duty to attend unless freed of this duty by a hearing.

Rules prescribe certain procedures in the conduct of the hearing.[9] The chairman must explain the grounds for the child's referral and ascertain whether or not they are understood and accepted by the child and his parents. If they are not both understood and accepted, the hearing cannot proceed and must either discharge the referral or refer it to the Sheriff Court. If the facts are established in the court, the hearing proceeds at a subsequent sitting.

The chairman must reveal the substance of reports which are material to the disposal of the case unless such disclosure would be detrimental to the interests of the child. The reasons for the hearing's decision and the family's rights of appeal must also be explained at the conclusion of the discussion.

The duration of a hearing varies according to the complexity of the case and its immediate purpose, but a forty-minute session is typical. If the panel members are unable to arrive at a decision without further investigation, they may remit the case to a subsequent hearing. Otherwise, they must either discharge the referral or make one of two kinds of 'supervision requirement'. The requirement may take the form of either an order to submit to domiciliary supervision or an order that the child reside in an establishment named by the hearing members. Both kinds of requirement may include conditions. Monetary penalties are not competent but regular school attendance, the performance of tasks, attendance at clinics and residence at a specified home address may be required. Of initial referrals to hearings in 1974, 41·9 per cent were discharged, 47·5 per cent resulted in non-residential requirements and 10·5 per cent in residential requirements (Curran 1977).

If a supervision requirement is not reviewed by a hearing within one year of its making it ceases to have effect but no termination date is specified at the outset, and, with reviews, the child may continue to be subject to supervision until his eighteenth birthday if this is thought to be in his interests. The supervising social worker may request a review hearing at any time and the child and his parents have the right to a review after three months in the first instance and after six months in certain other circumstances.

The hearing is intended to be a forum for open discussion and the sharing of information and opinion with full participation on the part of the family, in addition to being the venue for decision-making. The provision for review hearings, at which there is usually some continuity of panel membership, allows flexibility in the application of compulsory measures of care over a lengthy period of time.

The social work department

One of the regional social work departments' many statutory responsibilities is the fulfilment of their local authorities' obligations to the children's hearing system.

When the reporter has investigated a case and has decided that a child may require advice, guidance and assistance, the social work department must make this available. The child and his parents, however, are under no obligation to accept the help offered which is often referred to as 'voluntary supervision'. When the reporter refers a child to a hearing, he must request a social background report and the social work department must supply it. This may contain information from any source deemed appropriate by the reporter and social worker. Reports must also be provided for review hearings.

If, on referral, a child is seen to be at immediate risk, the police or a social worker authorized by a Justice of the Peace may have to arrange for him to be temporarily accommodated in a 'place of safety' until his case can be presented to a children's hearing. The social work department must provide such accommodation.

A key responsibility of the department is to 'give effect to a supervision requirement made by a children's hearing in their area' (Section 44 of the 1968 Act) and a child subject to supervision is, for many purposes, in the department's care. Although the department may utilize the resources of other agencies, the ultimate responsibility lies in its hands.

Although the 1968 Act does not explicitly require the department to be represented at the hearing, it may be assumed that this is essential. Not only should it be possible for a social worker to elaborate on his report but also he should be on hand to give an up-to-the-minute account of available resources and to convey the child into residential care should the hearing require it.

Other agencies

Space does not permit a description of the parts played by the many other agencies whose work may involve them in the hearings system. However, it should be appreciated that teachers, school welfare officers, child guidance psychologists, psychiatrists and officers of the Royal Scottish Society for the Prevention of Cruelty to Children frequently contribute to its operation. They may be called upon to furnish reports (as is the school in almost every case) and in many instances to attend hearings. They may also, of course, play a crucial role in providing care and treatment for children referred to the reporter and the hearings.

The social worker and the system in operation

What part does the social worker play at each stage in the Scottish juvenile justice system? The flow chart (Table 3 : 1) demonstrates diagramatically the referral process which we shall now consider.

Table 3:1   Procedural flow chart of the children's hearing system

REFERRAL
By police, education authority,
social work department, etc.

↓

REPORTER

No action

Investigation
inc. initial report from social worker

↓

Decision

No further
action

Need for compulsory
measures

Referral to local
authority for advice,
guidance and assistance

Full reports inc. school
and social background

↓

HEARING

Grounds for referral
not accepted

Grounds for referral
accepted

Decision

Referral
discharged

Sheriff
Court

Supervision
requirement

Referral
discharged

Grounds not
established

Grounds established

Accepted

Not accepted

Referral
discharged

Referral to
hearing

Implemented

Appeal to
Sheriff

Referrals to the reporter

Although social workers refer only a small proportion of all children reported to the reporter, the nature of these referrals often gives rise to difficulties. More often than not they are cases where the standard of parental care is in question, the child being either beyond parental control or likely to suffer from a lack of parental care. If a child is to be referred on the basis of the first of these grounds parental cooperation is usually required. Unless the parents agree that their efforts to control the child have been thwarted, there is likely to be difficulty in proving the facts of the case.

An even more sensitive area is where lack of parental care is alleged. Parents might well dispute the grounds for referral, and compulsory intervention could not then follow without a proof in court. Since action of this kind is likely to alienate the parents to some degree, there should be confidence that the facts can be proved. Failure to obtain the right to intervene might then be followed by the parents refusing the social worker all access to the child. It is advisable to seek the advice of the reporter as to the evidence required in these cases. The challenge for the social worker is to find a way to bring about change without creating fear and hostility on the parents' part. However, this is not an argument for avoiding confrontation when the child's needs demand it, nor is it justification to wait until the child commits an offence, a more easily established ground for referral.

There is good reason, then, for practising social workers to be familiar with the legal conditions which must be satisfied before a hearing referral can proceed, as well as with the circumstances in which he may remove a child to a place of safety prior to a hearing. These conditions are to be found in Sections 32 and 37 of the 1968 Act as amended by the Children Act 1975.

The reporter's investigation and decision

What the social worker actually does goes beyond the statutory requirements already mentioned. Although the reporter's right to a social background report exists only after he has decided to refer a child to a hearing, it is the policy and practice of many social work departments to provide reports when the reporter is first investigating a referral. A social worker is asked to write what is often called an 'initial investigation report' aimed at assisting the reporter to arrive at a decision. He normally sees the family and makes a recommendation after assessing the information available to him. If it appears to him that intervention is not likely to be required his report will be brief, but if there are manifest problems he may choose to write a comprehensive social background report which would obviate later duplication and delay. Such an approach would, of course, require the family's cooperation, and if the grounds for referral are denied, information should not be pressed for. In these circumstances, as in every investigation, the family's attitudes will be affected by how well the social worker can explain the nature and purpose of the system. The extent to which parents and child know their rights and understand the aim of intervention will surely shape their response to any subsequent proceedings (see chapter 8).

In making a recommendation the social worker will bear in mind the options open to the reporter. If 'no further action' is suggested, the absence of social work criteria for intervention should be made clear although the reporter may have other criteria for taking action. If the social worker believes that 'advice, guidance and assistance' would be more appropriate than compulsory measures, a reasoned summary of what can be offered will be helpful. The entirely voluntary nature of any such contract with the family has to be borne in mind. When the social worker indicates that a hearing referral is desirable his report should point to why an element of compulsion seems necessary, and also suggest any other known sources of information which the reporter might draw upon.

Initial enquiry reports are important in so far as the social worker can identify children in need at an early stage and influence the reporter in the use of his discretionary power. May (1977) has rightly stressed the 'de facto' power the social worker has through his control over, and interpretation of, the flow of information to the reporter and hearing.

Before the hearing
Once the reporter has decided to refer a child to a hearing the social worker's principal tasks are to compile the social background report and to prepare the child and his family for the coming hearing.

If the report is to assist the hearing to decide in the best interests of the child it must provide a comprehensive picture of him and his environment. At the same time, the worker should avoid unjustified intrusion into family privacy. The purpose of the report warrants the inclusion of material relating to: relevant family history; the child's own developmental history; the child's place in the network of family relationships; his physical, cultural and social environment and its impact on him, including socio-economic features, schooling, peer groups and recreational opportunities; and the child's perceptions and attitudes in the light of these factors. Also significant will be the social worker's view of how the grounds for referral relate to the information collated. How do the child and his parents see the events which have brought about the intervention? Have they had previous contact with social work or other professional agencies and what was their response? Is there motivation for change? What are the child's strengths and weaknesses and his met and unmet needs? The answers to these questions too, will be relevant. The report writer will need to be familiar with resources which could benefit the child and it is desirable that the hearing should know what is available as well as the ideal.

The report will be more valuable if its form of presentation facilitates discussion and is readily intelligible to both family and hearing members. The use of ambiguous expressions and clichéd generalizations will confuse rather than clarify and will diminish recognition of the child as a unique individual. The social worker should be able to cite evidence to support statements made, and his reliability as an informant may be tested in court on appeal. There are differing views on whether the report should conclude with a specific recommendation. It is my view that the formation and expression of a professional opinion should follow the collection and analysis of information. It is not the social worker's role to pre-empt the decision of the hearing but it should be possible to outline alternatives open to the hearing and at the same time indicate the direction in which the social worker's thinking leads. Further assessment, e.g. of a multi-disciplinary and/or residential nature, may be the only possible recommendation in some cases. As with any other recommendation, the reasoning behind the suggestion should be clear.

The prospect of attendance at a hearing is a threatening one for most families but the social worker can prepare the family in several ways. He can emphasize that they will be encouraged to express their feelings and views. He can explain the form the hearing will take, who will be there and why they are there. For example, that it is the panel members who have the authority to take decisions, and that the 'reporter' is not from the Press! The worker may also wish to describe the private and confidential nature of the proceedings when he is stating the hearing's concern for the child's welfare.

The family are entitled to know their rights and the social worker can help them ascertain these. He can tell them how to exercise them during and after the hearing and they can also be told of the legal advice available beforehand.[10]

A key to the social worker's approach is openness. To both protect the family's rights and promote understanding, it is good practice to let the family know the contents of the report which will be the basis for discussion at the hearing. One approach is to give them the choice of reading the report or having the contents read to them by the social worker.

At the hearing

The social worker is not a silent observer at the hearing but an active participant in open discussion. His written report cannot be his final word since it may require clarification and new information often comes to light during the hearing. The worker can draw attention to the principal points made in his report and thus encourage discussion of the most relevant issues. It may also be that what transpires during the hearing itself will require him to reconsider his recommendation.

The worker is in a good position to facilitate communication because he already knows the family and understands the hearing's goals. If the child or his parents do not contribute to the discussion, either through fear or lack of encouragement from the panel members, the social worker can prompt more family involvement by pertinent questions and comments. He also may assist by interpreting, when appropriate, non-verbal communication.

The social worker should not presume, or appear to have, a privileged relationship with the panel members. For example, seeking 'a word in private' with members beforehand is to be discouraged. He is a representative of one agency which provides information and professional advice and he has to reconcile himself to the fact that his advice will not always be accepted. On the other hand, he must be firm in his stance if the hearing members have unreal expectations of social work intervention and he should resist any attempt by the hearing to prescribe his day to day working. Occasionally a hearing, unsure of the action it should take, may seem to ask the social worker to decide the outcome. Such invitations to usurp the hearing's role should be declined.

The hearing must attempt to strike a balance between a degree of formality which would stifle any real communication and an approach so casual as to deny its serious purpose and be an affront to the family's dignity and self-respect. The way in which the worker relates to both family and hearing members will be one factor affecting this balance. He will enhance the prospects of a successful hearing, as Hiddleston has succinctly explained, by 'facilitating and clarifying but not dominating'. (1976, 113)

After the hearing

Useful work may be done immediately after the hearing. If the child is to be taken to a residential establishment, benefit will usually accrue from asking the parents to accompany the child and worker there to learn where the child is going and about visiting and leave arrangements. Inasmuch as every hearing is to some extent a family crisis, the immediate aftermath is an opportunity for the social worker. The implications of the hearing decision can be explained, and it is an ideal time to make arrangements for the early stages of supervision.

Although other advisers such as teacher, psychologist and psychiatrist may have contributed reports to, and attended, the hearing, the sole responsibility for giving effect to the requirement lies with the social worker. He may, of course, place some reliance on other workers, especially residential staff, but the ultimate responsibility to ensure adequate supervision remains with him. The social worker has a right which accompanies this duty, namely the right to request that a review hearing be arranged. It is possible then, for him to suggest that the hearing vary or terminate a requirement.

What form does supervision take? Within the limitations of the requirement and its conditions, this will depend on the social worker's own assessment of the child's needs. Work with the child and his family will be based on general principles underlying social work intervention and the worker may draw on skills, methods and strategies particularly appropriate to work with children. The advantages to be derived from mutual goal-setting, contract-making and task-centred work with the child and family, are relevant to supervision. The indefinite duration of the requirement does not preclude such approaches, and timely use of review hearings can provide a framework for them.

The nature of supervision will also depend, of course, on the availability of resources as well as on the worker's preferred mode of intervention. A heavy workload may make intensive home visiting and frequent one-to-one supervision sessions impossible. Opportunities for groupwork, community service and inter-mediate treatment may or may not exist.

The amount of residential provision available also varies from one region to another. Most authorities manage a variety of types of children's homes and hostels but the voluntary sector also plays a major part in the residential field. Scotland has thirty-two 'List D' schools which accommodate around 1,800 children. Most of these establishments, formerly known as 'Approved' schools, have independent boards of management and together offer a wide variety of regimes and settings although demand for places usually exceeds supply. The choice of school must be guided by the individual child's needs. It is both necessary and desirable that a supervising social worker maintain regular contact with a child subject to a residential supervision requirement. Apart from the obvious need to provide continuity of care and maintain the child's links with his home, the worker's duty to arrange review hearings means he must liaise closely with the residential workers. One problem posed by the nature of the review system itself is that the prospect of an early review at his own request can sometimes make it difficult for a child to settle.

It is fair to comment that a supervisor is to some extent an agent of social control because of the authority invested in him by the system. While this role may not appeal to all social workers, the use of authority, as Foren and Bailey (1968) have illustrated, can have positive aspects in casework terms as well as in the control of delinquency. In this context, it is worth emphasizing that, for the purposes of the children's hearing system 'care' is taken to include 'protection, control, guidance and treatment' (Section 32 (3) of the 1968 Act). It should help if the child and his parents are made aware of this aspect of their relationship with their social worker.

It would not be constructive to think of the social worker's role as supervisor in terms of casework alone. It may be that much of his energies will be focused on elements in the child's environment which are amenable to change. The worker may endeavour to promote understanding of the child's needs among the network of people to whom the child relates, including relatives and teachers. Efforts may also be directed towards an improvement in the child's immediate physical and material environment and in the services available in his community.

What can members of a review hearing expect to learn at the end of a period of supervision? They will want to know what supervision has taken place and what effect it has had, if any. They will require some description of present problems and information about changes in attitudes and circumstances. Should the requirement be continued without variation, varied or terminated? What does the social worker recommend and why? Effective collaboration with others involved in the child's education and development throughout the period of supervision will assist the compilation of a meaningful report.

Throughout his contact with the panel members, the social worker has the task of explaining what is possible. They, not directly involved in other branches of social work, may have unreal expectations and may not be fully aware of the worker's need to determine the priority of any one case relative to his own total workload and that of his agency. The worker, then, should be able to explain what the limitations of treatment are and his criteria for determining priorities.

Conclusions

Most social workers will find imperfections and drawbacks in various aspects of the children's hearing system. Too many children are still prosecuted in court, for example, and lengthy delays often occur between referral and hearing. There is frustration at some of the decisions reached by panel members and some confusion as to the boundaries between the roles of the professional and lay participants in the system. It may sometimes appear, too, that timely intervention is hindered by legal restriction on action and that a shortfall of resources denies the worker the opportunity to fully exploit the system's potential.

However, few Scottish social workers would ask for a return to the old system because the positive attributes of the new one are many. It presents opportunities for early identification of children in need, it removes the necessity for a child to go through a tariff system of court disposals before intervention can occur and it reduces the number of children stigmatized by formal proceedings. The system encourages communication and collaboration between the relevant professions and permits a flexibility in the provision of services appropriate to the child's changing needs. Above all, perhaps, is its capacity to focus on the interests of the individual child and to tackle problems in a manner which encourages the family to participate and retain its self-respect. There is room, no doubt, for improvement in the realization of its potential but a system which has such inherently strong welfare values must appeal to social workers.

How relevant are the ideological and theoretical issues which give rise to much criticism of this kind of approach to juvenile justice? Experience in the USA has illustrated the perils of neglecting children's rights in welfare-oriented systems (Fox 1974) and it is important that those who operate the Scottish system ensure adherence to the safeguards embodied in it. There is also danger in any view of delinquency which seeks to explain it in terms of personal and family pathology alone and ignores environmental factors which reflect weaknesses in social organization and institutions. It should be recognized, too, that any system of juvenile justice has the control of delinquency as one of its purposes, and where values associated with this goal conflict with welfare values, the internal contradictions of the system should be acknowledged. So, too, should the limitations of treatment. There is also a need to refine the concept of community involvement in order that the role of lay participants can be further clarified.

However, it is unlikely that any system of juvenile justice would be viable without compromise and an amalgam of conflicting values. Parsloe (1976) and Martin and Murray (1976), among others, have rightly noted that such inconsistencies and tensions reflect the ambivalence and conflicting demands of society.

Heated debate continues on whether the system can be described as successful, and yardsticks range from crime statistics to qualitative assessments in terms of humanistic values. Some critics press for the reintroduction of fines, others suggest that many children require punishment rather than treatment. Yet others see success as dependent upon a massive input to the resources available to the personal social services. There is certainly a need for more extensive research than has been carried out to date if sound evidence is to form the basis for any proposed changes.

Meanwhile, the present system continues to present a challenge to the social work profession to demonstrate what can be achieved through intervention with children in trouble.

Recommended reading

BRUCE, N. and SPENCER, J. 1976: *Face to Face with Families: a report on the children's panels in Scotland*. Loanhead: MacDonald.

CURRAN, J. H. 1977: *The Children's Hearing System: a review of research*. Edinburgh: HMSO.

MARTIN, F. M. and MURRAY, K. 1976: *Children's Hearings*. Edinburgh: Scottish Academic Press.

MORRIS, A. and McISAAC, M. 1978: *Juvenile Justice? the practice of social welfare*. London: Heinemann Educational.

Notes

1 This report, *Children and Young Persons (Scotland)*, contained the findings of a committee appointed by the Secretary of State for Scotland and chaired by Lord Kilbrandon, a Scottish judge.

2 *Social Work and the Community* Cmnd 3065. 1966. HMSO.

3 See, for example, Cloward, R. A. and Ohlin, L. E., 1960, *Delinquency and Opportunity,* Illinois: Glencoe Free Press. Matza, D., 1964, *Delinquency and Drift*, New York: Wiley. Becker, H. S., 1963, *Outsiders: Studies in the sociology of deviance*, New York: Free Press.

4 Figures derived from estimates given by Murray, G., 1976: Juvenile Justice Reform. In Martin, F. M. and Murray, K., editors, *Children's Hearings.* Edinburgh: Scottish Academic Press.

5 These figures, provided by Social Work Services Group, Edinburgh, 1978, are provisional.

6 This percentage and those that follow regarding reporters' decisions are derived from Social Work Services Group provisional figures for 1976.

7 See Section 32 of the Social Work (Scotland) Act 1968, as amended by the Children Act 1975, for the comprehensive list of these conditions.

8 This is a provisional estimate provided by Social Work Services Group.

9 Children's Hearings (Scotland) Rules 1971.

10 Legal advice about grounds for referral is available under the Legal Advice and Assistance Act 1972 in addition to the legal aid available when court proceedings ensue.

Chapter 4

The Social Worker, the Court and Some 'Life Decisions' about Children

Eric Cooper and Elwyn Owens

Every decision made by a court about a child is important.[1] Each one affects the child but some have more far-reaching consequences than others in that they may change his legal status and relationship with his parents, dictate with whom he should live and sometimes what he will be called. Courts in England and Wales have been able to make 'life decisions' about children in some form or other since 1889[2] and the most recent piece of legislation about children acknowledges and enshrines the lifelong importance of what is being decided when it stipulates that in adoption, and proceedings regarding the assumption of parental rights, 'first consideration' should be given to 'safeguard and promote the welfare of the child throughout his childhood' (Children Act 1975, S3 and S59). Ways of caring for children separated from their natural parents have been an interest of officialdom since the days of the poor law and through to the 1975 Act. This new Act reflects these evolving attitudes and practices and will have a bearing on a social worker's practice and his contribution to 'life decisions' about children.

The Act had its origin in the report of the Houghton Committee, published in 1972, which was set up in 1969 to consider 'the law, policy and procedure on adoption of children and what changes are desirable'. That its recommendations reached the statute book, and particularly that the provisions of the new law stretched beyond the specific issue of adoption, was attributable to three main factors:

1 At a time when fewer infants were available, adoption was being seen increasingly as a means of providing a substitute family for older children in the care of the local authority. The division between long term fostering and adoption became less pronounced and many social workers began to think not of one or the other but of substitute family care. The Act in

many of its provisions encouraged and reflected this development.

2 Media publicity and one notable piece of research drew attention to the plight of many children in care and the problems of local authorities in trying to meet their needs. The death of Maria Colwell and the subsequent report[3] showed the regard that must be accorded by courts to the feelings and opinions of the child, and provision is made for this in the Act. Jane Rowe and Lydia Lambert (1973) drew attention to the large number of children in care who were not protected adequately by law, and for whom life within a substitute family appeared to be most desirable, though all too often a remote possibility. The Act, by extending the grounds on which parental rights may be assumed, makes it easier for children to be safeguarded but its effect on professional practice is less certain and remains problematic.

3 The political and social climate was right. A law about children in need of substitute familes was acceptable, but a statute which might have been enacted at the same time, about the poverty of one-parent families, was just not possible (1974).

Attempts by an alliance of the National Council for One Parent Families, Gingerbread, and the British Association of Social Workers to persuade the Government to drop clauses such as those relating to time limits failed, and only time will tell whether the child-centredness of the Act penalises natural parents unfairly.

Social workers are used to contributing to courts 'life decisions' about children and the provisions of the 1975 Act are such that they are brought into a specially sharp focus. In this chapter three instances are selected for description and discussion. The obvious omission relating to the social worker's role in court proceedings concerning the assumption of parental rights is dealt with in chapter 2 on juvenile court work. Throughout this chapter the assumption is made that all the provisions of the 1975 Act referred to have been implemented.

The social worker in adoption proceedings

There is probably a no more profound 'life decision' which a court may make, nor a more complex set of circumstances for a social worker to handle, than those in adoption proceedings. The decision and the right to confer the order may belong to the court, but its quality, to be tested by time and the testimony of the adopted person, will depend upon the social worker's skill and judgment. Theirs is the primary professional responsibility for the whole adoption process, and upon their skills and expertise the happiness of many thousands of children depends. Fundamental issues such as personal identity and the role and concept of the family in society have a crucial bearing on practice, particularly in the placement of older children which is quite properly on the increase. In 1969 in its monograph 'Adoption: the way ahead' the Association of Child Care Officers said of adoption 'It is a legal pretence which can lead to confusion for the child and the loss of his identity rather than the gaining of it; and to confusion for the adopters, who are pressurized on all sides to pretend that the child is their own and that therefore their feelings should be the same towards him as if he were, and yet somehow they can never (should never) forget that he is not.' While the principles contained within this cautious statement remain as sound as ever the late seventies have seen a significant and courageous move forward in social work practice. Agencies and courts, in the spirit of openness enshrined in the new Act, are including adoption as one of the ways of providing a family for children of all ages who are separated from, and unlikely to return to, their natural parents.

As well as superseding all previous adoption legislation the 1975 Act places the onus on local authorities to ensure the provision of a comprehensive adoption service either by themselves or in conjunction with approved adoption societies. These will be subject to approval by the Secretary of State for Social Services. The concept of an adoption service includes arrangements for meeting the needs of children who may have been or who may be adopted, their parents or guardians, adopters and prospective adopters, and the provision of temporary board and lodging where needed by pregnant women, mothers or children, arrangements for assessing children and prospective adopters, and counselling for persons with problems relating to adoption. Section 3 has been described as the keynote of the Act.[4] It states that in reaching any decision relative to the adoption of a child, a court or adoption agency shall 'have regard to all the circumstances, first consideration being given to the need to safeguard and promote the welfare of the child throughout his childhood, and shall so far as practicable ascertain the wishes and feelings of the child regarding the decision and give due consideration to them, having regard to his age and understanding.'

The Act changes the role of the social worker in adoption proceedings. In some ways it is restricted and made more precise and in others it is considerably extended. In the past adoption placements could involve three or perhaps even four social workers each with different tasks definable by themselves but sometimes confusing to the prospective adopters and the child. One or occasionally two made the arrangements for the placement, one undertook the 'welfare supervision' for three months after the application to the court and then submitted a report to the court, and a third undertook the responsibilities of the guardian *ad litem*. The new Act envisages that welfare supervision will be undertaken by the placing agency and it will become the responsibility of that agency to prepare a report for the court about the suitability of the applicants and other relevant issues. All agencies will be subject to approval by the Secretary of State, and third-party placements are made illegal.

The present duties of the guardian *ad litem* in adoption proceedings show how extensively the court expects the guardian *ad litem* to make his enquiries.[5] They also illustrate how social workers undertaking that duty can have difficulty in integrating administrative attention to detail with sensitive casework skill. Basically the social worker is expected to act independently of other agencies and to investigate the circumstances of the proposed adoption in order to safeguard the interests of the child and to ensure that adoption is in fact in the child's interests. He is expected to obtain reports from and to interview all respondents to the application, making sure that parental consents are given freely, and where appropriate the views of the child are also reported to the court. The significance and nature of each investigation varies a great deal. What is required in the case of an infant of an untraceable father and a mother who willingly consents is totally different from what is involved in the adoption of an older child who has a clear recollection of his past experience and personal heritage and whose parents withhold their consent. Under the 1958 Act procedure a guardian *ad litem* was always appointed. The new legislation provides that a guardian *ad litem* shall be appointed in such cases as are prescribed by rules made under the Act.

Again in keeping with the recommendations of the Houghton Committee, there are now provisions which allow for the 'freeing of a child for adoption' (S14). The effect of this will be to place the child in the care of the adoption agency and the intention is to reduce the risk of a child being damaged by a parent's vacillation.

In this procedure, initiated by the agency, the 'reporting officer' will assist the court by witnessing agreements to adoption and ensuring that consents are given freely by parents. Reporting officers and guardians *ad litem* will be nominated by the court from local panels to be approved by the Secretary of State.

The Act extends social work responsibilities in adoption in two further ways. Section 10 (3) requires that where an application for adoption is made to a court and the applicant is a step-parent of the child then the court shall dismiss the application if it considers the matter would be better dealt with under the Matrimonial Causes Act 1973. This appears to come as a surprise to some who make the application but it reflects the spirit of openness with children which pervades the Act. For the social workers such an application, and the subsequent referral to the court making the original matrimonial order, will require the preparation of a report for the court. In addition he is expected to respond (skilfully) to adults who are sometimes in conflict with each other, to appreciate what is in a child's interests and how these can best be served by the court making an order for custody. Section 26 enables adopted adults to apply to the Registrar General to obtain a certified copy of the record of his birth. Local authorities provide a counselling service for people who make such an application, and if the adoption order was made before 12 November 1975 the Registrar General shall not supply the information unless the applicant has attended an interview with a counsellor. This work is important for adopted people and for social workers. At times it is a moving experience for both, because it is a time when a court's 'life decision' is seen in its true perspective.

The social worker in the separate representation of children

The concept of the separate representation of children in care is new in legal proceedings. It is related to the finding by the Committee of Enquiry into the Maria Colwell case that the role of social workers in care-related proceedings is, in fact, not one role at all but many, leading to possible partiality and conflict. In that Report, para. 227, it was felt that it would be of the greatest value for the court to have 'the views of an independent social worker' whose duty it would be to act exclusively as a representative of the child. Under the 1975 Act every child in need of such protection is to have a separate representative known as a guardian *ad litem*. The term is not a new one but in this context it carries extensive new duties. The process of appointing such a person falls into two main parts. First, the court has to consider making an order excluding the parent or guardian from representing the child. If it does that it must then decide whether to appoint an independent representative – the guardian *ad litem*.

The scarcity of resources, however, and the need to proceed cautiously, allowing time for a body of experience and knowledge to be built up, result in a distinction being drawn between those cases where the court *may* order the exclusion of the parent or guardian as representing the child, and those situations where the court *shall* take this action (DHSS Local Authority Circular (75) 21). The new legislation is contained in the Children Act 1975, Section 64, which inserts new paragraphs 32 (A) and 32 (B) in the Children and Young Persons Act 1969. Section 32 introduces the court's new power to order that 'in relation to the proceedings the parent or guardian is not to be treated as representing the child or young person or as otherwise authorized to act on his behalf'. This Order has already become widely known as an exclusion order. There is a subtle distinction, as we have already said, between Section 32 (A) (1) and Section 32 (A) (2) in the power of the court to exclude the parent.

In Section 32 (A) (1) (a) to (f) we are referred to Care Proceedings under Section 1 of the 1969 Act, and all those Sections of the same Act relating to applications for the discharge of Care Orders or Supervision Orders and powers to appeal against the dismissal of such an application. If in any of those proceedings 'it appears to the Court that there is, or may be, a conflict . . . between the interests of the child or young person and those of his parent or guardian, the court *may* order the exclusion of the parent or guardian as the child's representative'.

Section 32 (A) (2) has a narrower but sharper focus. It refers to those applications mentioned in Section 32 (A) (1) (b) and (c), i.e. applications for the discharge of a relevant Supervision Order (or a Supervision Order made under Section 21 (2) of the 1969 Act on the discharge of a relevant Care Order) or applications under Section 21 (2) of the 1969 Act for the discharge of a relevant Care Order (or a Care Order made under Section 15 (1) of the 1969 Act on the discharge of a relevant Supervision Order). In such proceedings under the provision of Section 32 (A) (2) where such an application is *unopposed*, the court *shall* order the exclusion of the parent or guardian *unless* 'satisfied that to do so is not necessary for safeguarding the interests of the child or young person'. The latter part of the same section indicates clearly that where a parent or guardian is excluded in this way, but where the application for the discharge of the relevant order was made by him, his exclusion 'shall not invalidate the application'.

It remains to be seen whether the knowledge of the court's responsibility in unopposed hearings will influence the practice of a local authority which, being the respondent to an application, has to decide whether to oppose or not. The court hearing will represent only a small part of what may be a very long and, one hopes, carefully thought out response to the needs of a child. Good practice will not deny the presence of conflict and this will be acknowledged and faced outside the courtroom setting. A hearing where adults who are significant to the child are seen to abuse and damage each other in public can be a deeply wounding experience for all the individuals involved. Sometimes, though, such an experience will be a necessary one as the only means of resolving otherwise irreconcilable and polarized strains within a child's life. Social workers will often be involved in the healing of wounds of children and adults which may go with and follow the facing of such conflict both within and outside the court. Practice which includes the ability to comprehend, respect and contain deeply opposing feelings is required, and sad a reflection as it is on current professional practice, it may be that these provisions in the Act will prompt the development of such skills.

The essential difference, therefore, between Section 32 (A) (1) and Section 32 (A) (2) is that under the former the court needs to be satisfied that 'there is or may be a conflict' between the interests of the child and those of his parents before the parent *may* be excluded, but under the latter, where the relevant application is unopposed, the court must assume conflict of interests and *shall* order the exclusion of the parent *unless* satisfied that it is not necessary to do this. It is, therefore, possible that a guardian *ad litem* may never be appointed even under this more demanding Section. The wording suggests that a parent or guardian shall have the opportunity to try to satisfy the court that it is not necessary to make an exclusion order, and for this purpose he may of course be represented. It also seems that even when an exclusion order is made under this Section a guardian *ad litem* may still not be appointed because Section 32 (B) (1) says that the court shall appoint a guardian *ad litem* 'unless satisfied that to do so is not necessary for safeguarding the interests of the child or young person'. In what circumstances the court might be satisfied that it is not necessary to appoint a guardian *ad litem* after an exclusion order has been made is not yet clear.

Section 32 (B) is the authority for the court to appoint a guardian *ad litem*. Sub-section 1 refers to those cases where an exclusion order has been made under Section 32 (A) (2). Sub-section 2 authorizes the provision of rules of court for the appointment of a guardian *ad litem* in those proceedings in which an exclusion order is made under Section 32 (A) (1). Sub-section 3 lays down the general duty of the guardian *ad litem* 'to safeguard the interests of the child or young person in the manner prescribed by rules of Court'. To carry out this duty the social worker requires a range of skills the most important of which is the ability to communicate with children, a skill with which everyone in the profession is not blessed, and the capacity to present evidence and opinion to a court.

The Magistrates' Courts (Children and Young Persons) Rules of 1970 are now amended by the (Amendment) Rules 1976. Rule 14 of the 1970 Rules related to the giving of notice of the proceedings, has now been amended in two important respects. First, there is now a firm requirement that any foster-parent or other person with whom the relevant child has had his home for a period of not less than six weeks, ending not more than six months before the date of the application, should be given notice of the proceedings. In the case of Maria Colwell such notice would have gone to Mr and Mrs Cooper who were not parties to the proceedings and were not called as witnesses. Such a person may henceforth play a crucial part in the hearing of any application. Secondly, the respondent to the application is now required to inform the Clerk of the Court within fourteen days whether or not he intends to oppose the application. It is clearly important here that if the respondent fails to reply, the court will be able to assume that the application is unopposed and the provisions of Section 32 (A) (2) will apply in relevant cases.

New rules 14A and 14B are now inserted into the 1970 Rules and their effect is far-reaching. They deal first of all with the appointment of the guardian *ad litem* from the 'panel of persons' established under Section 103 of the 1975 Act. The latter part of sub-section (2) Rule 14A makes it clear that the person appointed must be truly independent of the parties to the proceedings. The panel, when it is established, will consist of local authority social workers, probation officers and other qualified, but independent, persons. The appointment of a guardian *ad litem* from the panel 'shall be exercisable before the hearing of the application . . . by a single Justice or by the Justice's Clerk' (Rule 14A (4)).

The new Rule 14A (6) (a) to (f) sets out the duties of the new guardian *ad litem*. In pursuit of his overriding duty to safeguard the interests of the relevant infant, wide powers are envisaged to enable him to 'investigate all circumstances relevant to the proceedings and for that purpose shall interview such persons and inspect such records as the guardian *ad litem* thinks appropriate'. What action may be judged 'appropriate' by the guardian *ad litem* clearly depends on the individual case, but the Rules generally convey a feeling of thoroughness which ought to dispel any complacency that the duties would be interpreted simply as an extension of some existing responsibility. It immediately becomes apparent that the guardian *ad litem* will be required to make an independent assessment of policy decisions of the local authority in the case, and will require him on occasions to express an opinion about the best interests of the child which may conflict with the opinion of another professional social worker. It has already emerged that the power to 'inspect such records' will sometimes be resisted, and the complex issue of confidentiality will undoubtedly again come under minute dissection. It may be right in passing to reflect on the effect of this rule on attitudes towards recording in social work. There is clearly potential for professional rivalries to be played out on this new ground where the guardian *ad litem* and the relevant social worker represent different agencies or social work disciplines, but one would hope that the spirit of independent professional scrutiny will give rise to improved quality and care in the accurate recording of services provided and decisions made. It might also be said that even in those circumstances where the guardian *ad litem* is denied access to such records as he may require to see, his experience should enable him to elicit the reasoning, opinion and attitude he hoped to find therein, by directly interviewing the individuals who made the records or are aware of what they contain.

The crucial part of the duty of the guardian *ad litem* is the requirement to represent the views of the child. This can only be achieved effectively by going beyond the records and opinions of those adults involved, to actual communication and dialogue with the child concerned. It is an issue of which authorities nominating panels of guardians should be aware because skills in other fields of social work practice, perhaps with adult offenders or vulnerable elderly or handicapped people, are not an automatic qualification. Knowledge of normal development and first-hand experience of work with children are essential. To be allowed to enter into and share a glimpse of a child's perception of the world is a privilege for an adult at any time, and a comparatively rare experience within the context of a professional relationship. Time and personal security are probably the main prerequisites and they both appear scarce commodities. Children will communicate what they truly feel to adults with whom they feel safe, at times and in places where they feel comfortable. The same principle may well apply in work with adults but dangers lurking in the formal interview situation and the making of adult interpretations of childish perceptions must be acknowledged in working face to face with children.

At all times the work of the guardian *ad litem* is guided by the principle that it is the child's opinions and perceptions he will seek first to understand and then represent to the court. In the light of the work carried out by the guardian *ad litem* he must then make a decision 'in the infant's best interests' whether 'the application to which the proceedings relate should succeed'. When that decision has been made he must then 'decide how the case should be conducted . . . and where appropriate instruct a solicitor to represent the infant' (14A (6) (b) and (c)). If the decision is not to instruct a solicitor, then the guardian *ad litem* shall 'conduct the case on behalf of the infant', although the infant may 'otherwise request' Rule 14A (6) (d).

We have mixed feelings about the advisability of proceeding without instructing a solicitor. It might be argued that the guardian *ad litem* having made extensive investigations, and having arrived at his independent and professional opinion, would be hard-pressed indeed adequately to brief a solicitor to represent his views within the formal and adversarial court setting. It could be said that a solicitor would tend to reduce arguments to fit his accustomed mode, whereas a social worker, whilst recognizing the limitations of the court setting for his free expression, would nevertheless be more concerned to find ways of meeting the demands of the setting whilst in no way impairing the force of his argument. Against this it may be countered that if the guardian *ad litem* does not instruct a solicitor, then he himself has to be master of the legal process and the relevant rules of evidence, thereby increasing his burden rather than reducing it. It is too much, particularly in especially complex conflicts, to expect the guardian *ad litem* to conduct the case, using such legal and adversarial skills as he may possess, to the point at which the court makes its decision about the application, and then to become the independent caseworker and submit a confidential report which must be the product of different, and perhaps more subjective, assessment skills. Additionally it is possible that the laws of evidence may bias or restrain the development of certain aspects of the case during the hearing of the application, but that these could then be developed quite properly in the guardian *ad litem*'s report. The court may be in a dilemma if it has been satisfied, on the formal evidence produced, that an application to discharge a Care Order should succeed, but becomes less certain when influenced by the report. As the separate representation provisions were designed to give the court access to the opinions and feelings of the child through an independent person, it appears to be self-defeating for the court not to receive it until after it has made its decision. Probably the need to appoint a solicitor will only occur in those cases where the guardian *ad litem* decides to oppose the application; and this may result in a conflict between him and the local authority especially if it has decided to support the application.

Rule 14A (6) (e) together with its reference to Rule 20 (1) (a) makes it clear that only where the court is satisfied that the applicant's case has been proved should it consider any written report which the guardian *ad litem* may make available if he 'thinks that it would assist the court'. This is different from the position of the guardian *ad litem*'s report in adoption proceedings, which is available on completion of his investigation, but is quite consistent with all other proceedings and requirements relating to the use and purpose of Welfare Reports. In other words, any written report would be provided to assist the court to decide which of its powers to use in relation to the application. For instance an application for the discharge of a care order may be accepted by the court, which may then be persuaded through the provision of a written report by the guardian *ad litem* that a supervision order needs to be made in the interests of the child.

There seems to be no legal reason why the guardian *ad litem* may not become the supervisor of the child in those cases where a supervision order is the outcome. In fact, there would appear to be some justification for hoping that this may be the case, in view of the independent and extensive nature of his investigation, and the relationship and rapport which should have developed, on the other hand there may be many practical reasons why this may not be possible for reasons of geography or agency policy.

Rule 14A (7) lays down the guardian *ad litem*'s final duty in respect of the child. 'When the Court has finally disposed of the case, the guardian *ad litem* shall consider whether it would be in the infant's best interests to appeal to the Crown Court.' If so, he should then 'give notice of appeal on behalf of the infant'. In reaching this decision the social worker is guided by the feelings and opinions of the child to which he should have become highly sensitive, and if it is available, the expert opinion of a lawyer.

The social worker in custodianship proceedings

Custodianship (S. 33–46, 1975 Act) was introduced as a means of providing legal security for a child and the adult or adults with whom he lives. Unlike adoption it can be revoked and the child retains his name. It has its parallels in law, in guardianship and matrimonial proceedings. Section 33 (9) makes it clear that the principle enacted in section 1 of the Guardianship of Minors Act 1971 applies to applications for a custodianship order, namely that the court in dealing with such cases shall have regard to the welfare of the minor as the 'first and paramount consideration'. In this respect therefore, the provisions referring to custodianship are significantly different from others introduced by this Act.

With the consent of the person having legal custody of the child application for a custodianship order may be made by a relative or step-parent of the child, after the child has lived with them for three months, and by any person with whom the child has had his home for a period or periods totalling twelve months, including the three months immediately prior to the application. This second group includes foster-parents and house-parents of small children's homes. Without the consent of the person who has the legal custody of the child application may be made by any person with whom the child has lived for a period or periods totalling three years including the three months immediately prior to the application. The order, once it is made rests the legal custody of the child in the person or persons who made the application. They become the custodians of the child.

At the time of the hearing of the application or while a custodianship order is in force the court may make conditions about access to the child on an order, possibly against both parents separately, regarding a financial contribution towards his care. Application to revoke the order may be made by the custodian, the father, the mother or guardian of the child, or any local authority in England and Wales. If that application is refused another may not be made unless it appears to the court that because of a change in circumstances or for any other reason it is proper to proceed

hapter 5

ocial Work and
omestic Proceedings

ic Cooper

ckground

e range of social work demands which now arises from all kinds
domestic proceedings has, in the main, developed in relatively
ent times. Changing social conditions, and developments in
th law and social work, have led to the proliferation of statutory
ks required of social work agencies, notably in those aspects of
oceedings which concern the welfare of children.

In a less formal way, however, the relationship between
mestic Courts and social workers, particularly probation
icers and the former child care officers, goes back a surprisingly
g way. The range of problems experienced by the clients of
se workers inevitably provided them with wide experience of all
al remedies for family distress. In some cities the practice
veloped amongst probation officers of intercepting applicants
matrimonial summonses at local courts to offer a conciliation
vice. More formal opportunities came to be provided in a
iety of proceedings, when the means of the parties needed to be
estigated, and in applications for consent to marry, especially
ore the lowering of the age of majority. Intervention in all of
se both drew upon, and added to, the growing body of
owledge about marital and domestic dispute.

The 1960s and 70s have seen the advent of much important
islation. The Matrimonial Proceedings (Magistrates' Courts)
of 1960 brought together all the legislation which had
veloped in this field from the turn of the century, and with the
dition of some new provisions provided a framework in which
st aspects of domestic dispute could be resolved, at least in so
as any legislation is able to make provision for the complexity
domestic conflict. The Divorce Reform Act of 1969 and the
trimonial Causes Act of 1973 transformed the law on divorce

with the application. Before revoking a custodianship order a
court shall, unless it already has sufficient information, require a
report from the local authority or a probation officer. It is within
the power of the court, on the basis of information in such a report,
to make a supervision order or a care order.

A custodianship order may be made when an application has
been made by a relative of the child or by the husband or wife of the
mother or father of the child *to adopt* the child. Likewise when a
similar application is made by a person who is neither a relative
nor the husband or wife of the mother or father of the child, i.e. a
foster-parent, the court may deem that a custodianship order
would be more appropriate. In all circumstances where a court
considers making a custodianship order, for whatever reasons, it
may request a report from the local authority or the probation
service in whose area the applicant or applicants reside.

Custodianship is going to have resource implications in local
authority social services departments particularly as far as the very
limited resource of skilled manpower is concerned. In addition it
requires of those social workers involved with families and
children for whom custodianship may be considered a need to be
very clear in their own thinking about legal statutes and the
needs of children. A legal procedure can be used in various
circumstances to achieve different ends. Prior to the implementation of this measure the chief ways of providing security
for a vulnerable child were through a care order, the assumption of parental rights by the local authority, or adoption.
Custodianship provides another alternative and the Houghton
Committee anticipated that it would be the most appropriate
provision for children being cared for by relatives and step-
parents. Some people have expressed doubts about this (Terry
1976, 78) and argue that it would be unacceptable to relatives
because it would not 'cancel the reality of the family background'
nor result in a change of name. It is impossible for legal provision
of any kind to remove the reality or the recollection of family
background and there are ways, other than adoption, of changing
a child's name if it is in his interests. Sooner or later every child asks
the question 'who am I?' and 'where do I belong?' and especially
when he is with members of his own family he will seek the answer
in his own way from amongst his own feelings and recollections.
Legislation will seem peripheral to his experience. 'Tug of love'
conflicts between foster-parents and natural parents which
sometimes attract public attention are tragic for several reasons. It
is regrettable that a child is subject to such conflict, that adults

experience and inflict such wounds, and that social work practice has failed to cope with the strains involved before what is sometimes a public explosion of anger and distress. There must be grounds for concern that custodianship, rather than reducing the number of 'tug of love' conflicts may well cause more. It gives to one of the parties involved the option to take a legal step which will shift the balance between substitute and natural parent. While this is worrying for the social worker because he is in the midst of the conflict, there must be special concern for the child because it may be that legal processes will pronounce decisively about an issue about which he feels ambivalent, for at least some of the time. Custodianship may lead to a polarization between foster-parents and social workers who should work together. This will be particularly unfortunate because what will be at stake will be the credibility of a social worker's practice. It would appear to us that in most situations where there is sound rapport the child and his foster-parents are adequately protected by the provisions of other existing legislation providing they are used properly.

If foster-parents do apply to a court for such an order the child cannot be moved by the local authority before the hearing unless there are grounds for a place of safety order. The court report in such a hearing is prepared by a local authority or probation officer not directly involved with the child and his family. The department responsible for care contributes to the hearing as it will be party to the proceedings. It may be that the authority concerned will not oppose the application, in which case all the concerns about conflict are irrelevant. If the custodianship order is granted to foster-parents the child ceases to be 'in care' and it may be that this will be helpful for some children. If it is thought to be appropriate there is provision for local authorities to continue financial contribution towards the maintenance of the child and for a supervision order to be made.

The report prepared for the court in custodianship proceedings is important. The skills required and the qualifications of the individual who prepares it have already been described in this chapter. What is apparent and what emerges more clearly with every stage of the implementation of the 1975 Act is the urgent need for social workers of considerable stature to contribute effectively to the making of 'life decisions' about children.

Recommended reading

TERRY, J. A. 1975: *A Guide to the Children Act* Lo
    Maxwell.
PACKMAN, J. 1975: *The Child's Generation* Lon
    Robertson.

Notes

1 The term 'child' is used throughout the chapter and
   under eighteen who may be adopted.
2 The Prevention of Cruelty to, and Protection of Chil
   first great children Act. It introduced the 'fit pers
   removal of children neglected or ill-treated in their
3 Report of the Committee of Enquiry into the car
   provided in relation to Maria Colwell. London: HM
4 House of Lords (1975). Volume 356 col. 18. The I
   Lord Elwyn Jones.
5 They are well set out in the second schedule to the
   Court) Rules 1959, as amended by Rule 7 of the
   Court) (Amendment) Rules 1963.

breaking away from the notion of guilt and innocence (still the crucial test in the Magistrates' Court where a matrimonial offence has to be proved) to a compromise position whereby the sole criterion for divorce is the irretrievable breakdown of the marriage. The Probation Service had been pioneering a Divorce Court Welfare Service since the early 1950s and it was natural that this new legislation should place upon it heavy responsibility for continuing to provide this service, with extended powers and duties. The Guardianship of Minors Act 1971 and the Guardianship Act 1973 also gave magistrates the power to make orders relating to children in cases outside the scope of the earlier legislation, and the Children Act 1975 added new principles and further refinements. In this way, Magistrates' Courts, County Courts and the Family Division of the High Court, are all involved in work arising out of matrimonial and family disputes, which involve social workers in a variety of roles and duties.

Domestic proceedings in magistrates' courts

Magistrates' Courts are able to hear complaints by married persons and may make a wide variety of decisions. Proceedings at this level are based upon the notion of the matrimonial offence, which has to be admitted or proved, and for this purpose one spouse must lay a complaint against the other.[1] This may be done at any time from the date of marriage, unlike a petition for divorce. In some areas probation officers work among those spouses making applications for summonses at local courts, to offer an advice or conciliation service to those applicants who are unsure, or reluctant to proceed.

At the hearing of such a complaint the magistrates may make a Matrimonial Order (commonly known as a Separation Order). This may contain a number of clauses depending upon the needs of the situation. These will relate to such matters as maintenance, non-cohabitation, custody of, and access to, children of the marriage.[2] Magistrates may sometimes call for assistance in their decision-making about maintenance by asking for a Means Enquiry Report.[3] This requires the social worker to investigate all aspects of the financial position of the party or parties referred, and to report his findings to the magistrates in writing. Undoubtedly the most frequent and demanding task required by the court is the preparation of a 'Welfare Report' on the background of applications relating to the custody of children. A report may be requested at the hearing of the original application for a Matrimonial Order, or on a subsequent application for a variation in any previously ordered arrangements. Custody reports may be requested by magistrates in two types of proceedings: Matrimonial[4] and Guardianship.[5] A report is usually only required when the question of custody is in dispute, but by no means all contested applications lead to such a referral. These reports are normally provided by the probation service, but exceptions may occur if a local authority social worker is already involved.

Custody reports (matrimonial proceedings)
That part of matrimonial proceedings which relates to the custody of children and related matters, will usually be separated from the main application and dealt with on another date, particularly if the issue is contested. A report may only be requested in these proceedings after the court has reached a decision on the matrimonial complaint, even if its decision is that the case has not been proved. The probation officer may often, therefore, find that he has a substantial period of time in which to make his enquiries and report, but the complexity of such situations will sometimes make even that length of time appear inadequate. Custody reports relate only to those children who are under sixteen years of age.[6] It is now generally agreed that the report should have only one author, even though the parties may be living at some distance from each other, and the children may be living with one party only, or be shared between them, or staying with a third party. Clearly, in some circumstances considerations of distance and expense may make this impossible, but the value of all aspects of a situation being appraised by the same person is self-evident. The report will often be allocated to the worker for the area in which the children are resident, but practice will vary from area to area and case to case. The report will be made available to the court, and to each party, but the author need not attend the hearing unless required to do so by either of the parties or their legal representatives.[7]

Custody reports (guardianship proceedings)
Magistrates may be faced with the need to make similar decisions about the welfare of children in applications under the Guardianship of Minors Act 1971 (this Act enables proceedings to be brought at Magistrates' Court, County Court and Divorce Court levels). Such applications differ from those brought before

magistrates under the Matrimonial Proceedings Act in that the court is not required to adjudicate on the state of a marriage, but solely on those aspects of the welfare of children which are referred to in the application. This enables applications to be made by parents who are not actually married, or those who are married but intend to obtain a divorce rather than a Matrimonial Order and require a decision in the interim to establish or ratify suitable arrangements for the children of the relationship. Additionally these proceedings enable the court to appoint a guardian for children who have no parents. In this Act we have a clear expression of the principle on which all similar proceedings are based, namely that the court must regard the welfare of the child as the first and paramount consideration.[8] As in matrimonial proceedings, the court may call for a report on any matter which appears to be relevant to the application,[9] although in practice most requests require a full survey of all the available alternatives. When a guardianship application is received by a court, a single magistrate or a Justices' Clerk may call for a report to be prepared in time for the initial hearing of the application, thereby often avoiding unnecessary delay in reaching custody decisions.[10]

Divorce proceedings
Divorce proceedings are shared between certain designated County Courts, presided over by a Circuit Judge, and the Divorce Court (Family Division of the High Court). In general terms the County Courts deal with undefended divorce petitions, and contested cases are heard by the High Court. Under new arrangements introduced in April 1977, a decree may be granted in all undefended cases without the need for the Petitioner to attend court. When children under sixteen are involved, however, the Petitioner must discuss with the Judge in Chambers his Statement of Arrangements (filed in all divorce cases when children of this age are concerned).

All contested divorce applications are heard by a High Court Judge who may, when he has ruled on the disputed application, refer ancillary matters for hearing in the County Court. The principle operating in divorce proceedings is that of the irretrievable breakdown of the marriage, which is the sole ground on which the petition may be presented and the decree granted. The grounds on which it may be accepted that the marriage has irretrievably broken down are set out in the Matrimonial Causes Act 1973 (Section 2 Part 1).

The volume of work which is referred by these courts for the attention of social workers and probation officers is very great and increasing constantly, and for each Divorce Court or group of Courts a Divorce Court Welfare Officer is appointed (usually a Senior Probation Officer) to coordinate and administer all the necessary arrangements. In some divorce petitions an interim order will already have been made by the Magistrates' Court[11] about the welfare of the children, and the higher court will not normally interfere with these. When this has not already happened, the County or Divorce Court will first deal with the petition and then remit the child-related matters to a private hearing in chambers at which only the parties are present.

A Judge or Registrar is empowered at any time to refer to a court welfare officer for investigation and a report on any matter arising which concerns the welfare of a child.[12] When such enquiry is referred to a social worker or probation officer the Divorce Court welfare officer will send him copies of relevant documents from the file, but particularly copies of the parties' affidavits and the Statement of Arrangements made for the children. Requests for Welfare Reports will usually fall into one of the following categories:

1 *Satisfaction Reports* are requested when the Judge does not feel that he has enough independent knowledge of the arrangements made for the children to express himself satisfied. Such reports may often be relatively brief.

2 *Custody Reports* are requested when the parties are in dispute and proposing alternative arrangements for the welfare of the children. These reports are invariably the most demanding of all, and are usually lengthy because of their complexity.

3 *Access Reports* are usually requested when the custody issue is agreed or settled but help is required in determining the details of the access arrangements. These will often be complex, even intractable, especially when the dispute arises out of the parties' inability to cease hostilities.

4 A fourth category of report occurs when the Statement of Arrangements indicates that a child or children is under supervision or in care. The relevant supervisor will be required to report on the origin and progress of supervision, but as this will usually be requested before the hearing of the relevant matters and because of the relatively narrow focus, such a report would not normally preclude the possibility of a welfare report being required subsequently in any of the other circumstances described.

The grounds on which decisions are made to ask for welfare reports to be prepared, or to proceed without them, seem to vary enormously in practice and give cause for concern. A recent study (Oxford Centre for Socio-Legal Studies 1977) indicates that regional variations in practice are extremely wide. On the basis of statistics alone it is clear that the situation of many thousands of children who are affected by the breakdown of their parents' marriage is given no adequate professional attention. The recommendations of a recent working party on the subject include provision for greater involvement of the Divorce Court welfare officer in decisions about which cases require full investigation (Chief Probation Officers' Conference 1976). Such a measure would undoubtedly help to overcome the worrying inadequacies of current decision-making on this vital matter, and would in no way detract from the responsibility of judges. The availability of professional advice and support, both to courts and to families, would seem to depend on a more effective partnership between the judiciary and the Probation Service in the initial but all-important task of scrutiny.

Some attention now needs to be given to the definition of 'Custody' which has so far been used in this chapter in a very general way. In legal terms custody actually means the possession of legal rights over the child, whereas day-to-day possession of, and general responsibility for, a child is indicated by the term 'Care and Control'. 'Access' means the right to visits or meetings with the child. An Order made by a court will, therefore, tend to be one of three types. Possibly the most common of these is for custody and care and control to be granted to one parent with access to the other. Sometimes care and control will be given to one, with custody to the other, who will therefore have to be consulted over major decisions relating to religious and secular education, consent to marry, etc. The third situation would occur where each parent is granted custody so that major decisions would have to be shared, with care and control to one only. Some aspects of the law on these matters impart greater authority and discretion to judges than to magistrates, but these considerations lie outside our scope.

All the courts with authority in these matters may make a supervision order in respect of any child who is the subject of a custody decision when the court feels it appropriate to do so.[13] There is no lower age limit for the making of such an order, and it would expire on the child's sixteenth birthday in the case of an order made by a magistrates' court, and at the age of eighteen when made by a Divorce Court. The court may specify that supervision should be exercised by a probation officer or by the local authority. In the magistrates' court a supervision order may be varied or discharged by application by the supervising officer, or one of the parties.[14] In the Divorce Court a similar procedure is available, or in cases where his decision to discharge the order is not contested by the parties, the supervisor may simply refer the matter to the Judge via the Divorce Court welfare officer, stating his case in the form of a letter.

In exceptional circumstances a court may place a child in the care of a third party or in the care of a local authority, and in that situation the local authority must be given the opportunity to be heard.[15]

The professional task

To be involved in any of the proceedings mentioned in this chapter presents a complex professional task to the probation officer or social worker. With the possible exception of Satisfaction Reports where the worker's task may simply be to confirm that the situation is satisfactory and as described in the Statement of Arrangements, the demands that will be made upon him will almost invariably be more extensive than the question of custody may seem to imply. The worker needs to be aware of the tremendous significance which his intervention will have in the minds of the parties concerned. For them, the question of custody and access will be another stage in the decomposition of their most intimate relationship, providing opportunities for old scores to be settled, or previous defeats to be reversed. In many cases, the worker's presence provides the first opportunity for the un-interrupted expression of hurt, anger, guilt, etc., and the worker may have to spend many hours with the parties before he is able to engage in discussion of the precise purpose for which he is involved. It is crucially important for the worker to appreciate that the sole principle on which decisions will be made about the custody of children is that paramount consideration will be given to the welfare of the child. The worker will usually be aware of the needs of the parties themselves, but should beware of playing the game, so easily and unconsciously entered into, of 'awarding' the child to the parent who is the most distressed, or deserving, or innocent. The emotional burden which the worker may often be required to carry can bring about such a degree of distortion or subjectivity that professional consultation and supervision should be provided or sought in most cases. When the family unit is in the process of dissolution the feelings of parents and children will be understandably confused, and possibly destructive. The form that the future will take for all of them may be quite uncertain and the need to gain the support of the worker for a particular arrangement or point of view may give rise to a fair degree of manipulation and pressure. For many workers the plight of the children themselves will be the most stressful aspect of the enquiry. Exposed to the inconsistency and bitterness of the parents, or simply to their confusion and unhappiness, the children may have suffered consequences which will demand of the worker acute perception and finely balanced judgment. Much will depend on the age of the child concerned, but wherever possible the feelings and opinions of the child should be sought, as these will assume importance in the making of decisions about him, in proportion to his ability to understand and express them.

In order to arrive at a comprehensive assessment of what constitutes the welfare of the child, the worker will need to have discussions with a wide variety of people. General practitioners and teachers are probably the most informed sources of information apart from the parents themselves, but sometimes grandparents or other relatives may be considered as well as the local authority, the police and the education welfare service. Very great care has to be exercised in decisions about potential sources of information, but discussion of these with the parties will usually make one's responsibilities in this direction clear. In all cases the worker should make it clear to his contacts that the information given, if included in the report, will be seen by the parties.

The worker will need to examine carefully the implications of any proposed arrangements for a child. For example, one parent may be proposing that the child should live with him or her at an address other than the matrimonial home, and the worker will need to consider the impact on the child of another environment which may be strange to him and which may involve a change of school, etc. Wherever possible, the worker should see the child in the circumstances to which it is proposed he should go, and where this would involve a change from a situation which may have been relatively constant prior to the hearing of the application, great care will need to be exercised. It is clearly important to see the child in the company of any person who may acquire 'Care and Control'.

Some of the most difficult and intractable situations arise where the only outstanding matter is that of access by the party not having care and control. The worker may be called to report on the possibility of defining access quite precisely in those situations where the parties cannot agree. Such a definition might be so detailed as to specify the frequency, timing, duration and place at which access is to be made available, and may even require the presence of a third party acceptable to both parents. The court may often seek a way out of such a dilemma by making a supervision order, with the specific intention of dealing only with the access problem. It is sometimes tempting to collude with the desire of one party to exclude the other from access altogether, which may be presented as a deceptively commendable way of simplifying matters and relieving the strain on the child. It is helpful to reflect that the right of access is as much the child's as the absent parent's, and denying the child that right carelessly is a denial of an essential part of the child's personality. It is, in any case, extremely rare for a Court to deny access to a natural parent, and such a step would normally only be taken when a real element of risk to the child existed.

Supervision in domestic proceedings has no clear definition; unlike other forms of supervision there are no statutory conditions or sanctions, although the matter can be referred back to the court for clarification or variation. The court needs only to decide that it is 'desirable' that the Order should be made. Usually, however, the making of Supervision Orders will follow an extensive period of contact between the worker and the family for the purpose of a report of one type or another, and in most cases the Supervision Order will be made on the advice of the author of the report. It follows, therefore, that the meaning of supervision in that particular situation will already be clear to the worker, and it will obviously be to everybody's advantage that the implications of such an Order should have been discussed during the enquiry with the parties. This is particularly important in view of the fact that although the legislation clearly envisages that the supervisor should be a person of some influence in the total situation, no statutory rights or powers are given to him, not even on access to the child. Supervision in most cases would probably provide for the continuation of discussions begun during the enquiry, with a view to establishing and confirming those developments which have been identified as in the best interests of all concerned.

It is clear that there are a number of persistent anomalies in the field of social work in domestic proceedings. The Probation Service, by virtue of its role as social work agent to the courts, has become responsible for a steadily increasing volume of Welfare

Reports in the Divorce Courts, whilst paradoxically its com-mitment to matrimonial work has steadily declined. Opinions vary about the propriety of allowing a Service which has become increasingly identified, in the eyes of many, with the penal system, to have total responsibility for the provision of the Divorce Court Welfare Service. There seems a strong possibility of the stigma which often attaches to probation officers in the mind of the ordinary citizen, proving to be a huge impediment to helpful communication with the divorcing parent. Nor is enough known about the way probation officers view and approach this expanding, non-criminal, proportion of their workload in the context of demands, also expanding, for the provision of alternative measures to imprisonment. The Service's unique relationship with the judiciary could possibly satisfy one of the criteria advanced in the Finer Report (1974) for a specialist Court Welfare Service, but its divided loyalties and idiosyncratic preferences from area to area would fail to meet other requirements. It is, however, undeniable that a wealth of appropriate experience exists in the Service which could be used to great effect in all family-based court business. The Probation Service should decide, at national level, whether it can, and should, demand resources for the adequate and organized provision of such a service, based perhaps on the secondment model. Such a course could enrich the experience of the clients, courts, and workers themselves, when they meet to resolve the difficulties of families in disarray.

Postscript

The Domestic Proceedings and Magistrates' Courts Act 1978, when implemented, will repeal the Matrimonial Proceedings (Magistrates' Courts) Act 1960. Its effect will be to simplify the conditions under which a Matrimonial Order may be made, and bring the spirit of domestic proceedings in Magistrates' Courts much closer to that which prevails in divorce proceedings in higher Courts. There will be some adjustment to the rules govern-ing the making of Supervision Orders in certain proceedings, and the circumstances in which Courts may request Welfare Reports will be extended. Magistrates' Courts will have a new duty placed on them in some proceedings to consider whether there is any possibility of a reconciliation between the parties and may adjourn the proceedings and request a Probation Officer to attempt the work of reconciliation.

Notes

1 Matrimonial Proceedings (Magistrates' Courts) Act 1960 S1.
2 Matrimonial Proceedings (Magistrates' Courts) Act 1960 S2.
3 Matrimonial Proceedings (Magistrates' Courts) Act 1960 S4 (2).
4 Matrimonial Proceedings (Magistrates' Courts) Act 1960 S1.
5 Guardianship Act 1973 S6 (1).
6 Matrimonial Proceedings (Magistrates' Courts) Act 1960 S2 (1) (d).
7 Matrimonial Proceedings (Magistrates' Courts) Act 1960 S4 (3) and (4) as amended by Children Act 1975 S91.
8 Guardianship of Minors Act 1971 S1.
9 Guardianship Act 1973 S6 (1).
10 Guardianship Act 1973 S6 (6) As amended by Children Act 1975 S90 (2).
11 Matrimonial Proceedings (Magistrates' Courts) Act 1960 S6. Guardianship Act 1973 S2 (4).
12 Matrimonial Causes Rules 1973 Rule 95 (1). Guardianship Act 1973 S6 (1) As amended by Children Act 1975 S90.
13 Matrimonial Proceedings (Magistrates' Courts) Act 1960 S2 (1) (f). Matrimonial Causes Act 1973 S44 (1).
14 Matrimonial Proceedings (Magistrates' Courts) Act 1960 S10 (1). Matrimonial Causes Act 1973 S44 (5). Magistrates' Courts (Matrimonial Proceedings) Rules 1960.
15 Matrimonial Proceedings (Magistrates' Courts) Act 1960 S8 (1). Guardianship Act 1973 S2 (2) (6) and S4 (1) and (2). Matrimonial Causes Rules 1973 Rule 93.

Chapter 6

Professionals in the Magistrates' Courts: The Courtroom Lore of Probation Officers and Social Workers

Pat Carlen and Margaret Powell

The office of Justice of the Peace originated late in the twelfth century, but it was not until the sixteenth century that the work of the justices began to take on many of its present-day characteristics (Milton 1967). The Justices of the Peace Act 1361 described their duty as being 'to pursue and arrest' offenders – they were, in short, detectives and prosecutors. Acts of 1554 and 1555 added the taking of depositions to their duties, and, later, the responsibility of administering the Elizabethan Poor Law also fell to them. When the 'police' courts of the large urban area came into being in the late nineteenth century the ominously prophetic words 'Police Court' were often inscribed on the walls of the uniformly bleak court buildings. But not for long were these buildings to remain the sole domain of magistrates and police. Already psychiatry, social work and probation were encroaching upon the classical model of criminal justice (Beccaria 1964; Taylor, Walton and Young 1973) and, with the vast majority of defendants pleading or being found guilty, much of the decision-making in the lower courts soon came to be centred on questions concerning the *type* of person who had committed the crime, rather than on questions of guilt or innocence. The new penology, therefore, attempted to fit the punishment to the person rather than to the crime, but the tension between retributive justice and reformative treatment has still not been resolved. It is daily reactivated in the magistrates' courts as magistrates try to satisfy both the classical (and popular) demands that justice should be seen to be done *and* the current rhetoric that offenders should be viewed as individuals amenable to treatment *after* professional assessment by either psychiatrists, probation officers or social workers.

Magistrates' courts as professional workshops

The primary mandate of the magistrates, whether they be unpaid lay magistrates or paid stipendiary (professional) magistrates, is the same: the hearing and determining charges of lesser offences according to the principles of law in a democratic society. In addition they also hear matrimonial and affiliation cases, as well as evidence from fine defaulters about their financial position. The administrative work of magistrates includes the granting of summonses and warrants for arrests, the taking of declarations, the witnessing of documents and the granting of liquor and betting licences. Nor is their criminal jurisdiction limited to the summary disposal of cases. Nearly all criminal cases come before the magistrates, if not to be heard summarily, at least for preliminary inquiry. Surrounding the magistrates are the teams of competing professionals who assist the court in reaching its decisions. The formally prescribed and legitimate interests of these professional teams can be set out quite simply; in theory they are not even opposed.

The magistrate is expected to dispose judiciously and lawfully of all matters brought before him; other teams of professionals are expected to provide information which will assist the court in reaching its judicial decisions. In criminal matters the two decisions of paramount importance are the determination of the guilt or innocence of the accused and, in the event of a finding of guilt or a conviction, the determination of the appropriate sentence.

The prosecution and its witnesses (police, sometimes solicitors and sometimes witnesses of the alleged crime) and the defence and its witnesses (sometimes a solicitor, sometimes a friend or voluntary organization conducting a defence, more often the accused person on his own or with witnesses) assist the magistrate by providing evidence as to the guilt or innocence of the defendant.

Assisting the magistrate by providing 'knowledge' of the defendant found or pleading guilty are the police who provide 'antecedents' of the defendant. Sometimes a solicitor makes a plea in mitigation, and occasionally recommends a sentence. Similarly, sometimes probation officers, who in their social inquiry reports provide items of information about the defendant's past and present circumstances, assess his attitude towards the admitted or attributed offence and make a recommendation as to sentence (see chapter 7). On occasion social workers can provide additional information. The pervading mode of inter-action between the different professional groups in the magistrates' courts – and the words most frequently used to describe that mode – is one of 'uneasy compromise'. The policemen, the probation officers, the social workers, the magistrates and the solicitors in courts are nowadays working in multi-professional workshops. The court setting which is so alien to the defendant (Dell 1970; Carlen 1976; Christie 1976; Newman 1966; Parker 1974) is the daily workplace for the professionals who regularly come there to practise their professional expertise, and who, in so doing also establish working relationships which will enable the court to get through its business. There are three distinct features of these judicial and professional workshops which infuse these inter-professional relationships with unease.

First, there is the awareness that the goals of the various professional groups are often in direct opposition to each other. Second, there is an uneasy acknowledgment that inter-professional strategies designed to 'do the best we can in the circumstances' might be (or sometimes could be) construed as actually being infringements of the law or the professional ethic (cf. Parkinson 1977). Third, there is among courtworkers an uneasy awareness that many of the decisions they make are based on either an instrumentality or a forced economic expediency which violates both their own and popular conceptions of justice. These three features of their courtroom situation provide the inter-actional context within which professionals engage in the strategies which, without detracting from their own professional interests, will secure the best outcome for their clients. The informal rule-usage thus engendered results in a *courtroom lore* which enables the job at hand to be done with a minimum of inter-professional conflict. The admission by the professionals that they often have to say that they are doing one thing when in fact they hope that they are doing something entirely different leads many of them to talk about the magistrates' courts using terms taken from the theatre or the games field. Defendants also complain that court proceedings are 'just a game' and this generalized tendency to compare the courtroom with the games field converges with the practice of sociologists who have also used games theory to highlight some of the inter-actional features of the lower courts (Blumberg 1967;

Carlen 1976; Emerson 1969). The analyses have usually stressed that the games being played in courts are primarily information games.

> Information games arise whenever one actor wishes to uncover information from another who wishes to conceal it. Some persons and categories of persons must play information games almost all the time, or as part of their occupations. Among the former are those possessing discreditable identities; among the latter, all those charged with keeping institutionalized secrets. (Lyman and Scott 1970)

Within and around magistrates' courts several different information games are being played at once, and, in the remainder of this chapter we will be discussing how probation officers and social workers account for their own professional gamesmanship.

Probation officers in court

The tradition of probation officers providing the court with background information about a defendant, and further, urging upon the court a particular course of action, dates back to the earliest days of the police-court missionaries at the end of the last century (Jarvis 1974, 108; Herbert and Mathieson 1975, 10); they explicitly and without embarrassment pleaded on behalf of certain defendants. When the probation order was formally introduced, it was to be used 'having regard to the character, antecedents, age, health or mental condition of the person charged' (Probation of Offenders Act 1970 S1) thus implying some form of report or provision of information. As the probation officer's role with adult offenders developed, so the 1927 Report of the Departmental Committee on the Treatment of Offenders showed that reports were being prepared by probation officers on many juvenile cases. Subsequently, the 1933 Children and Young Persons Act provided for the court to obtain the fullest possible information on young persons. This principle was carried through to the 1969 Children and Young Persons Act, although the responsibility for providing such information is now being transferred to the Social Services Departments of the local authorities.

So, the probation officer is an 'officer of the court' (Cmnd 1650, 1962) but who is his client? Is it the court? Or is it the defendant? If the client is the court, then how does the probation officer stand in relation to court and defendant? Whose side is he on? Is he, by definition, a formal agent of control, or is he a professional offering his services to the court? The Departmental Committee on the Probation Service defined the probation officer as a 'social caseworker who is an officer of the court' (Cmnd 1650, 1962). Certainly *his* professional status, unlike that of the solicitor or policeman, is ascribed by the court, although the structure of the probation service gives him his own professional hierarchy. Yet the bulk of the work, and the work in which probation officers claim to be most interested, is in practising their 'treatment' or 'diagnostic' skills with clients. Because of this Ms W, a probation officer, thought that probation officers should be striving to develop the role of 'independent' professional rather than taking their status from the court: 'I don't feel the probation service is professional enough about the role it plays in court. I think the court abuses our role; the magistrate can do so by using us as servants of the court rather than as providing a service to the court.'*

Some probation officers solve the control/treatment problem by seeing the court as the 'referral agency' to whom they have a responsibility to provide information concerning diagnoses and treatment of a client, whilst seeing the client's 'interests', as defined by their professional judgment, as being determinant of the *kind* of information and diagnoses which they provide. For other probation officers however the nature of their relationship with the court in general and with solicitors, police and magistrates in particular is a constant source of strain. The practices they engage in with each of these groups depend to a large extent upon their definitions of the probation officers' courtroom role, though in interaction with other professionals this role is defined and redefined time and time again. At different times and with different groups, different role-definitions tend to be dominant, though the range of courtroom strategies engaged in by probation officers tends to centre on four possible major definitions of their courtroom role. We have categorized these dominant definitions as: (1) the servant of the court; (2) the political educator of the magistrate; (3) the 'McKenzie friend'; (4) the independent professional.

1 The servant of the court

The probation officers we talked to very seldom described themselves as being simply 'officers of the court'. Much of their talk did, however, centre on the question to what extent they should stand on their professional dignity when magistrates ask them to

* All quotations are taken from published or unpublished work by the authors unless otherwise stated.

do something which is not strictly their job. 'They ask you to phone round to see if there's a hostel and you have to say "No, I can't do that this morning"' (*probation officer*). But not all probation officers took this hard line concerning the specification of their professional tasks: 'Sometimes magistrates ask us to do things which aren't our job. I often think, "That's not my job", but then, at the same time, I'm glad they're seeing that we can be useful.' The probation officers who took this softer line about the range of their court duties tended to do so because they gave priority to one or more of the three other possible role definitions, the favourable negotiation of which was seen to be dependent upon the maintenance of credibility with the magistrate.

2 The political educator of the magistrate

It's our job to educate them [magistrates]. These two are willing. Younger generation, I suppose. (*probation officer*)

So long as you're not subservient. Respect their position, but know that in some ways they haven't the first idea. They're profoundly ignorant, even when they're being most benevolent, they come out with some ideas that sound so childish. But you can take opportunities of going up to see them. The ones here are only too willing to talk to you. They almost seem to have an inferiority complex about certain social issues as if they suddenly realize that they're really out of touch and that you're going to come out with some long-winded sociological, psychological statement. You can see them wince. It always gets too near to the bone, back to themselves. (*probation officer*)

Many of the probation officers we interviewed expressed gratification that magistrates, often totally perplexed and depressed by the complexity of some of the social problems revealed to them during court hearings, seek out probation officers in order to discuss issues of general social interest: 'It starts out about a particular case, and in no time they want your views on things in general' (*probation officer*). The views are not always welcome. No probation officer expressed any generalized antagonism towards magistrates but some magistrates certainly felt that a few probation officers were totally unappreciative of the magistrates' own particular courtroom problems. Note below the two versions of just one occasion when a probation officer undertook to 'educate' the magistrate.

Probation officer to P. Carlen: You have to explain to them [magistrates] that all people aren't the same, particularly West Indians. You have to tell him that what he sees as cruelty they see as disciplining their children.

Later, Magistrate to P. Carlen: It's all very well the probation officer coming in here and telling me that West Indians come from a different culture. I *know* that. But when a nine-year-old boy is beaten so severely that he jumps out of a window! There has to be some limit. To protect the weak against the strong must be a major aim of the court.

The very few probation officers whom magistrates characterized as 'way-out' or even as 'Marxist' were usually those who either violated every commonsensical notion held by magistrates or who showed contempt for the magistrates' concern that 'justice must be *seen* to be done'.

3 The 'McKenzie friend'

Most dominant of the definitions applied to the probation officers' courtroom role by defendants as well as by solicitors, policemen and even, on occasion, by magistrates, was that of 'McKenzie friend', a lay person speaking on behalf of the defendant. Undoubtedly, many defendants, bereft of legal representation, are grateful that somebody (the probation officer) is there to articulate some of the background features of the case. Undoubtedly, too, many legally represented defendants find that their probation officer does a much better *de facto* defence job than the Legal Aid solicitor who is *de jure* defending them (Bottoms and McClean 1976). By tradition, also, everyone knows that 'the police knock 'em off, the probation officer gets 'em off'. Probation officers do not find this definition of their role to be totally unpleasing. At the same time it is not a definition which they can unequivocally embrace.

All the probation officers we interviewed stated quite categorically that their duty is to provide unbiased information about the defendant to the court. Again and again, also, probation officers followed up this recitation of their statutory duty by immediately distinguishing between the writing of a report for a client whom they had known previously and the writing of a report on someone previously unknown to them:

If a person is under supervision to you, to my mind he is my client, and my report would be written in that sort of vein. If it's a report where I've never known the chap before and it is just purely and simply a report for the court, then one can regard the court as one's client in a sense. Now, one can say, how does it make a difference? Well, in actual fact it shouldn't make much difference at all – one would hope one would be as equally impartial.

Yet the definition of the probation officer as a 'friend' to the defendant is so ingrained in courtroom lore that their 'impartiality' was sometimes seen as 'harshness' by the very magistrates for whom probation officers felt a need to maintain a veneer of impartiality *vis-à-vis* the defendant:

> Then sometimes they ask for reports on a girl – she never turns up and we can't trace her – and we say, 'You'll have to remand her in custody if you want reports' – and they're shocked. They hate sending anyone to Holloway. They think we're hard then and that we shouldn't be like that – being probation officers, I mean'. (*probation officer*)

On the other hand, probation officers constantly have to bear in mind that they must maintain professional credibility with the magistrate if they are to do the best they can for *all* their clients. Probation officers cannot afford to be seen by magistrates as being mindlessly 'soft'.

> If you start soft-pedalling with those whom the magistrate feels, and society feels, shouldn't be soft-pedalled with, *then*, when you have a genuine recommendation going against the grain, then it wouldn't be accepted, unless they feel that you as a probation officer are not flinching from the more difficult ones that come along. (*probation officer*; Carlen 1976)

Yet even those probation officers who operated with a predominantly 'adversary' model of criminal justice felt that they should occasionally 'speak for' the defendant in court. For the administration of justice in the magistrates' courts, where the majority of defendants are not legally represented, continuously violates most common-sense conceptions of adversary justice (Carlen 1976). The following statement was echoed by many probation officers:

> Part of my role is to get over to the court what the defendant thinks, what *he* thinks is important, even if I go on later to say that I disagree with this. It's extremely difficult for someone who's standing in the dock with all the paraphernalia of the court – in an unfamiliar situation – very often not versed in procedures in court – maybe not represented. Then I see it as part of my role to be able to facilitate what he wants to say to the court – a sort of intermediary. That's part of it, if he's not represented. (*probation officer*)

So the problems associated with the 'McKenzie friend' definition of the probation role exactly specify the ambiguous position of the probation officer in court. As one probation officer put it, 'we're sitting on the fence, really, between court and defendant, and whichever way we jump we're likely to come a cropper'. Maybe so, but probation officers are not totally at the mercy either of other people's expectations of them or of the contradictions incorporated into the production of magistrates' justice. They have acquired a set of knowledges, tacit rules-of-thumb and routine strategies directed at achieving a measure of professional control over their courtroom work. These knowledges and strategies are part of their professional competence.

4 The independent professional

All probation officers seemed to be aware of the foregoing three possible definitions of their courtroom role. They might reject a particular definition as being 'irrelevant' to their 'real' work, but nonetheless they indicated that they knew that other courtroom participants held such a definition of their role. They also indicated that whether or not they *agreed* with these definitions of their courtroom role they had to take account of them within the courtroom setting. A favourable definition was to be enhanced, a negative one was to be negated. This explicit recognition by probation officers that, within the courtroom, they could act to achieve their own ends; that they could engage in forms of active rule-usage designed to activate their own definition of the situation; that they did not have to engage in totally reactive rule-usage in order to counteract definitions of the situation unfavourable to them – all of these knowledges activated their fourth role-definition, that of independent professional. So the remainder of this chapter on the gamesmanship of probation officers will be directed at examining, first, their courtroom strategies, and second, the operative definitions of their role which make possible the success of such strategies. The complex of formal and informal rules by which probation officers play the law game constitutes their courtroom lore.

The courtroom lore of probation officers

Probation officers operating with what we have called the independent professional definition of their role know that the success of their gamesmanship depends upon their competent manipulation of all the courtroom rules both explicit and implicit (Carlen 1976). Their major concern, of course, like that of the other professional groups, is to maintain credibility with the magistrates, but a secondary interest is to maintain good relationships with the other professionals working in the court. In ascending order of importance they have to maintain good relationships with solicitors, policemen and magistrates.

Probation officers and solicitors

That's another world of its own, the world of solicitors. *They* can just look at the individual and consider him, but we've got to think more of the community. We're more on the same side as the solicitors – we both have our battles with the magistrate – but we do have to think more of the community than do solicitors. Domestically, as it were, there's a lot of frustration on the part of probation officers, conscious that although they're getting paid for their reports it's not on a piece-rate basis. There's a solicitor getting paid for it, and he picks up your report, and providing he goes along with your recommendation he'll make a lot of capital out of it, without doing any work himself, which probation officers find very frustrating. (*probation officer*)

The greatest bone of contention between probation officers and solicitors concerns social inquiry reports and solicitors' usage of them. Probation officers resent lazy solicitors who, although being paid a substantial fee, use social inquiry reports to script pleas of mitigation. There is a suspicion too that the reports will be kept and used for purposes for which they were not intended:

It's barristers who don't do their homework and that's why I insist on getting my reports back because in three years time the client may have changed tremendously. And the solicitor may use your old report if he's got it. Therefore I insist on getting my reports back. They nearly all try to keep the reports. (*probation officer*)

Yet solicitors can be useful, particularly when, for reasons of their own, probation officers wish to reject the 'McKenzie friend' definition of their role:

When they tell me they were not guilty I advise them to get a solicitor. I explain to them that we are not barristers and therefore do not defend. They ought to get a solicitor. Especially people who have known you for years think you are a defence counsel. (*probation officer*)

Once a solicitor has been recommended by a probation officer a distance has to be maintained:

Professionally, I'm very cagey about solicitors. I am particularly careful not to be involved with a solicitor whereby he might later get me in the box and ask me something which in fact might be to the benefit of his client.

Solicitors know that it is to their advantage to maintain good relationships with probation officers:

They'll let you see their reports if they trust you, if they know you won't abuse the information they have. (*solicitor*)

Probation officers vetted solicitors more closely than that. Repeatedly they used the phrase 'those with a social conscience' to distinguish 'good' from 'bad' solicitors, and having a social conscience means that the solicitor will act upon the probation officer's advice, rather than upon the instructions of his client:

> Like if I say 'I want him kept in a couple of weeks . . . I want to find him a hostel place' – they will go along with me to persuade the guy that this is a good idea rather than doing what may be in the guy's short term interest. (*probation officer*; Carlen 1976)

In courts which are situated near to a local solicitors' firm, the firm in fact that handles most of the local court cases, a *modus vivendi* can develop between solicitors and the more experienced probation officers.

> We get a lot of help from them in domestic cases, legal advice and so forth, and in return we pass a lot of people over to them. A lot of people come in to see us and if reconciliation is a non-starter we refer them straight to a solicitor and that's business for them – so obviously that's a two-way thing. (*probation officer*)

Relationships between probation officers and policemen were always viewed as being more problematical.

Probation officers and police

Although most probation officers would reluctantly (and not too regretfully) agree that often their clients see them as substitute defence counsel, none of them wanted their clients to see them as being on the same side as the police. The areas of conflict are many and breed a mutual suspicion between policemen and probation officers.

First, probation officers try to dissociate themselves from police-views of defendants which they find distasteful and which result in policemen violating probation officers' ideal notions of due process.

> When you go out of the court to see a man remanded for social inquiry reports the police officer will often come up there and chip in comments in front of the bloke, like He's a right thug this one, you know. We've got fifty other charges we want to book him for but we can't get him. 'He's got to go down on this one.' That sort of conversation very often goes on. (*probation officer*)

Probation officers retaliate. Due process becomes part of a game between professionals with opposing goals:

> The police are concerned with preventing crimes, that's the end product. So therefore it's just a matter of course going through the court, getting a conviction . . . and of course the quicker and easier they can do this the easier and better . . . and therefore a certain

amount of plea-bargaining goes on. Therefore if we come into it and say, 'Look here, if you're not guilty don't be silly, don't plead guilty' . . . they get a little bit upset about it. (*probation officer*)

Second, police often see probation officers as withholding information from them, information about clients which the police need. They see probation officers on these occasions as 'trying to be funny', and, as one police officer pointed out, 'We can be funny too'. A probation officer bore witness to this police 'humour':

> I went to Anytown Court and I asked the police – they're very choosey about who goes down to the cells – and they took me down but said I had to speak through the grille and I insisted on going in – so they locked me in and then went off for twenty minutes and had a cup of tea or something. It was just spite.

The third area of conflict is engendered by the police view that probation officers not only *are* but should be *soft*. A probation officer explained:

> They don't take a breach of probation seriously. I took out a warrant, it took four weeks for the police to arrest him and he was at the address I gave. And I kept having to ring the police and say, 'Will you arrest him?' But their standard image is that probation officers are soft and then whenever you do anything that shows that this isn't the case they are pleasantly surprised.

Recognition of police power in the courts, however, is a prerequisite of successful performance by any other professional team. Encounters have to be managed so that police respect for probation work can be increased:

> When they let their hair down they [the police] are quite sympathetic to us, feel that we work with impossible villains, against all the odds and all that. But once you can get them talking and get them to agree that one needs a doctor, that little Johnny isn't *totally* bad, then you're getting somewhere. *They* like to talk too. (*probation officer*)

and, never snub a policeman!

> You do occasionally get a policeman ringing you up to get information about a client that it would be dangerous to give. But, on the other hand, I never sort of say to them 'No, I'm not going to give it to you,' but I say to them, 'Look, if you like I'll ask so and so if they'll come round to see you or if you can contact them.' And often, if they are genuinely interested in contacting someone they'll be ready to accept the situation. (*probation officer*)

There's a pay-off for careful handling of the police – easier access to the cells to see a client, background information about a case the details of which appear to be hopelessly muddled, and sometimes discreet help when a client or his family are in non-criminal 'trouble'.

Probation officers and social workers

Professionals who work regularly in the magistrates' courts often criticize all those who appear there less regularly. In particular, there is a tradition of criticizing the courtroom performances of social workers. Anecdotes abound about social workers' maladroitness in court. Specific criticisms concern the in-appropriateness of their reports and their demeanour. More generally, their attitude to the judicial process is seen to be cavalier and lacking in judicial finesse. To attribute these poor per-formances to either ignorance or indifference would be unjust. Social workers have but limited opportunities to observe the workings of the magistrates' courts.

Local authority social workers appear in magistrates' courts only when someone already 'known' to them in their professional capacity appears as a defendant: a juvenile appearing with an adult; a young person over the age of seventeen but still in care; a physically or mentally-handicapped person; someone known through social work in a family situation. Social workers from voluntary agencies appear in court if their particular specialist help is being offered or utilized. Appearances in the magistrates' courts constitute only a minute proportion of all social workers' duties. Local authority workers in England and Wales do indeed have court experience but in a very different setting – the juvenile court.

Social workers appearing in magistrates' courts are often disadvantaged because they bring to their work in the adult courts an alien and displaced expertise. The juvenile court, as a professional workshop, has its own structure, ideology and rules of professional discourse and gamesmanship. Insofar as social workers fail to adjust their behaviour to the culture of the adult courts they attract the same type of criticisms as do those barristers who provoke some nice magisterial sarcasm by forgetting that a magistrates' court is not the High Court, still less the House of Lords! Social workers' different expertise and limited experience of magistrates' courts engender much of the criticism related to their apparent failure to appreciate the reality of judicial power:

Social worker: He [the magistrate] can't remand him in custody.
Probation officer: He *can.* You must argue that he *shouldn't.*

In juvenile courts much power resides with social workers. A juvenile court may make a care order, but it is a social worker who decides whether the child stays at home or goes into residential care. In the adult courts magistrates can and do make decisions that force the hands of probation officers and social workers. The recognition of magisterial power is one reason why probation officers seek to establish their authority in a multitude of practical ways. Social workers are not familiar with such a balance of power in the juvenile courts and some of them are resistant to its display in the adult courts. Additionally they are often unwilling to enter into any discourse dependent upon the concept of punishment, a concept inherent in most forms of magistrates' court disposals. Refusal to enter into the discursive practices which 'gloss' the whole 'treatment versus punishment' debate, a debate so central to the concerns of the magistrates' courts, diminishes the professional stature of social workers in the eyes of many of the other courtroom professionals. Reluctance to acknowledge judicial power has also resulted in a reluctance to employ judicial discourse.

In the juvenile courts in recent years there have been many developments of a quasi-judicial nature. Perhaps this is why so many social workers appear to be unfamiliar or impatient with notions of 'due process' or other specifically judicial concepts. Derisive probation officers tell how social workers recommend that a case be 'dropped' – even after the defendant has been convicted! Equally irritated social workers describe their dislike of courts – 'it's a parade of all your failures'. Maybe this is the source of the professional rift between probation officers and social workers: whereas the probation officer depends upon the adult courts for his clientele, the social worker too often sees them as at least an encroachment upon, if not a reproach to, his own previous professional efforts. This antipathy towards adult courts has unfortunately resulted in some social workers failing to acquire even the minimum of judicial expertise necessary to efficient operation within them. Against that, it must be pointed out that some social workers act as they do knowingly and with theoretic intent. They hope that by ignoring the rules they will change the nature of the game (Mungham and Bankowski 1976). That said, however, it remains true that, in the present state of the game, social workers' frequent mistakes and misconceptions make them subject to hostile stereotyping and prejudice from the other professionals. Further exclusion from courtroom processes is the result.

Probation officers and magistrates

It is of paramount importance to all professionals who appear regularly in the same courts that they should be 'in good standing' with the magistrates. Many probation officers felt that, as far as their relationship with the magistrates went, they had a head start on other courtroom professionals.

> Probation officers are a bit jealous of the tradition that they have such a very easy access to the clerks and to the magistrate. It's something we treasure. (*probation officer*)

The rewards for being in such 'good standing' are threefold. First, where magistrates are 'pro-probation' they will always look across at the probation box before they remand anyone for social enquiry reports. Second, where magistrates know and respect particular probation officers they will give them opportunity in court to support their reports. Third, probation officers thought that if they had maintained credibility with a magistrate *then* he would follow the occasional unusual recommendation which otherwise he might have considered as being either risky or bizarre. It was in explaining to us how best to influence magistrates that probation officers most frequently cited social workers as examples of how *not* to behave in court. We have formalized their comments into a set of precepts for maintaining credibility with magistrates.

Get your face known

> If there's a new magistrate we all tend to go with our reports – everyone – at least until he gets to know us. (*probation officer*)

Prior to gaining any credibility at all within the courtroom the new probation officer has to be *seen*, and seen to be working competently!

> Even if they don't let you into the Box I think they know that you're prepared to stand by what you say. (*probation officer*)

Social workers, on the other hand, often just fail to turn up.

> They can't find the court, or they sit at the back and don't tell anyone they're there. (*probation officer*)

A probation officer told us about a Clerk at one court:

> If he knew a social worker was appearing in court he'd say, 'For God's sake see that she knows what she's doing.'

The following scene recorded in court was typical of a number of occasions when social workers certainly did not appear to know what they were doing.

Magistrate: Is the social worker here then?
Policeman: He's in the public gallery, sir.
Magistrate: Well . . . shouldn't he be round here?
  (*Policeman brings social worker to stand in front of the dock*)
Magistrate: Are you looking after Brown's interests?
Social worker: Well, I'm a social worker.
Magistrate: Then you're looking after his interests aren't you?
Social worker: (*raises eyebrows and shrugs*) Yes.

Magistrate: Then perhaps you should be here so that you can hear
what is going on.

Talk to the magistrates out of court

In this court we have monthly meetings with them. But you often get
further with them when you go up before or after court, and talk to
them on their own (*probation officer*)

The reason given for talking to magistrates on their own was
usually that something in a Social Enquiry Report could be
explained.

Very occasionally, if you're suggesting something a bit out of the
normal it might be politic to go and say to the magistrate, 'Look, I'm
suggesting something a bit outrageous here, do you want to ask me
anything about it?' It makes a lot of difference once you get to know
the magistrates. (*probation officer*)

Dress for the part

It may seem remarkable to those unfamiliar with the professional
lore of the courts that 'what to wear' in court is mentioned so
frequently by probation officers and social workers. Yet most
probation officers and social workers recognized (even if
reluctantly) that, in the formality of the courtroom, cues as to
character and respectability are often taken primarily from
demeanour and dress. Ms X summed up the irritation and eventual
capitulation that many other probation officers and social workers
described to us when they touched upon this issue.

We are told to be deferential. The dress you wear in court – and to
some extent I go along with this. If you are a person in some
authority and with power, then you dress neutrally, you don't draw
attention to yourself – because you're not there to be the focus of
attention. But all this business about you have to wear suits in court –
there's a lot of pressure on young officers to do this – you know – 'tut,
tut, tut, you should get your hair cut', and 'tut, tut, tut, you shouldn't
wear jeans in court'. Well, as far as I'm concerned, so long as the
person looks tidy. . . . But it's interesting, if I'm going to court with
a client in front of a magistrate whom I know to be very much of the
old school, I will tie my hair back and I would wear a skirt, simply so
that he's not antagonistic to the visual picture I present. Now that's
daft if you think about it logically – the fact that I'm bothering about
how I dress up for a Magistrate. But if it's a court where I don't know
the magistrate I tone down because I think there's more chance of his
taking what I say seriously. If he can dismiss me as a slip of a girl or
an unrealistic hippy, then there's less chance that he will read my
recommendation seriously. (*probation officer*)

Applaud the magistrate's performance

Again and again probation officers mentioned to us that often they were the magistrates' best (and only) audience.

> They need encouragement . . . to do good things maybe . . . but often they just look over at us when they say something silly, or if they shout. You know, they're looking to see how we take it. Well, it *is* embarrassing because often you're sitting there thinking, 'You bloody bully . . .' (*probation officer*)

Another probation officer thought that the probation officer's response in these situations could affect the effective relationship with the magistrate.

> Because of the in-group thing, if a magistrate makes a funny about a guy in the dock and you *don't* laugh – or you look away, or you look disapproving – then, and this again is lack of professionalism I think – that magistrate is going to feel less warm to you, and I think very often accepting your recommendation or not accepting it is for far more personal reasons than I like to think. (*probation officer*; Carlen 1976)

These four prescriptions for gaining and maintaining credibility with magistrates were often described to us wryly and with a certain degree of professional self-censure. 'Games?' queried one probation officer. 'Arselicking!' Probation officers were hardly enthusiastic about the games they play in magistrates' courts, but a failure to win at each round of the game can have dire results as Mr Z pointed out to us:

> *Probation officer:* Actually, I had a case on Friday where I'd wanted to talk to the magistrates about it, didn't get the opportunity and there was a hell of a mess as a result. On Friday there was a new magistrate that I didn't know. I went up to him and he had about seven social inquiry reports in front of him. He made very busy noises and I spelled it out in some detail in the report that this bloke was homeless and probably suicidal and that he should be remanded in custody until I could fix him up with hostel accommodation. Whether the magistrate didn't read that or whether he disagreed with it, I dont know. But he put him on probation there and then, so I've been all the weekend getting him in and out of hospitals and God knows what – so I'd have welcomed a bit more contact with the magistrate on that one.
>
> *P. Carlen:* Couldn't you tell the probation officer on duty to say something in court?
>
> *Probation officer:* Actually, I was in court myself but I didn't really know what to do. By the time it got to the point where I felt that I ought to stand up and say something, it had all been tied up and the man was being ushered out of court.

The major channel for probation officer/magistrate communication, however, is the social inquiry report itself. Here we
have a situation where probation officers, whilst having their own
professional assessment of the most appropriate disposal of a case,
at the same time operate with a knowledge of the tariff system of
sentencing (Davies 1974) and its specific usage by particular
magistrates. Where the view attributed to the magistrate and the
professional view of the probation officer do not coincide some
form of adjustment is necessary. In writing the report a probation
officer has to show that he is realistic (i.e. knows the going rate of
punishment for a specific crime) even though his diagnostic skills
lead him to make an alternative recommendation. Hardiker calls
this 'manipulating the court towards a social work decision'.

Strategic report writing
We will deal here with three types of strategy. First, there is *filtering*,
the redefining of character to suit the recommendation, and the
persuading of the magistrate to adopt an individualized rather
than a tariff sentence. A failing in the client can be excused, or
factual information can be skimmed over. Of course, probation
officers may not admit that they are filtering, which suggests deceit
and dishonesty, instead they invoke the concept of 'relevance'.

> You know, I don't necessarily filter the information to make it
> appear that my recommendation is right. I rather say my recom-
> mendation is right and then give . . . I write the report in a way
> to, you know, keep it relevant. (*probation officer*)

Another justification for filtering is the prevalent belief that reports
should not be too long. Magistrates and probation officers often
claim that social workers write reports that are too long. While this
can make sense, especially in courts where magistrates read the
reports for the first time in open court, it can also serve to
legitimize the practice of excluding certain material. Magistrates,
however, are often a move ahead. Listen to one magistrate's
comments on what surely must have been one of the crudest ever
attempts at filtering.

> *Solicitor:* If you've read the social inquiry report, sir . . .
> *Magistrate:* I must tell you straight away that I'm not impressed with
> the social inquiry report. When you read it as I have – and analyse it –
> you realize that between the lines there are different meanings. For
> instance, it talks of his being 'separated' from his common-law wife.
> It's not true to say he's separated. In 1971, April, when he was
> supposedly 'separated' from her he was sentenced at the Inner
> London Sessions for assaulting her. Since then, understandably,
> she's refused to live with him.

'*Tickling*' is a further piece of craftsmanship.

> There are two ways of catching trout – you can cast a fly or you can 'tickle' them. I 'tickle' magistrates. (*probation officer*)

In 'tickling', a probation officer's report lulls the court into a sense of security by arguing in terms acceptable to them and by not appearing to suggest anything that the court did not have in mind already. Recognition of the court's point of view is indicated: 'Whilst not underestimating the seriousness of the offence, I feel . . .' Respect is made overt: 'I would respectfully suggest'; and the client is accorded 'defendant', rather than 'client' status:

> A minor point, do you call a male defendant Jones or Mr Jones? Now, as a personal preference he rates a Mister, you know. *Anyone* rates a Mister. But if I'm writing a report for a magistrate who gets uptight because you call him Mister – well, I'll act in the interests of the client. (*probation officer*)

Tickling is to do with the court's ultimate authority to dispose of a case and is therefore 'respectful'. Social workers were often mentioned as professionals who see themselves as being above 'tickling':

> They insist on calling their clients by their first names and the magistrates don't like it.' (*probation officer*)
> They lecture the magistrates. Students do sometimes.
> They don't *persuade* the magistrate, they *tell* him what to do.

Not that probation officers felt that they should be servile in court. What they did recognize was that their own authority had to be continually re-established and this involved them in a third set of strategies which we have called *staking claims*.

Embedded in the courtroom lore which establishes their professional competence are the sets of discursive practices which establish probation officers' authority. Reports provide a medium by which probation officers can 'stake their claim'. These discursive practices embody sets of knowledges and their legitimated modes of invocation and organization. They are a series of strategies involving appeals to either abstract virtues, higher authorities, or lastly, commonsense knowledge of the way the world works. Appeals can be made to 'reasonableness' or 'fairness':

> The court may feel that it is reasonable for him to continue his present efforts to establish himself in the community.
> He surrendered himself voluntarily to the police.

Reference can be made to higher authorities:

> Mr X has been given a chance by the Inner London Crown Court.
> The psychiatrist commented that . . .

and, lastly, to the therapeutic effects of 'normal everyday life':

Since he last attended this court he has been fully employed. He was married in August and his wife is expecting a baby in the New Year. The court may feel that with these responsibilities . . .

It is *not* admissible to incorporate social criticism into the social inquiry report:

One probation officer made reference to Capitalism and Marxism – you know, Capitalist Society, that sort of thing, you know. And I had to say, 'This won't do.' I don't care about the politics of a probation officer, but the defendant has to see that report and that kind of thing isn't appropriate to a relationship of – uh – treatment. (*Magistrate*; Carlen 1976).

But some probation officers, and even more social workers, (Pearson 1975) think that such criticism *is* appropriate.

So what of the strategies of filtering, tickling and claim-staking? Are they unethical? Do they merely reproduce judicial settings celebrating professional powers, jealousies and rivalries? Whether they do or not, a neophyte probation officer made it quite clear that she had quickly learned the material facts of life in magistrates' courts:

I think you have to play them, play them at it, see who they are and what they go for and what they don't. That is what people definitely did at Anytown Court. They played all of them – all of the time.

Finally, a magistrate acknowledged the crucial part such negotiations play in getting the work of the court done. Replying to the comment that 'we all play games in court', she said: 'Not games, my dear – professional expertise.'

Recommended reading

BLUMBERG, A. S. 1967: *Criminal Justice*. Chicago: Quadrangle.
BOTTOMS, A. and McCLEAN, J. D. 1976: *Defendants in the Criminal Process*. London: Routledge & Kegan Paul.
CARLEN, P. 1976: *Magistrates' Justice*. London: Martin Robertson.

Chapter 7

The Role of Probation Officers in Sentencing*

Pauline Hardiker

The role of probation officers must be considered in the context of changes in the penal system of some industrial societies towards the end of the nineteenth century. As Taylor *et al.* (1973) point out, traditionally justice has been based on classical utilitarian principles which considered offences rather than offenders when fixing a punishment for the crime. Classical justice principles were difficult to implement in practice, however, because frequently the circumstances of the individual offender seemed relevant. For example, age, past record, mental condition and social situation were gradually seen as limiting free-will, thus making some offenders seem less responsible for their crimes than others. This is probably one reason why, during the nineteenth century, some courts had begun to experiment in a piecemeal fashion with other sentences, such as reprimands, bail and conditional discharge (Bochel 1976).

Social enquiry reports reflect the increasing importance of experts within the courts. This in turn owes itself to the individualization of justice, which allows other things to be examined besides a strict tariff. If sentencers are to consider the circumstances of *individual* offenders, they need information which can be taken into account either in mitigation of sentence (probation instead of custody) or as a pointer to a rehabilitative measure (psychiatric treatment rather than borstal training).

The extent to which sentencing has gradually come to be based on considerations of individual circumstances is illustrated by the fact that the probation service presented 217,923 social enquiries to the criminal courts in England and Wales in 1974 (HMSO 1976). These, alongside the reports presented by psychiatrists and other social workers, must present a significant contribution to social

* This paper reports on work which was conducted as part of a project funded by the Social Science Research Council. I should also like to acknowledge the help I received from Philip Bean and David Webb in the preparation of this paper.

work in the courts (Bean 1975; Davies 1974). However, the nature and function of these reports remain controversial. Bean points to their dangers as 'character assassinations' and thinks that social enquiries should be abandoned (1975), whilst Mathieson discusses probation officers as 'sentencers of the future' (1975, 1976, 1977). Davies (1974, 32) makes more modest claims for social enquiry reports, calling them, 'descriptions of circumstances', which 'help the sentencer choose a sentence appropriate to the offender's apparent circumstances'.

Probation officers sometimes make recommendations in their social enquiry reports (Ford 1972), but this is viewed with some ambivalence by officialdom because of its suspicion of interference with the judiciary. Nevertheless, in 90 per cent of the 1,024 reports prepared by an intake team between 1976 and 1977 (Hardiker 1977a), specific recommendations were made. The material in this chapter is derived from an analysis of these reports. The quotations are taken from either research interview transcripts or actual social enquiry reports. The circumstances in which probation officers saw themselves as playing different roles when they made particular recommendations to the court will be examined.

A framework for recommendations – a tariff in reverse

Individualized sentencing involves two types of decisions: either a punishment for the offence has to be fixed, given the nature and circumstances of the crime, or a treatment for the offender has to be selected, given the criminal's needs and situation. This distinction is too neat of course, but it will be helpful to keep it in mind during this discussion. Thus probation officers have to consider a form of *tariff* in which punishment is set against offence, as well as the individual's social or psychological *needs*. It is extremely difficult to identify precisely the decision-making process at work in these situations, but Davies has advanced the following hypothesis (1971, 18):

> In my submission, and it is no more than a hypothesis for testing, the combined effects of individualization, the growing influence of the probation officer and the lack of any firm evidence to provide a scientific basis for reductivist sentencing . . . leads to the imposition of a tariff system in reverse in which once the primary decision is taken . . . the sentencer through the medium of the social enquiry report determines *where on the continuum of social need the offender stands*. If the need is minimal a fine or conditional discharge will be

recommended. If problems exist then a probation order is made. If problems are severe or previous probation has failed, custodial measures are considered [my italics].

The 'continuum of need' does appear to be a factor in probation officers' recommendations to the court (Table 7 : 1). Conditional

Table 7 : 1   Recommendations and needs of the offender

Recommendation	Low	Need rank High	Total
Conditional discharge	13·1	5·8	9·7
Fine	38·6	5·5	23·4
Probation	2·5	49·7	24·2
Custody	12·3	14·7	13·4
Other	22·3	14·8	18·8
No recommendation	11·2	9·5	10·4
	100	100	100
	N = 511	433	945

X^2 349·70   df 5   p < 0·001

discharge and fine cases were more likely to be given low need ranks, i.e. the social problems facing these individuals were not seen as serious, whereas probation and to a lesser extent custody recommendations were given high need ranks. Some examples may help to illustrate this point.

A youth aged sixteen was charged with possessing a loaded air weapon under age and had no previous convictions. The probation officer thought there were no undue problems in this case and the youth was at the threshold of a new way of life, having just started work. These feelings were reflected in his recommendation to the court:

X comes from a good home and has the support of interested parents. On the whole he seems to be a well-adjusted person, who is able to cope with the pressures of everyday living without recourse to supervision. These court proceedings are causing him anxiety and it is felt that this has been a salutory reminder that he must behave in the future. Therefore, it is respectfully suggested that this case is dealt with by means of a *conditional discharge*. (my italics)

The recommendation for conditional discharge seemed appropriate, given the offender's personal strengths and family supports.

Another offender, aged twenty-one, was charged with theft of watches valued at £110, and had a previous conviction for theft.

The probation officer thought he was a capable and intelligent man who knew what he should and should not do, could make decisions and take the consequences. These points were brought out in the social enquiry recommendation:

> Y is a pleasant, well-mannered young man who is quite capable of organizing his affairs in a manner which is acceptable to society. He can readily distinguish between what is permissible and what is not, and he recognizes, albeit reluctantly, that he has to accept the consequences of his transgressions. Supervision is not indicated therefore. *A financial penalty* would probably have a deterrent effect on him [my italics].

Again, this was a case in which the probation officer thought needs were minimal, and a fine was appropriate since no social work help was deemed necessary.

The offender's circumstances appeared to be very different in a case where probation was recommended. A man, aged twenty-one, was charged with theft of £20, and the probation officer summarized the offender's needs in the recommendation to the court:

> This young couple are currently struggling against severe financial hardship, coupled with poor housing conditions and two small children. Mrs Z appears to be quite a competent mother but is obviously quite depressed by her present circumstances. It seems likely that this offence was committed as a direct response to the financial difficulties in which Mr Z had found himself. He lacks the guile to deliberately and with forethought seek for material gain in this way but he also lacks the knowledge of how to seek for help for his difficulties. This family undoubtedly needs help if it is to survive as a unit. Such help could be offered via a *Probation Order* and in the circumstances it is suggested that this would be an appropriate course of action to take.

Clearly, probation seemed relevant in this high-need case given the problems which existed.

Probation was not feasible in some of the high-need cases and so custodial measures were suggested. For example, a man, aged twenty-six, was charged with several offences including theft, possession of drugs and taking cars without consent; there were twenty-five other matters taken into consideration and the offender had previous convictions. The probation officer thought he was the 'black sheep' of a stable working-class family, could have been a professional footballer and coped well in between his criminal and drug escapades. He realized that the court was thinking of a custodial sentence, thought the man needed either treatment or containment, but decided that probation was not feasible. Accordingly, he said he tried to give the court a comprehensive view of the offender and to advise them of their options in his recommendation:

B's contradictory patterns of behaviour create problems in diagnosis and the court may feel that medical reports would be useful. It is recognized that the nature and extent of current offences, together with the breach of the previous disposal, will cause the court to consider an immediate and relatively substantial sentence of imprisonment. Conventional supervision has not been helpful in the past, partly because B has lacked motivation, and this enquiry does not suggest that the situation has changed to any marked degree. Should an immediate sentence to prison be considered necessary, it is thought that B might benefit from the treatment facilities available at *HM Prison, Grendon Underwood.*

This did seem to be similar to the situation Davies (1971) had in mind – that custodial measures are considered when previous supervision has failed and there are serious problems.

It does seem that at one level social enquiry reports are a vehicle for describing the offender's needs to the court. The categories of 'low need' and 'high need' which have been used are extremely crude, of course, but the illustrations convey some of the flavour of the situations probation officers have to handle during their social enquiries in deciding whether 'treatment for the offender' is indicated.

Offenders on whom social enquiry reports are prepared appear before the court because they have committed offence(s), and they may have previous criminal convictions (tariff). This considera-

Table   7 : 2   Recommendations and seriousness of criminal history (tariff)

		Seriousness		
Recommendation	Low	Medium	High	Total
Conditional discharge	38·0	6·2	0	9·9
Fine	19·6	30·5	6·0	23·5
Probation	19·0	27·3	16·2	23·6
Custody	1·3	8·0	38·4	13·4
Other	12·0	18·6	24·5	18·8
No recommendation	10·1	9·5	14·8	10·8
	100	100	100	100
	N = 158	630	216	1004

X^2 354·98   df 10 $p < 0.001$

tion also seems to be very relevant in probation officers' recommendations and a further parameter to the decision-making process. The need for punishment may be minimal in conditional discharge cases, whereas custodial sentences constitute a very heavy punishment. Financial penalties and probation typically lie somewhere between these extremes. This is an interesting phenomenon in itself, and the cases described above seem to illustrate this pattern: a minimal sentence for possessing a loaded air weapon under age, a maximum sentence for theft, possession of drugs, taking without consent, with previous convictions and several offences taken into consideration; moderate punishments for thefts of varying amounts. Therefore, Davies' hypothesis about 'a tariff in reverse' seems to miss out an important dimension; not only are offenders' 'needs' considered but the relative seriousness and circumstances of their offences ('tariff') are taken into account too.

However there was some evidence that 'need' and 'tariff' are associated (Table 7:3), because the more serious an offender's criminal history, the more likely it was that he would be considered to have personal and social problems. 'Need' may somehow contribute to people's inability to keep to this side of the law. (See Hardiker 1977b for a discussion of similar findings.)

When 'need' and 'tariff' are combined to make what may be called a 'reverse tariff rank', this appears to be a relatively precise means of pinning down the association between recommendations, personal problems and criminal histories (Table 7:4). Davies' hypothesis can be modified accordingly.

The sentencer through the medium of the social enquiry report determines *where on the continuum of tariff and social need the offender stands*. If tariff and need are minimal, a conditional discharge will be

Table 7:3 Need and seriousness of criminal history (tariff)

| Need | Tariff | | | Total |
	Low	Medium	High	
Low	66·0	55·8	38·9	53·9
High	34·0	44·2	61·1	46·1
	100	100	100	100
	N=150	585	193	928

X^2 27·9   df 2 $p < 0.001$

Table 7:4   Recommendations, criminal history and offender need (reverse tariff)

Recommendation	Low tariff	Reverse tariff rank Low need Medium tariff	High tariff	Low tariff	High need Medium tariff	High tariff	Total
Conditional discharge	43·4	7·1	0	28·6	4·2	0	9·8
Fine	27·3	48·3	10·5	2·0	8·0	2·6	23·4
Probation	1·0	3·7	1·3	53·1	58·4	28·2	24·4
Custody	2·0	8·3	42·1	0	8·0	35·9	13·4
Other	16·2	22·8	28·9	4·1	13·7	21·4	18·9
No recommendation	10·1	9·8	17·1	12·2	7·6	12·0	10·2
	100	100	100	100	100	100	100
N=	99	325	76	49	262	117	928

X^2 695·61   df 25 $p < 0.001$

recommended; if the tariff is moderate and needs are minimal, a fine will be indicated; if the tariff is moderate and needs are evident, probation will be suggested; a maximum tariff and serious personal and social problems will be a pointer to custodial measures. The following diagram illustrates this situation:

Figure 7:1   A reverse tariff

NEED	TARIFF		
	Low	Medium	High
Low	Conditional discharge	Fine	
High		Probation	Custody

Sentencing roles

Some of the ways in which probation officers appeared to advise sentencers by operating a 'tariff in reverse' in their social enquiry work have been described above. Their reports were a vehicle for presenting information about an offender's personal and social circumstances, and recommendations were based on these assessments. But what role did probation officers think they were playing in their court reports? As Ford points out (1972, 6), there seems to be some uncertainty about their function in sentencing.

> In addition to official ambivalence, probation officers themselves have shown uncertainty as to their proper function in sentencing. Are they humble servants, respectfully giving their opinions only when asked? Dedicated social workers using their casework skills on paper to manipulate the court? Or professional penologists, telling a bench of lay magistrates how to do their job? Elements of all three views are to be found in s.e.rs.

The probation officers studied here also seemed to perform multiple roles in the way Ford described. In 80 per cent of the cases, they thought they were advising sentencers (Table 7 : 5),

Table 7 : 5   Recommendations and sentencing role of probation officer

Recommendation	Sentencing role Classical justice	Advising sentencers	Social work	Total
Conditional discharge	2·2	11·3	5·2	9·8
Fine	5·6	27·7	7·3	23·7
Probation	0·0	22·5	49·0	23·2
Custody	31·5	11·1	14·6	13·5
Other	5·6	20·0	20·8	18·7
No recommendation	55·1	7·4	3·1	11·2
	100	100	100	100
N =	89	816	96	1001

X^2 294·89   df 10 $p < 0.001$

whereas in the remainder they saw themselves as either leaving a case to classical justice or influencing the court towards a social work decision respectively.

They also appeared to play different roles depending on the recommendations they were making (Table 7 : 5). Their classical justice role became evident in the custody and no recommendation group, whereas their social work role emerged in the probation cases. It was when they recommended conditional discharge, fine, or 'other' sentences (e.g. attendance centre, community service order, deferred sentences) that their advisory role became most apparent. Some of the activities probation officers were involved in when they were playing these different roles will now be examined.

1 Advising sentencers

In many cases, it appeared that probation officers advised in a relatively straightforward manner. They used the social enquiry report to present a 'factual' picture of the offender; for example, a probation officer who recommended a *fine* for a man charged with theft said, 'I was trying to give the court some kind of picture of the guy and his relation to the offences, and to advise them as to the best way to deal with it.' The picture they presented was likely to be based on 'tariff in reverse' too, because it has been shown that a social enquiry may determine where on the continuum of 'need' and 'tariff' an offender lies. The 'reverse tariff' may provide an acceptable framework within which circumstances can be described, and the majority of social enquiry recommendations probably fit into this category (see Figure 7 : 1.)

On the other hand, probation officers sometimes played a rather more active role when they advised sentencers. They presented an explanation (diagnosis) for an offence and a recommendation about which sentence would be most effective in preventing further offences (prognosis). When they did this, they were more concerned with reforming than helping an offender. Davies, though, is suspicious of these attempts at reductivist sentencing (i.e. to reduce crime). He thinks they are a charade of social engineering, because probation officers are social workers not correctional agents (Davies 1974). Even so, probation officers did sometimes drift into reductivist sentencing (Fay 1975). For example, a man aged twenty was charged with theft as trespasser, he had previous convictions and had spent a period in an approved school. The probation officer thought he was growing out of an unsettled adolescence despite irregularities in his work, housing, and family situation. He told the court that 'the present offence does not fit the previous pattern and I assume it owes more to drunkenness than need for goods'. This *diagnosis* formed the basis of his recommendation to the court for non-intervention and that a fine would be a suitable punishment.

The probation officer explained his role in the following way:

I was pushing the court here rather than advising them mutely. I was advising them that this was nothing like as bad as it might appear in terms of his offence and record; I was emphasizing that there were grounds for not being too worried about him and just punishing him for what he did.

Similarly, a probation officer performed a diagnostic and prognostic function in a case where a community service order was recommended. A man aged forty-four was charged with theft of

£1,588, which he had embezzled from the working-man's club where he was a steward; he had previous convictions for similar offences. The probation officer thought he needed help because he had been rejected by his wife and family, was lonely and isolated, and needed to be accepted. Sentencers needed to be advised that:

> Here was an offence which was really a factor of his personality and circumstances, as previous offences had been. His own self-image needed to be raised and that was going to be the most effective way of preventing further offences.

The probation officer told the court that a community service order would improve Mr G's self-image and preserve his social base.

Advising sentencers was the role probation officers played in the majority of cases, and this was particuarly evident when they recommended either conditional discharge, fine or 'other' disposals such as community service orders. They sometimes played a relatively straightforward advisory role, by providing reports which were little more than descriptions of circumstances. However, in some situations they did also appear to perform a rather more active role. They presented the court with an explanation of why the offender committed offences, and suggested a sentence which might have a deterrent effect, given his circumstances. As Davies reminds us, probation officers have little justification for taking on such a diagnostic function when they advise sentencers, so it is important to try to understand some of the decision-making processes at work.

A different aspect of their role will now be examined.

2 Influencing the court towards a social work decision

So far, the relatively straightforward situations in which probation officers advise sentencers have been described, and the 'reverse tariff' seems to be one means of summarizing these processes. However, it is apparent from Table 7 : 4 that many cases did not fit into these neat patterns. For example, conditional discharge and fine were recommended in some high-need cases and probation was suggested even when tariff and need were given high ranks, and previous supervision had failed. Part of the explanation of these findings seems to lie in the fact that probation officers were attempting actively to influence the court towards making a social work decision in these circumstances.

But why did probation officers adopt such an active role in these cases? It appears that they were typically high need cases, frequently with particularly high tariff ranks (Table 7 : 6). In 50 per

Table 7:6   Sentencing role and reverse tariff

| Role | Reverse tariff rank Low need | | | High need | | | |
	Low tariff	Medium tariff	High tariff	Low tariff	Medium tariff	High tariff	Total
Classical justice	9·2	5·0	19·8	0	7·4	12·0	8·0
Advising sentencers	90·8	89·4	71·2	86·7	81·0	60·4	81·9
Social work	0	5·6	9·0	13·3	11·6	27·6	10·1
	100	100	100	100	100	100	100
N =	98	320	74	49	258	116	915

X^2 93·07   df 10 $p < 0.001$

cent of the ninety-six cases where this social work role was played, probation was recommended (Table 7 : 5). And in 88 per cent of these ninety-six social work cases, an attempt was being made to keep the offender out of prison. So part of the explanation for probation officers adopting a more active social work role in their social enquiry reports was that the offender's criminal record and personal circumstances were so serious that custody was likely, but an attempt was being made to keep him out of prison. A recommendation for probation was a typical and classical means of doing this, but a variety of sentences – conditional discharge, fine, suspended and deferred sentences, community service orders – served a similar purpose.

The probation officer's social work role was clearly illustrated in a case where *probation* was recommended as a means of keeping out of prison a man charged with two offences of incest with his daughter. This was a high need case, because the probation officer thought the offender had had a deprived history of unsettled institutional care, had a low IQ, suffered poor health and was estranged from his wife who had colluded with the offences. He explained why he tried to influence the court.

This was clearly a case where the man had very great needs which needed to be stressed, and I felt fairly strongly that a punitive response would be a harmful one. It was a case where I felt justified in sticking my neck out, even at the risk of losing some credibility.

This was a very difficult decision for him, as he went on to elaborate.

I was really stuck. From a social work point of view I knew he needed help and I knew that we could offer him that sort of help; whether it is effective or not is a different matter, but I knew we had something to offer him. From my own previous experience I knew that the court had made a probation order in an incest case, so I knew it was possible. Therefore that led me to believe it was worth sticking my neck out . . . the alternative would have been to make no recommendation, to have played safe and kept cool but I felt so strongly about this man that I couldn't do that.

However difficult probation officers find a particular recommendation, they still have to choose an acceptable way of communicating their views to the sentencers. In this case the officer realized that the likely sentence would be custodial, given the sentencing policy of the court. However, the conclusion to the social enquiry report was a plea for probation.

If the Court is in any way minded to consider an alternative to imprisonment then it is suggested that Mr Brown would respond favourably to a period of *Probation* which would aim to help him rebuild a life for himself. He is currently in voluntary contact with the Service and calls weekly at the office. Whatever the outcome, it is envisaged that he will need help and support for some considerable time.

Historically, probation was always meant to be a classic means of keeping some offenders out of prison. However, it seems that other recommendations (e.g. conditional discharge, fine and suspension of a custodial sentence) serve a similar purpose if for a variety of reasons probation is not indicated. For example, a woman and her co-habitee were jointly charged with conspiracy to defraud after making a false insurance claim for £5,000. The probation officer did not feel that the woman should go to prison even though the offence was premeditated and serious; he thought that she was unlikely to do it again and seemed to have enough about her not to need the intervention of the probation service. For these reasons, he considered that suspension of a custodial sentence was appropriate and made the following recommendation to the court:

Miss D is only too aware of the gravity of the perpetrated offence and that it could result in the loss of her liberty as well as that of her co-accused's. It is considered that the defendant had sufficient inner resources to cope with the demands of life and therefore probation does not seem to be indicated. Should the court be considering a *custodial sentence* it is felt that its *suspension* may well be a sufficient deterrent to prevent any repetition.

Surprisingly, conditional discharge was sometimes recommended as a means of keeping an offender out of prison. For example, a man, aged twenty-three, with previous convictions, was charged with theft of heavy-duty cables valued at £200. The probation officer thought that neither intervention nor immediate imprisonment was necessary, but this left him with a difficult decision about a recommendation, given the man's previous criminal record. During the research interview, he said that a probation order was a waste of time as the man would think he had been let off; his financial problems ruled out a fine; a community service order would be difficult to meet because of his working hours and he would probably benefit little from it anyway. He elaborated his reasons as follows:

> I was arguing against a custodial sentence and I suppose I tried to be a bit cute really. I recommended what I thought was best although I realized that as far as the court was concerned I would have to argue very well to get it. The gist of my conclusion therefore was, here is a guy who has been a criminal in the past but who does not seem to be any more. He has done very well without the help of anybody at all, let us leave him alone and carry on doing this. The present offence was an isolated lapse. If you accept that and give him a *conditional discharge*, if I am wrong then you can hammer him for both next time he goes into court.

Accordingly, the probation officer told the court that either a financial penalty or supervision was inappropriate whilst a conditional discharge would perform the dual functions of rewarding Mr F for his past progress whilst reminding him of the punishment he might expect if he offended again. Mr F was sent to prison for six weeks. The probation officer acknowledged that his recommendation might have been accepted had it been for the suspension of a prison sentence, but he just could not bring himself to accept that such a conclusion was appropriate. His recommendation did not appear to be so unrealistic given the arguments on which it was based.

In another case, a man aged fifty-six was recommended for a financial penalty instead of a custodial sentence after being charged (with others) with deception and falsifying his clock card. The probation officer said he tried to cool the situation and present the men as they were – just perfectly normal, constructive, respectable citizens before the courts for offences which could probably be levelled at 90 per cent of the community. He felt he had to say that to the magistrates without appearing to condone their behaviour. Accordingly, he pitched his recommendation in the following way:

> The practice for which Mr G appears in court is unfortunately very widespread on all sides of industry and it would seem that he unthinkingly followed established patterns of behaviour. It is likely that he did not fully consider the implications of his activities and detection has made him realize that the practice was illegal and

morally dishonest. The risk of further similar incidents would seem to be minimal. Mr G's offences would seem to represent a lapse in a lifetime of hard work and honest endeavour. In the circumstances, the court may feel that imprisonment would not be an appropriate response and *monetary penalties* may represent the proper disposal.

In each of these cases, probation officers felt that their role was actively to influence the court towards making a social work decision against custodial measures. Placing offenders on probation has been a traditional means of keeping criminals out of prison, but there are other ways of doing this if, for example, supervision seems inappropriate.

3 Classical justice

The variety of roles probation officers thought they played in sentencing has not been exhausted yet. There were some cases in which they said they were leaving the sentence to classical justice and this was particularly evident in the cases where either a custodial sentence or no disposal had been recommended (Table 7 : 5). Their reasons for playing such a role were that no strong arguments for suggesting probation could be found. Furthermore, in many of these situations custody was inevitable. A combination of low need and high tariff ranks (Table 7 : 6) in a significant number of classical justice cases may be further evidence of the same point. If a probation officer said he could not identify needs to support a particular treatment recommendation, he was faced with little alternative but to return a case to classical justice. Again, he could play a relatively passive or active role in this respect.

Sometimes probation officers had little option but to accept the inevitability of a custodial sentence. For example, a man was charged with the murder of his wife's lover, and the officer said in discussion that he accepted a classical justice role because, 'whatever I felt his needs might have been or might not have been, the offence was so serious that it had to be left to the court. Prison was so inevitable that I just had no role in commenting on that.'

Why did he prepare a social enquiry report then in this case? He said it was mandatory because of Home Office policy and that reports were used by prison and parole board personnel. If this is so, the purpose of social enquiry reports at the sentencing stage may be in need of clarification.

Probation officers were sometimes quite actively involved in deciding whether or not to return a case to classical justice. For example, a man aged thirty-eight was charged with theft, damage and handling stolen goods; he had many previous convictions and had served several prison sentences. The probation officer noted his previous criminal record, that he was rootless, homeless and said to be a typical recidivist. He knew that a custodial sentence was inevitable, given the sentencing policy of the court, and acknowledged this in the conclusion to his social inquiry report. He explained during the research interview why he had *returned* the case to classical justice:

> I accepted the fact that he was going to prison for these offences. I couldn't produce any good arguments against it and didn't feel strongly about it anyway. I found it difficult to come to this conclusion because of the lack of treatment resources for alcoholics and the inevitability of prison. Alcoholism was his way of life and I felt some obligation to try to help someone in this position, and the difficult thing to accept is that there is nothing that we can do. I think we have to bow to the inevitable in cases like this; it would be very silly – in terms of safeguarding your own credibility – if we were to try to con the court that we could do something.
>
> I don't think it was a waste of time doing the enquiry, because there are occasions when one begins to see something positive and then that is worth pursuing. I think we should go through the motions just in case something does come up.

So even if the social inquiry report seemed to have little bearing on the sentence passed in such cases, at least the offender has been given some consideration. His circumstances could have changed and the probation service might have been able to meet his evident needs. It is these possibilities which are open to exploration at the social enquiry stage.

Therefore, probation officers could either *accept* a classical justice role, when for example the charge was murder, or they might *return* a case to classical justice after having explored needs and found none especially in cases where custody was inevitable. It has been argued elsewhere (Hardiker 1977b), that they are faced with the dilemma that a man will face a punishment for his crime if needs cannot be identified to support a recommendation for treatment for the offender. As one probation officer put it, 'I knew he was going to be punished because I had not recommended that he needed help.'

Conclusion

The framework within which probation officers make recommendations in their social enquiry reports has been described. In the majority of cases, they appeared to advise sentencers by determining where the offender was on the continuum of need and tariff. Their reports in these circumstances were often relatively straightforward descriptions of circumstances, though sometimes they included diagnostic and prognostic statements. There were other aspects of their role in sentencing. They sometimes used a report actively to influence sentencers to make a 'social work' decision, especially when they attempted to keep an offender out of prison. Probation officers also played a classical justice role, by either accepting the statutory penalty in murder cases, or returning a case for an inevitable custodial sentence.

Social enquiry reports should be considered in the context of neo-classical criminology. This enables individualized consideration to be given to selected criminals, so that sentencers can choose a 'treatment for the offender' rather than a 'punishment for the crime'. In this schema, most offenders are still held to be responsible and accountable for their actions; the neo-classicists, 'merely sketched in the structures which might blur or marginally affect the exercise of voluntarism'. (Taylor *et al.* 9). This seems to be the legitimization for probation officers to have a role in sentencing. They can present sentencers with details about a person's offences, past record, age, personal and social circumstances. In doing this they may inform the court that there seem to be few problems or they may present a picture of an offender in severe personal and social stress. Even so, their activities do not seem to be confined to commenting on the offender's responsibility for an offence. They play a more active role in some situations, by either diagnosing offence behaviour, recommending a reductivist sentence, or attempting to keep an offender out of prison.

Much more evidence is needed before judgments can be made about the appropriateness of some of the roles probation officers play in their social enquiry work. It does appear that they sometimes go beyond the bounds of the revisions to classical justice which, 'remain the major model of human behaviour held to by agencies of social control in all advanced industrial societies' (Taylor *et al.* 9–10). They also seem to be ahead of official policy in this respect (Streatfeild 1961; Morison 1962; Home Office Circulars, e.g. 194/1974; Mathieson 1977).

Probation officers straddle judicial and welfare systems, and their social enquiry reports often encapsulate this dual aspect of their role (Hardiker and Webb). Their task is to sketch in the limits of both free will and determinism. Their credibility is at stake if they exaggerate their roles either as servant of the court or as social worker. Even if they end up playing a classical justice role, at least the offender has been given some consideration at the social enquiry stage. When they actively attempt to manipulate the sentencers towards making a social work decision, there will always be boundaries to their influence, given their structural location in the courts.

Unless probation officers have a theory of practice in their social-enquiry work, they will have few professional principles to guide them in their sentencing roles. It is then too easy to indict them for 'hack work' (Bean 1975; Perry 1974) and violations of due process (Blumberg 1967) in these circumstances.

Bean (1975) suggests that social-enquiry reports should be abandoned because they raise so many problems. I do not agree with such a view for three reasons. Firstly, probation officers *are* crucial implementers of the reverse tariff, where individualistic recognition of the person is affirmed. To write off such an important role seems to be too simple, even though the structure and process of the reverse tariff must be scrutinized. Secondly, treatment ideologies may be liberating (Hardiker 1977b) and as Cohen observes (1975), radical non-intervention may be a euphemism for benign neglect. Thirdly, the ethics, skills and knowledge of the social work profession may be used to ensure that social-enquiry reports are constructed appropriately. These reports are not casework assessments but documents for the court. Probation officers do sometimes get themselves involved in diagnostic sentencing, but when they overstep their brief in this respect, they are not served very well by social science and criminology. They do on occasions attempt to manipulate sentencers and their function in these circumstances must be carefully examined. When they are involved in classical justice, they are sometimes asked to prepare reports for purposes other than sentencing; perhaps it is multi-purpose social enquiries which have been a source of so many of the problems in this area (Curnock and Hardiker).

An attempt has been made to document some of the activities engaged in by probation officers in their social enquiry reports, and to analyse some of the processes which appear to be at work. It has not been possible to evaluate the practices described. Such an exercise clearly needs to be the focus of a separate study. Perhaps as more evidence becomes available and theories of social practice are developed, there will be less need for probation officers to play the games with the court analysed in chapter 6. Then, sentencing will be restored to its proper place – the court.

Recommended reading

COMPTON, B. R. and GALAWAY, B. 1975: *Social Work Processes*, Illinois: Dorsey Press.

DAVIES, M. 1974: Social enquiry for the courts. *British Journal of Criminology*, 14 (1), 18–33.

HARDIKER, P. 1977: Social work ideologies in the probation service. *British Journal of Social Work*, 7 (2), 131–54.

HOGARTH, J. 1971: *Sentencing as a Human Process*. Toronto: University of Toronto Press.

TAYLOR, I., WALTON, P. and YOUNG, J. 1973: *The New Criminology*, London: Routledge & Kegan Paul.

Chapter 8

Client-Defendant Perceptions of Juvenile and Criminal Justice

Howard Parker

Social work has been described as the 'unloved profession'. Part of the problem undoubtedly stems from the fact that social workers by and large deal with society's official deviants, misfits and inadequates. Such a 'class' is unpopular in society and receives more by way of abuse, accusation and blame than help or concern from the bulk of 'the public'. Social workers are consequently tainted, their energies regarded as misplaced, their compassion naïve and their politics perhaps even dangerous.

Yet if social workers are tainted, client-defendants and convicted criminals are poison. Their position in the prosecution process in particular is one of massive inferiority. Their deal is lousy. The 'beginning' social worker might be forgiven for asking 'well, isn't the social worker or probation officer there to help the client, identify and attempt to alleviate his personal and social difficulties and also report them to the court and so make the client's position less inferior, less lousy?' In this chapter I shall try to hold on to this ideal but in so doing must demonstrate that tremendous pressures, demands and even contradictions militate against the 'helping' role.

It is of course a fact that some social workers/probation officers regard themselves merely as servants to the court and therefore without a major responsibility for 'helping', in the broadest sense, the client. The assumption in this paper is that a helping and facilitating role, fundamental to all social work, must remain inalienable in the court context, whatever other tasks are demanded by law. A further assumption in the provision of social services is that 'there are reciprocal and complementary elements in social worker-client exchanges, and that ideal practice is characterized by shared but different activities aimed at the attainment of a common goal' (Rees 1974). Do social workers carrying out statutory tasks in general, and tasks required by the courts in particular, enter into reciprocal and complementary exchanges with defendants and convicted persons as a matter of course? We will explore these difficulties by focusing upon the view from the receiving end of juvenile and criminal justice.

The context of the social work-client relationship

First, a general feature of social work-client relationships which must be recognized concerns *social status*. In general the social worker is well-educated (even if not qualified) and from a higher social group than the client (Collison and Kennedy 1977). This status differential is in fact magnified and highlighted in the court setting where social workers and probation officers are at their most formal, wear their 'best' clothes and are on their 'best' behaviour in terms of their written and spoken English and disseminate their knowledge and opinions with esoteric or elaborated style.

A second general feature of worker-client relationships concerns the inherent *power differential* present in them. Consumer-based research almost universally identifies clients' awareness of this. An associated feature of this awareness concerns clients' apprehension and nervousness at the prospect of contact with a social worker.

Mayer and Timms (1970) identified this condition as did Reith (1975) in his study of clients who were bold enough to contact one social work department in 1971. Reith identified much heart-searching and indecision amongst intending clients. He documented comments such as: 'I was frightened to death. You get worked up having to go to such places.' 'I was terrified of going but I was desperate. My nerves were terrible.' The limited rights of appeal open to clients concerning their (compulsory) treatment from social work agencies is a further demonstration of the relative powerlessness of clients. 'Client rights' is not a familiar slogan and indeed it is only recently that critics of present juvenile justice have proposed punishment as a preferable alternative to treatment. The rationale behind such a proposal is not difficult to understand when we consider the indeterminacy of a care order imposed on, say, a girl 'in moral danger' or a school refuser. Powerlessness amongst client-defendants in the courtroom is, as we shall see, a central feature of their feelings about the criminal process.

Thirdly, *confusion* seems to pervade the majority of worker-client contacts. Nearly all consumer-based research emphasizes that clients and defendants when consulted about their contact with social care and control agencies admitted confusion and ignorance. The work of Mayer and Timms (1970) demonstrated this forcibly. Similarly a small study in Scotland found that the majority of the general public interviewed had little knowledge of what social work is about. '74 per cent of respondents did not know what services Strathclyde Social Work Department provided nor had they any idea of what social workers actually do. Only 4 per cent of those interviewed had considered going to see a social worker and only 6 per cent knew where the local social work office was located' (Graham 1976).

Stuart Rees makes the distinction between worker-client contact and contract. His research suggested that contact rather than contract epitomizes social agencies' relationship with poor families. Rees' interviews with clients of social workers found that they were understandably confused by the stream of official visitors so typical of the State's approach to poor families. These clients 'often did not know what the social worker's job was with reference to them. In their eyes he seemed immediately or eventually to become no different from other officials who passed by' (Rees 1974). As one respondent told Rees: 'These people come here and ask you all sorts of personal questions, they get you telling them all about your personal troubles and then you don't see them again.' Rees' work was centred on the views of poor families mainly with material problems. Their confusion can be all the more comprehensible when we see that misunderstandings about the function of social services and social security departments reach as far as the producers of ITN news. The reorganization of social services and the reorganizing of statutory responsibilities between the local authorities and probation services has of course exacerbated these confusions. As we shall see this confusion is multiplied amongst those processed through the courts as well as through social work structures.

My final contextual point may appear obvious but it is no less important for that. Whilst all the available research indicates that there is a spectrum of attitudes amongst clients and defendants concerning their experiences with social agencies and the courts, it also emphasizes that there is a large note of dissatisfaction, disenchantment and even alienation at the receiving end. It is equally obvious that compulsion and dissatisfaction will be closely associated. Given that the clients of probation officers and local authority social workers are increasingly clients by decree rather than by desire we must accept from the outset that the worker-client relationship is likely to be difficult. The social work role with client-defendants therefore presents major communication 'contract' difficulties almost as a matter of course. Social work, in and around the court process, perhaps more than anywhere else highlights the dilemmas State-sponsored social workers must face.

It is as well therefore that we count this large pile of chips already stacked up against communication and mutual goal-setting between client/defendant and social worker, given that they are possibly both pushed into a contact which they must make something of. The social worker has his obligatory duties and hopefully his kindred professional goals. The client-defendant (and perhaps prisoner) probably has to cope with apprehension, fear, confusion and ignorance, a sense of powerlessness and consequently suspicion. These debilitating constraints, as we shall now see, are as real for work in a juvenile court as for work in adult criminal courts.

Receiving juvenile justice

What little available research there is concerning the perceptions from the receiving end does suggest, without exception, that young defendants and their families expect criminal procedure and disposition in juvenile court to be based upon principles of justice. Matza's insightful classification of the delinquent's demands can be our basic guide.

> It is only fair that some steps be taken to ascertain whether I was really the wrongdoer (cognizance); it is only fair that I be treated according to the same principles as others of my status (consistency); it is only fair that you who pass judgment on me sustain the right to do so (competence); it is only fair that some relationship obtain between the magnitude of what I have done and what you propose to do to me (commensurability); it is only fair that differences between the treatment of my status and others be reasonable and tenable (comparison). (Matza 1964)

To a large extent these demands are consistent with the principles of traditional English justice, although everyday practice rarely achieves such standards.

Theoretically a welfare or treatment approach concerned with the 'best interests of the child' could satisfy these requirements although not without a monumental·reorganization of our whole machinery for dealing with deviant or 'at risk' youth. In practice an 'individualized' treatment orientation, based as it is on problematic social scientific and medical knowledge, in fact satisfies few of the delinquent's demands. *Cognizance* and *commensurability* are seriously relegated since delinquency is viewed as a symptom of deprivation requiring individualized 'sentencing' or treatment; similarly those 'at risk' who have committed no offence are also regarded as suitable cases for treatment. *Consistency* is difficult to achieve with an individualized treatment approach, particularly where for instance medical and psycho-social diagnoses and thus *competence* become questionable and *comparison* hard to make. All available research findings support the conclusion that the 'natural justice' model is firmly implanted in the judgmental equipment of those on the receiving end. Findings by Scott and Voeckler ante-dating the 1969 Act showing that parents and children expected the juvenile court to administer retributive justice have been duplicated by recent small scale studies. Morris and Giller (1977) showed that not only did children in the main expect their disposition to be linked with the seriousness of their offence but objected to any disparities in the offence record of a co-defendant not being reflected in their disposition. This study also found that parents and children questioned the validity of the use of additional information such as reports on their home circumstances. As one interviewee put it: 'They shouldn't look at your home, they should look only at the offence. At home you don't do wrong. They should only look at your home if you've done something wrong there.' Perhaps surprisingly therefore, at a theoretical level at least, the working principles demanded by those on the receiving end are much closer to those found in a justice or punishment model expounded, although often not adequately practised, by professional groups traditionally associated with the Right. Thus despite the increasing significance of the welfare or treatment approach in juvenile justice philosophy, operationalized by social workers, those on the receiving end would still expect justice principles to operate in most facets of juvenile-court work. This does not mean that the social worker's presence in the proceedings is seen as redundant by the receiving end. What it does mean, however, is that given that the juvenile court is associated with the finding of guilt and punishment in the broadest sense, then the social worker can be viewed either as a client advocate or at the other extreme as a prosecutor or official control agent.

Hapgood in a small on-going study of defendants' perceptions of juvenile court, is finding, for instance, that younger and 'first-time' defendants and their families often perceive the social worker or probation officer as their advocate (we have no research attempting to assess the distinctions clients make between these two social work styles) to the extent that they give this as their reason for not seeking legal aid. They are doing this with a perceptual framework which anticipates a system of retributive justice.

This finding does, however, have to be juxtaposed with my own previous research amongst older adolescents already immersed in the hard end of the tariff system (which undoubtedly operates) in both juvenile and magistrates' courts. In this group of adolescents and eventually young adults, 'the boys', social workers and probation officers were viewed with much greater suspicion mediated only by unexpectedly good service, in their terms, from the social worker.

In keeping with Hapgood's sample 'the boys' also judged the prosecution process in terms very similar to Matza's classification. When measured against their demands, however, the administration of justice to which they were subjected fell far short of acceptability. The cause of 'the boys'' alienation was not based on rejection of social control agents or the need for 'law and order' *per se*, but on a rejection of the administration and operation of the system, in short, the behaviour of those in Authority. 'Authority' was an umbrella term for almost any of 'them' with the ability to impose rules from 'outside' their normal social network, and most especially anyone involved in the prosecution process. Thus juvenile liaison officers, education officials, police, magistrates, solicitors, court officials and social workers were all seen as components of one conspiratorial chain – the laws on the law's side. This procession of officials who trade in trouble is closely comparable with that similar procession that knocks on the doors of 'problem' families – rent collectors, 'tick' men, health visitors, housing officials and any other representatives of 'the welfare' we mentioned earlier. According to a report by some children in care (Page and Clark 1977) they do sense this procession of passing workers of an anonymous local authority whether it be during their passage through court, assessment centre, case reviews or children's homes.

The research projects quoted here are too small and distinctive to allow elaborate comparison. However, we can tentatively hypothesize that, particularly in relation to criminal proceedings and care proceedings for either an offence or truancy, children and adolescents do expect a set of 'justice' rules to operate, and that within this frame they regard social workers diversely, with their views ranging from seeing the social worker as an advocate through to seeing him as just another control agent running an oppressive system. Client/defendant views vary amongst other things in relation to experience of the system and the operation of a punitive tariff system. The more often a youngster appears before the court the less of an advocate role the social worker can (even if he wishes to) play, and maintain his credibility in the court (see chapter 6). The more often an adolescent is 'processed' the more punitive the disposition and the more likely he is to observe or 'feel' malpractice of some sort during his prosecution. The social worker-client relationship may well get caught up in this escalation to its detriment. One worker-client relationship from my research illustrates this forcefully. In this case the worker had finally (had) to recommend detention centre. As he put it:

> It was odds-on for Borstal. I recommended detention centre because it was only three months. I would have been laughed out of court if I'd got up again and said he was a good lad. If I'd rubbed old . . . [the magistrate] up the wrong way he might well have used Borstal. As it was we probably got off lightly with three months DC.

Tank, the youngster concerned, didn't see it like that. He sensed a betrayal from an adult who had previously always helped him 'get off'. His response when I visited him in detention was 'He just worked to get rid of me so he didn't have as much work to do.'

These feelings amongst defendants are liable to be most extreme where (as increasingly is the case) a defendant is legally repre-sented. In this situation, as Williamson (1977) is finding in his on-going research in Cardiff, the defence solicitor is almost certain to challenge custodial recommendations as part of his mitigation brief. In such a situation the social worker is liable to be seen as the prosecution counsel, rather than the advocate.

The administration and maladministration of justice then is the point of departure between those on the receiving end and those advocating the justice approach in dealing with young offenders. No doubt the majority of arrests of adolescents by the police, the charge and their treatment whilst in custody, is of a technically acceptable standard. No doubt in non-stress areas of the country where police-community relations are good, malpractice is rare. In the urban conurbations however, where the conflict between control agencies and the urban poor is explicit, malpractice at all stages of the prosecution process is rampant. Urban adolescents soon collect a memory bank full of incidents of official deviance. It is upon these experiential foundations that the administration of justice is judged, is found guilty and its moral authority negated.

> You can just be walking down-town with millions of shoppers and they'll stop *you*. If they know your face you're fucked. If they know you've done a bit of robbery and they don't like your face, that's it. (Arno)

> I hadn't done nothing I was just walking around like, but these plainclothes busies, they pulled me in. They made up all sorts of lies in the station and said I was trying door handles and that. But they gave themselves away. They kept saying 'Plead guilty, plead guilty.' You'd have thought I was up for murder. They gave it away doing that, they had nothing on me so they made it up. (Fatch) (Parker 1974)

Once adolescents talk together and pool their experiences, whether in a pub, a youth club, an assessment centre or a community home, and perhaps with a degree of exaggeration, then any police malpractice in the system becomes highlighted. The same procedure operates for court-hearing experiences where a solicitor's inefficiency, clerk megalomania or magisterial madness occur. Thus unless the young person is a first-timer or a complete loner, then what may be a first exchange (e.g. to prepare a social enquiry report) for the 'new' social worker is, for the accused and his family, more a continuation of events. For the client here is yet another official asking questions and 'nosing around'. Of course this is but a general statement but it should lead to a general rule for our idealistic worker mentioned in the introduction. The rule to be consistent with the mood of the adolescent must be, 'I shall assume that my client does *not* trust me, does *not* have a clear understanding of my role and does *not* take for granted, perhaps because of prior experience with other members of my, or allied, professions, that I am trying to help him.' From this beginning progress can be made; fail to accept this handicapped start, and misconception and misunderstanding are liable to interfere even further with an already poor communication channel.

In setting out the context of worker-client relationships we highlighted powerlessness and confusion as generalizable features of many relationships. These conditions are widespread amongst those receiving juvenile justice. Morris and Giller, for instance, found that, in the court setting, 'the majority of children could not correctly identify who the magistrates were, let alone who had actually made the disposition decision'. The 'Who Cares' group of youngsters in care felt very strongly that social workers failed to explain to clients their rights under the law, particularly in relation to Section 1 Care Orders and variation and discharge of Orders. They advise social workers to remember that,

> They should look down the list of the children they have got and they should think: these children are in my hands. I make decisions for them. I think that whatever I do they should be consulted. They should know what's going on, even if they are too young to have a fair say in the matter, they should know what's going on. They should get the information firsthand. (Page and Clark 1977)

Easier said than done of course, but the task of providing client-defendants with a working knowledge of their rights and obligations and of demystifying the court process are functions which as far as many of those on the receiving end are concerned are greatly needed. Willock (1972) in an unpublished study of panel hearings in Dundee found that the majority of parents who had attended the hearings with their children and felt that they had understood the proceedings, invariably credited their comprehension to pre-hearing discussions with their social worker.

Providing an advocacy service for the defendant or youngster in care or detention is obviously not easy, given the weighty caseloads of many social workers. It is even more difficult when, from the alienated adolescent client's point of view, 'good' social workers should also be around regularly to be abused or stunned with silence. Visiting clients in assessment centre, remand, children's home, distant community home, or detention centre is a time-consuming and often apparently unproductive job. And yet listen to the kids in these institutions and they obviously badly need such visits, perhaps as a demonstration of consistent care, perhaps because they need to know where they stand, and, yes, even perhaps because they need to be mean to someone involved in determining the quality of their life. What is more depressing is that they might need that visit from the field social worker because someone is being mean to *them* during their 'treatment'. The roundabout goes on of course, since the youngster who doesn't get *anything* from the social worker, will the next time round not trust the next social worker, maybe not even trust the next adult. Once youngsters get on to this circuit, even skilled, detached youth workers working full-time with 'difficult' youth need many months to develop any rapport (C. Smith *et al.* 1972).

Ericson's study of youngsters sent to detention centre (Ericson 1976), provides further evidence of the constraints that *compulsory* social work supervision places upon a client-worker relationship. Ericson worked with, interviewed and listened to some fifty male adolescents, both during and after their detention. He demonstrated clearly that these detainees thought the probation officer's role in court and the prosecution process was in the main that of helper. However, Ericson found that as the period of detention progressed an increasingly negative attitude towards the Probation Service developed. The root cause of this alienation, according to Ericson, was an apprehension and resentment of the compulsory licence period upon release. Ericson noted that the detainees greatly resented the failure of their probation officer to visit them or explain to them the nature of their after-custody 'second sentence' (as they saw it). As one detainee Graham, put it: 'If I don't hear from him on the out I won't go and see him. He's never wrote to me, just to the social worker. He should have seen me. If I've got to see him on the outside he could have at least come and seen me once while I'm in here.' Had the probation officer actually visited Graham, however, other criticisms might well have been made about how he didn't stay long enough, or how he wouldn't go, etc. Nevertheless, the likelihood that such a visit would have proved useful is quite high since Ericson also found that once on the outside again licencees did feel that they could *use* the Probation Service, given they had a personal contact there. As Mike put it: 'If they just kick you out of the gate, you're bound to go back to court. Probation can give you guidance, get you used to the way on the out. I need him to tell me about the law, get me onto a course, get a job.' The function derived from listening to the receiving end in relation to after-custody supervision may not suit the social worker's 'professional' image but nevertheless I state it as one possibility: that the worker persist with a client through a period of detention, despite being given a rough ride, in order that the client may have a personal contact with a social work agency that he can *use* in terms of *his* requirements. In summary, parents and their children expect retributive justice. Where justice is meted out without maladministration and within certain principles they are satisfied with the system (whether social workers with their particular knowledge base find this position acceptable or desirable is another matter). However, because of the complexity of the court system and the nervousness and feelings of powerlessness it creates in defendants, and most of all because of malpractice by various allied officials, there is a degree of either dissociation or alienation from the whole process amongst adolescents, those on the receiving end. The social worker and probation officer have a variety of difficulties functioning within this system. First, they may be regarded as being part of a corrupt system and so be viewed with suspicion. Secondly, their official functions and credibility amongst the other 'professionals' may restrict their freedom to act in the best interests of their clients as they see them. Thirdly, the inadequate and inappropriate 'treatment' facilities and resources back-up places the worker in bad faith in that he cannot always fulfil his ideal contract with the client and thus loses credibility. Finally, the welfare or treatment philosophy espoused in social work education and held by many field-workers is neither well understood nor readily accepted by either magistrates, police or those on the receiving end.

Receiving criminal justice

Moving on now to English adult criminal justice, we must inevitably start with the deflating fact, for social workers and probation officers, that the social work role in criminal proceedings is, generally speaking, a relatively insignificant one. Indeed Bottoms and McClean in their study of Sheffield Magistrates' Court concluded that 'probation officers at present have little direct influence over the various decisions that have to be made by defendants in the criminal process' (Bottoms and McClean 1976). They point out that only 6·5 per cent of their sample of defendants spontaneously mentioned the help of the Probation Service. These researchers also concluded that most defendants did not see the probation officer as a worthwhile substitute for a defence lawyer (not that we need share the assumption that this is an appropriate function anyway).

While Bottoms' and McClean's conclusions are based on incomplete information and a questionable methodology, their point must be accepted. The majority of criminal cases in lower court proceed without either 'verbals' or reports from a social work agency. This may not be a situation approved of by advocates of individualized sentencing, but it is at present a simple fact. Consequently in this section we shall look at defendants' perceptions of the criminal process more generally and with less emphasis upon social work intervention. There are obviously identifiable defendant groups where reports are either mandatory or usual, although as the National Association of Probation Officers have found in their recent attempts to withdraw from preparing pre-trial reports for not-guilty pleas, judges may in such circumstances dispense with adjournment on the finding of guilt, and sentence without a social enquiry. This is perhaps another indication of the still limited function and power of social work in criminal justice.

Even more significant than in the juvenile court and the panels must be the impact of the courtroom atmosphere. The grandeur, the mystique, the esoteric language, the in-group atmosphere created by the regular professionals, the degradation ceremonies, all build into a setting which disables the majority of defendants. Obviously the nature and the degree of disablement vary greatly, and certainly some old hands will be relatively at ease during their prosecution. At present, however, we simply do not have adequate knowledge in this area to make definitive statements about the causes of diverse reactions to prosecution, the court hearing and disposition. Indeed without detailed information about a defendant's cultural background, personality and ideological leanings, as well as details of the arrest and crime categorization, prediction would be most unreliable.

One attempt – that of Bottoms and McClean – at a typology of defendants' approaches and reactions to the criminal prosecution process, despite its methodological limitations, is a useful beginning, and worth summarizing. They suggest that, broadly speaking, defendants in magistrates' courts fall into the following categories. *Strategists* in court are the rational planners. They make acquittal or reduced sentence their primary goal. Included in this category are many 'recidivists' and middle-class defendants with an 'alternative society' approach. *Respectable first-timers* make up a separate remorseful group. They tend to accept guilt and overtly seek to receive due punishment without fuss. This group can be juxtaposed with the 'mistakenly indicted citizen' who strongly denies the charge and also has no criminal record. *Right-assertive defendants*, as a small proportion of the research sample, were identified by their not guilty pleas and their persistence and emphasis upon their legal and civil rights. *Passive defendants* tended to submit to the criminal process, and adolescents were in particular represented in this group, a point to which I shall return. *Other-dominated defendants* were defined by the fact that they were largely influenced by the advice of others, whether police, solicitors or relatives.

Obviously any classification based on the findings of one case study is ideally only beginning its useful life, since further testing will adapt and modify it (or else show it to be redundant). Taken at face value this classification immediately suggests a vast variety of responses to the prosecution process. It also suggests that only a minority of defendants make a 'struggle' of their situation. The majority appear to remain relatively passive throughout their prosecution even when they feel aggrieved or outraged by the treatment they receive from the regular officials. Many critics feel that the present system of criminal justice enforces this passivity in more complex structural ways than we have elaborated here by merely focusing on its disabling effect. We cannot discuss these arguments here. An issue which must concern our discussion of 'the receiving end' however, concerns methodology. If we listen to 'offenders' talk amongst themselves about their views of criminal justice, rather than formally interview them, as I was able to do in my Liverpool study, our understanding changes. 'The boys' for instance, would fall squarely into Bottoms' and McClean's 'passive' category dissociating themselves from the courtroom dialogue. Without a doubt they would not have found professorial research interviews anything other than yet another set of officials asking questions, a view confirmed by the Sheffield researchers themselves. However, if we listen to 'the boys'' 'natural' reasons for presenting as 'dumb' and passive, we may wish to reconsider (Parker 1974).

1 Silence may be tactical at a remand hearing in terms of personal freedom.
Arno's father: Why didn't you speak up about them keeping you in nick all weekend and tell them you didn't do it?
Arno: I pleaded not guilty, didn't I? It's no good shooting your mouth off. That does no fuckin' good. They'd only have kept me in till February 15th then [date of hearing proper].

2 Silence may be necessary to maintain self-esteem and dignity in the courtroom if answering prosecution counsel questions previously had involved the counsel retorting: 'When you say you didn't say nothing, do you mean you didn't say anything or you did say something?'

3 Silence may be necessary to prevent oneself 'exploding' to one's cost during the hearing. Only after the hearing, with your mates, can you release the hatred against the prosecution process.

This clerk to the court feller, you know the one that sits near the judge. He says have you got £20 to pay the fine and I says no. Then he says why not? Why fuckin' not, I ask you, why fuckin' not. Honest to God. He wouldn't fuckin' know why not, the silly old cunt. I should have gone . . . (smack) that's why not.

It is not intended here to dwell upon issues of classification development. What I wish to illustrate is the present embryonic nature of formal understanding of the perceptions of those on the receiving end of criminal justice, particularly those who are regularly processed, the majority of whom come from the ranks of the urban poor. My main suggestion is that the apparent lack of 'struggle' amongst defendants and offender groups is to be found in the structure of the criminal process. Dissociation from the criminal process by defendants blends at one extreme of the spectrum into alienation. Alienation against the administration of the control apparatus of the State. The issue for many of the urban poor, who readily admit to criminal activity, is not that there are police, courts, and punishment – they accept these control mechanisms. The issue is that these control mechanisms are themselves manned by officials who indulge in malpractice, who fail to satisfy the very standards or keep within the boundaries they themselves patrol. In short, not only is the criminal process a mystification, a professional's game, but for many defendants those processes are but camouflage for a more sinister conspiracy. Passivity may be merely a final line of defence. 'I am obedient because I can do nothing else and that gives pseudo-legitimacy to the sovereign' (Sartre 1960). The sovereign is the State and its control apparatus.

This 'ideal type' defendant perception is of course an extreme, but one reached by many defendants and it is a condition that many defendants and 'offenders' move towards. Official denials of malpractice, or even incompetence and inadequacy of the system, are of course always available when accusations, or perhaps studies in the alienation of the urban poor, are made. Time and again complaints on or on behalf of the receiving end of criminal prosecution are refuted or ignored or diverted by talk about the victims of crime as if a knowledge that *someone* has committed a nasty crime justifies putting the boot in to anyone from 'the criminal classes'.

One piece of consumer research, *Crime in the City*, commissioned by a Liverpool City Council (1974) steering group, illustrated this process succinctly. The high-powered steering group (including the Chief Constable and stipendiary magistrate) which initiated the report was, after a period of denial and contention, stunned into silence and inactivity. The findings of the group of local men, who spent three months of part-time research and study in the inner city, simply did not come up with simple clear-cut and apologetic solutions that the steering group could digest. Instead they produced a hard-hitting report which began by admitting that there were high rates of crime, delinquency, vandalism and minor violence in the down-town areas, went on to accept the need for efficient policing and prosecution, but then turned their attention to the feelings and attitudes of inner-city residents. The researchers identified in their own neighbourhoods a high degree of poverty, unemployment and multiple disadvantage. Further, they found residents had great dislike and distrust of the police, not simply because of their power position but because of their attitudes and behaviour to down-towners. Similarly, the courts were regarded as unjust, particularly in relation to the standard of legal (aid) representation and the disproportionately high status of police evidence during the proceedings.

The report received little credence from the steering group although it did provoke the Chief Constable into several pages of considered denial of all charges made against his force. This was obviously a totally predictable and understandable response given the 'hearsay' nature of the evidence. Yet despite claims by control agencies that there are 'proper channels for appeal' we know only too well that these are quite unmanageable for most lone defendants and in fact perceived simply as more mystification of the system by the system. Powerlessness often leads to alienation.

A recent study of plea-bargaining in Birmingham Crown Court (Baldwin and McConville, 1977) encountered similar denials, this time from the Bar Council. The study was based on interviews with defendants who were expected, and themselves expected to, plead not guilty but who changed their minds and pleaded guilty, often at the last minute. In keeping with other studies the researchers found a spectrum of responses to the criminal process, ranging from satisfaction through to specific complaints and towards fundamental alienation. The characteristics we found so typical in the defendant in juvenile court were mercilessly repeated in Crown Court. The sense of non-involvement and feeling of disablement appeared routine.

> Everything's stacked against the accused . . . I had an argument with my barrister about who was going to be called as witnesses and who wasn't – they didn't want to call anyone as witnesses. He refused to ask lots of questions owing to the fact that he's one of the flag-wavers. I don't know whether he wants to be a QC or what. I was just dissatisfied with them all in general – putting it bluntly, they all basically piss in the same pot. (Case 82)

> I never made any decisions, they were all taken for me. I felt like I wasn't controlling things with the solicitor and barrister; I was just dragged along. I just had no say in what was happening. I was just carried along on the tide of what they said. I had to follow a set route

all the way through. I couldn't say 'No, I don't want to go that way', the way it was put there was only one route to follow. It's just like a blindfolded man being guided through a maze: I had to go but I wasn't sure where I was going. (Case 148)

Over half the Birmingham sample who had pleaded guilty in Crown Court felt that in effect this decision had been taken by their legal advisers. For some this was perfectly acceptable, although many other cases in the sample felt that they had been put under recognizable pressure, which they were not happy about. At the extreme the undue pressure that some of the sample claimed they were put under produced a severe nudge towards alienation, towards a rejection of the validity of the criminal process, towards a negation of its moral authority. Case 136 illustrates this:

My barrister pleaded guilty for me. I told him that I was innocent but he said I was a bloody nuisance and that nobody would believe me. He said, 'The judge and others will never believe what you say in court; they will always believe the police.' I said, 'How can this be so? What I am saying is *true*.' He said I must plead guilty. I even argued with him in court. This was wrong; the barrister decided my plea for me. I always remember in my mind saying, 'You should not plead guilty for me.' I was forced to plead guilty by my barrister; it was wrong of him.

Baldwin and McConville's study is methodologically sophisticated although it will be criticized for merely listening to 'criminals' with a gripe against authority. In fact it shows quite clearly and in fairly subtle ways that the sample of defendants were not merely nihilists. Significant numbers of defendants, who had received reduced sentences through plea negotiations between judge and lawyer, despite being satisfied with the outcome of the case were still highly aggrieved by the system through which they had been processed. The Birmingham study documents a mass of grievances across the whole breadth of legal representation. Further, it found a considerable minority of defendants pleading guilty whilst privately claiming their innocence. It also found defendants bitterly aggrieved by the nature of police evidence and prosecution practice. In short it found a condition of alienation amongst many defendants.

The social work role in criminal justice

Why should we be concerned with the social worker-client relationship? Could it not be argued that the social worker function in and around the courts is determined and defined by statute, and that therefore concern over the quality of relationships is misplaced? Other court officials can perform their professional functions, if necessary, despite the defendant. To be sure, in practice, social worker-defendant contacts *are* often merely the fulfilment of the minimum mandatory requirements. Yet we proposed at the outset that social work is in essence about facilitating, enabling, about a package of helping processes. It is in the pursuit of these goals, often submerged in statutory work, that we must consider the social worker-client relationship.

The possibilities of achieving 'essence' objectives do seem bleak when placed in the context of criminal process, and for this reason we might well be grateful that social work is not even more deeply implicated in defendants' imagery of the prosecution process. To return to the 'here and now', however, what tentative ground rules are available for those social workers who do serve or service the courts and who ponder upon the impact of the court setting on their relationship with clients?

First we should be clear that where there is significant social work involvement the worker or officer will mostly be viewed as one of the court regulars, the professionals who trade in words in the courtroom (Carlen 1976). The probation officer in particular (social worker in Scotland) is likely to be seen as part of the syndicate of officialdom, and will be to some extent 'tarred with the same brush' whether it be a pleasant or unpleasant shade. Where there has been no previous social work involvement with the defendant his preconceptions are likely to be few and more open-ended. Where there has been previous experience his perceptions will depend on the quality of that exchange and its significance in answer to his overriding question – how has this social worker affected the passage through and outcome of this prosecution I have been subjected to? The defendant who is knowledgeable about the tariff system will have a stronger perception of the social worker's (report's) significance. If defendants have reached this degree of comprehension then the worker/officer cannot expect to be 'cosy' with the other court regulars and assume that his client won't notice. The social work function will be viewed as part of, not apart from, the rest of the criminal process.

The most negative possibility as we have seen is that the social worker will be totally rejected as yet another agent of official (unjust) control. Certainly with this possibility in mind the rule mentioned in relation to work with juveniles is worth recalling. The worker should assume that the client is confused, apprehensive and possibly highly aggrieved. This begs the question of advocacy. Certainly the question is an open one. I am of the view that in the light of the evidence presented, the defendant, probationer, or parolee should be presented with the fullest information about the processes, the law, the rules and legal rights involved in his situation. Such 'help' may not be overtly asked for or graciously received but is nevertheless a potential function in the criminal process and disposition. It is a function which over a period of time could, if the quality of advice is high, both improve and clarify the essence of the social work task. Obviously many workers already include this function in their repertoire, but if consumer research is to be heeded there is still much to be done in terms of at least reducing the confusion and misunderstanding which dog the client caught in the criminal process.

Finally, whilst this paper has dealt, in the main superficially, with the receiving end of juvenile and criminal justice up to the point of disposition, it should be remembered that the social work function in supervision and after-care and control is an increasingly important one and obviously yet another aspect of the continuation or culmination of a chart of events. Phyllida Parsloe to some extent deals with this area in chapter 9.

Recommended reading

BALDWIN, J. and McCONVILLE, M. 1977: *Negotiated Justice*. London: Martin Robertson.

ERICSON, R. 1976: *Young Offenders and their Social Work*. Farnborough: Saxon House.

PARKER, H. 1974: *View from the Boys*. Newton Abbot: David & Charles.

Chapter 9

After-Custody: Supervision in the Community in England, Wales and Scotland

Phyllida Parsloe

This chapter is concerned with the contacts and responsibilities which probation officers in England and Wales* and local authority social workers in Scotland have with people who have served a custodial sentence. The contact may be voluntary so far as the former inmate is concerned or may be a condition of the licence which authorizes the offender's release from custody. In all the cases it follows from the fact that at some time in the past, be it the near or distant past, these people have pled or been found guilty by a *criminal court* and have received a custodial sentence. Similarly the involvement of social workers and probation officers in after-care supervision stems as much from their position as officers of the court as from their role as social workers in the penal system.

Release on licence may result automatically from the type of custodial sentence passed by the court, may be the result of a decision taken by penal administrators, or may follow from a recommendation made by the Parole Board or local review committees in England, or the Parole Board for Scotland. In the latter case the period of licence is often called parole. What any licence period means for an ex-offender is a continuing connection with the penal system. It is a feature of all types of licence that this connection is made through the person of a probation officer or a social worker. Those on licence have no contact with anyone employed in the penal system unless it is believed they have broken some condition of their licence. Then the prison administration or the parole boards come back into the situation to consider the question of recall. Thus licence for a former inmate of a penal institution means living in the community under the after-care supervision of a probation officer or social worker, and being

---

* In future reference to England should be taken to include Wales.

liable to recall to custody at any time for breach of the condition of licence or for committing a new offence.

The development of after-care

The present arrangements for after-care in Britain date back to the report of 1967, usually referred to as the ACTO Report (HMSO 1967). The Council surveyed the then existing jungle of after-care provision, some voluntary and some statutory, some provided by voluntary societies and some by various branches of government, and developed four principles on which they based their recommendations.

1 After-care must be designed to meet the needs both of society and of the individual offenders.
2 The nature and quality of the after-care service provided should be fundamentally the same and available for all offenders, irrespective of the particular type of sentence which they may have served.
3 After-care is a form of social work which requires in those undertaking it special qualities of personality and special training and experience.
4 After-care, to be fully effective, must be integrated with the work of the penal institutions in which the offender serves his sentence, and must be conceived as a continuing process throughout his sentence and for as long as necessary after his release. (HMSO 1967, para. 59)

The Council also committed themselves (in para. 22) to the view that the primary function of after-care is the rehabilitation of the offender. On the basis of these principles the Council suggested that the main changes needed were to amalgamate compulsory and voluntary after-care, employ professional social workers on after-care work in institutions and the community, decentralize the arrangements for after-care and strengthen the links between social workers in the institutions and those outside, and increase the understanding in the community of their role in the rehabilitation of offenders.

The Council thus placed after-care fairly and squarely within the context of social work and in fact stated, 'wherever after-care is undertaken the primary responsibility for it should be in the hands of those with an appropriate social casework training and outlook'. The 'treatment model' was to be followed for after-care

(May 1971). The results of this thinking were that the functions of the Central After-Care Association, a component of central government from which all compulsory after-care had been organized, were handed over to the probation services which changed their name to Probation and After-Care Service. The many voluntary societies, known as Discharged Prisoners Aid Societies, which had provided voluntary after-care for prisoners also lost much of their function to the Probation and After-Care Service. Interestingly, however, they reorganized into the National, and the Scottish, Association for the Care and Rehabilitation of Offenders and now fulfil a role as a pressure group. No one looking at the former highly conservative DPAS could have guessed that they would give birth to NACRO and SACRO which have been responsible for the development of some of the most original of the new approaches to after-care, such as voluntary associates and new careers.

Although not recommended by ACTO, the Probation and After-Care Services in England also assumed responsibility for social work in prisons, and local authority social work departments eventually assumed similar responsibilities in the Scottish prisons. This has created problems of its own, particularly in defining the task of social workers in institutions whose primary task is custodial, but these are outside the scope of this chapter. It does seem, however, that in England communication between probation officers inside and outside the prison is better than was communication between the former welfare officer and those responsible for after-care in the community. Whether the same is true of Scotland is questionable. The early findings of one research study at Aberdeen University suggest that the relationships between the staff in one prison social work unit and the local authority area teams in their region are more characteristic of those between strangers than between colleagues. The prison social work unit seems to seek its support within the prison rather than with social workers outside and so perhaps may run the risk of being co-opted into the prevailing prison ideology.

The ACTO Report led to the localization of after-care within the Probation and After-Care Service and to its being defined as a social casework activity. The report also gave some support to a quite different trend which was the development of voluntary associates to work with ex-prisoners under the direction of probation officers. There were at least two reasons for this development. One, it was a way of 'involving the community' – that nebulous but apparently desirable objective – in the rehabilitation of offenders. And second, it was suggested that volunteers could provide all that many prisoners needed. 'The main need of many offenders is for simple encouragement, friendship and human understanding, which could be given by sincere and warm-hearted auxiliaries who had sound common sense and the ability to make themselves acceptable to those whom they sought to help' (HMSO 1967, para. 21). In England the Probation Service, with considerable help from NACRO, were able to recruit and use voluntary associates, although this was not such a straightforward matter as the ACTO Report seemed to imply. Not only do trained social workers have, at best, mixed feelings towards volunteers, but the voluntary associates themselves had difficulties in finding acceptable and appropriate ways of offering help to former prisoners. In Scotland no such scheme has developed and despite frequent exhortation from the Parole Board in its annual reports (HMSO 1972), volunteers are noticeable only by their absence in the after-care field in Scotland.

Voluntary after-care

Any prisoner whose sentence does not carry with it a requirement of licence and who is not released on parole may request after-care assistance from the probation service, or, in Scotland, from the local authority social service. Many older prisoners who are not paroled may be in particular need of such assistance. Their unstable or non-existent home circumstances, lack of employment and perhaps a pattern of repeated imprisonment may be the reason why they were not selected for release on parole, but are also reasons why they may need the greatest help with re-entry to the community. It is an ironic but, given the dual responsibility of parole and prison to protect the community as well as to rehabilitate the offender, understandable situation that the prisoners most in need of graduated release and after-care are those least likely to be selected for it.

Prisoners can ask for voluntary after-care either by approaching the social worker in the institution who will make a link for them to the outside social worker or by waiting until they are released and then getting in touch with the probation officer or social worker. The numbers seeking voluntary after-care have increased quite markedly since 1963 and in particular there has been a significant increase in the numbers making contact before release. The following figures, updated to the end of 1974, show the trends in England:

Table 9:1

	Nos. seeking voluntary after-care	% of all after-care	% of total probation caseloads
1963	594	4·5	0·6
1967	5,393	23·7	4·5
1971	9,288	29·1	7·2
1974	18,500	42·9	13
		1965	1971
Enquiries or contacts made by PO before release		7,484	30,912
After release		12,008	24,556

The 1974 figures refer to the situation on 31 December 1974, when 13,403 voluntary after-care cases had been seen pre-release and 5,258 post-release.

The figures suggest that the aim of the ACTO Report to close the gap between social workers inside and outside institutions may be reflected in increased use of voluntary after-care by prisoners. The majority of voluntary after-care contacts are either a single interview or extend for less than one month, although the statistics also suggest that there is an increase in the proportion of longer contacts. It is much more difficult to form an impression of the content or quality of the contact. Talking to·probation officers one gets the impression that voluntary work of any kind carries a lower priority than does work with those people who are statutorily required to maintain contact with the probation service. There seem to be two reasons for this: first, officers feel a greater responsibility towards those who are compelled – or entitled (according to the way one wishes to define it) to receive after-care supervision, and also consider that if they fail to provide such assistance they could be criticized for falling short in their duty. Secondly, it is my impression that probation officers are much more comfortable within a 'compulsory' relationship. To encourage a voluntary client to keep in touch a social worker must believe they have something useful to offer to the client and be able to explain what this is. Some probation officers, accustomed as they are to compulsion providing the reason for contact, find it hard to have such confidence in what they offer or to explain it adequately.

In Scotland no figures are available to show the extent of

voluntary after-care undertaken by local authority social workers, but judging by the service provided to offenders in Scotland in general it would be wishful thinking to imagine that voluntary after-care is extensive or of a high quality. Here, former prisoners compete for service not only with those subject to compulsory after-care and probation, as do their English equivalents, but with all the multiplicity of human need which comes to local authority area teams. Against children at risk and old people liable to die of cold, a prisoner seeking voluntary after-care has low priority. This situation may change if the Scottish regional authorities follow what seems to be an emerging trend towards specialism within their social work departments. Several regions now have regional or district teams of officers specializing in work with adult offenders. These social workers may begin to feel that they have a special responsibility to the courts and the judiciary. This is something which, for good or ill, has been lost in Scotland since 1970, but which is strongly marked amongst English probation officers and which has implications for the nature of voluntary after-care relationships.

Despite such nebulous but powerful links with the courts, voluntary after-care still lies clearly within the mainstream of social work. Contact depends upon a mutual willingness between client and worker to meet and to accept and to offer help. Either side is free to end the contact at any time. There are certainly questions about the type of social work help which is needed by the many different kinds of people who seek voluntary after-care but again this is the type of question raised by any client group in social work. Compulsory after-care, however, raises other issues which are considerably more complex because they highlight the question of the balance in the social services between care and control.

Compulsory after-care

Who is subject to compulsory supervision upon release from prison? Table 9.2 summarizes the position, and shows the various administrative differences. Broadly speaking there are two separate groups: One comprises those whose original sentence carried with it a period of compulsory supervision after release. Such sentences are largely those to which young adults and older adolescents are subject; detention centre orders, borstal sentences and sentences of under eighteen months passed on young offenders. In addition young persons detained during Her

Majesty's pleasure and life-sentence prisoners are subject to supervision on release for the rest of their lives. The exact time when a prisoner in one of these categories is discharged on licence may be fixed at the time of the sentence and varies only if the prisoner loses time because of bad behaviour. This is the situation with detention centre orders, and prison sentences of under eighteen months passed on young offenders. Alternatively, the date of release may depend upon an administrative decision taken within the borstal institution or in the case of those held during Her Majesty's pleasure, life-sentence prisoners and young people convicted of certain grave crimes, by the Home Secretary or the Secretary of State for Scotland on the recommendation of their respective Parole Boards. For those held during Her Majesty's pleasure, or sentenced to life imprisonment, supervision is part of the original sentence should they ever be released, but there is no certainty that they will be, and they can be held in custody until they die. Juveniles convicted of grave crimes are supervised only if they are released before the end of their sentence. This causes problems for the Parole Board who may believe a young person needs as long as possible in custody and yet also requires help in settling back into the community.

Licensing has been a feature of British penal policy throughout this century. Its use was reduced when the sentences of corrective training and preventive detention were abolished and it became largely a measure used with younger offenders. Licence on parole, however, is a newcomer to the British scene, having been introduced only as lately as 1967 by the Criminal Justice Act. It is based on a different set of assumptions from those underlying other forms of licence. These assume that all prisoners of a particular type need help to resettle into the community and avoid further offences. Supervision, it is thought, can combine help with the problems of re-entry with the sanction of recall which will strengthen the former prisoner's determination to avoid reoffending. Licence is a right – or an obligation – for certain prisoners but is in almost all cases unavoidable. Parole, however, is widely held to be a state which a prisoner can earn. Here the assumption is that when sentencing, judges cannot predict accurately the way a man will respond to imprisonment. Many men and women will reach a point where, it is said, prison can do no more for them either by way of deterrence or rehabilitation, and when they no longer constitute a serious risk to the public (Hazelrigg 1968). Such prisoners should then be able to continue their sentence in the community under supervison, thus reducing

Table 9:2 The Categories of offenders subject to After-Care Supervision

Age when sentenced	Institution from which released	Length of sentence	Period served	Decision made by	Statutory Base England	Statutory Base Scotland	Period of licence or supervision
14–20 yrs (England) 16–20 yrs (Scotland)	Detention Centre	3–6 months (England) 3 months (Scotland)	Two thirds	—	Sec. 4 of Criminal Justice Act 1961	Sec. 11(1) of Criminal Justice (Scotland) Act 1963	12 months from date of release
15–20 yrs (England) 16–20 yrs (Scotland)	Borstal	Up to 2 yrs	No fixed point in sentence	Institution Board and visiting committee	Sec. 1 of CJA 1961	Sec. 4(2) of CJ (Scotland) Act, 1963	12 months from date of release
Under 21	Young prisoners' centres (England) Young offenders' institutions (Scotland)	Under 18 months	Two thirds	—	Sec. 63 of Criminal Justice Act 1967	Sec. 12(1) of CJ (Scotland) Act, 1963	12 months from date of release
Under 21	Prison (England)	18 months and over	From one third or 1 yr whichever is longer up to two thirds	By Home Secretary or Secretary of State for Scotland on the recommendation of the English or Scottish	Sec. 60(1) of Criminal Justice Act 1967		Unexpired portion of total sentence

Young offenders institutions (Scotland)			Two thirds if not paroled before	Sec. 60(3)b of Criminal Justice Act, 1967	Unexpired portion of total sentence
Over 21	Prison	18 months and over	One third or 1 yr up to two thirds	..	Sec. 60(1) of Criminal Justice Act 1967	Until date on which two thirds of sentence would have been served
Under 18	Any	HMP (Indeterminate)	Indeterminate	..	Sec. 61(1) of Criminal Justice Act 1967	Life
Under 18 (England)	Any	Sec. 53(2) of the Children and Young Persons Act 1933	No fixed point in sentence	By the Home Secretary or the Secretary of State for Scotland on the recommendation of the English or Scottish Parole Board	Sec. 61(1) of Criminal Justice Act 1967	To end of sentence
Under 16 (Scotland) (for certain grave crimes)		Sec. 206(2) of Criminal Procedure (Scotland) Act 1975				
Over 18	Prison	Life sentence (Indeterminate)	Indeterminate	..	Sec. 61(1) of Criminal Justice Act 1967	Life

the burden on society of their imprisonment and allowing them to rebuild a useful life outside. A highly complicated administrative structure has been created to decide when a man or woman should be released on parole. Prisoners become eligible for consideration for parole when they have served one year or one third of their sentence, whichever is the longer. They then have a choice whether or not to put themselves forward for consideration. The Parole Boards of England and Scotland concern themselves greatly about those prisoners who refuse to be considered, and certainly in Scotland the fall in the percentage of those who 'self-reject' is considered to be a sign of the success of the system. It is an interesting feature of the system that prisoners are free to complete the sentence given them by the court (minus one third remission for good behaviour) and that those who choose to do so seem to be seen as a threat to the idea of parole.

The purpose of after-care

After-care is the word used to describe the supervision provided by probation officers and social workers for those who have been in custody. It has no one purpose and it means different things to different people. Martin Davies suggests that it can be seen as 'society's apology for the hurt inflicted', an 'apology for vengeance', and thus makes clear that after-care cannot be divorced from the compulsory custodial and punitive nature of the prison experience which precedes it (Davies 1975, 4).

If prisons really provided rehabilitation then no apology would be necessary, but as anyone who has visited a prison knows, even if it is possible to rehabilitate people compulsorily, and that is at least debatable, the physical and human environment of a prison is not conducive to rehabilitation. The feeling roused in most people by their first visit to a closed prison is one of horror and guilt that fellow humans are caged in such insanitary, crowded and deadening conditions. Such feelings can lead to a wish to provide something for the prisoner to make good the damage done.

Closely linked to this idea of after-care is another which emphasizes the problems of moving from a closed community, where all decisions have been made for you, to the outside world where you suddenly resume responsibility for feeding and housing yourself and finding friends to ease the loneliness. This situation is not faced in its most stark form by those prisoners who return to families and often to employment. Such men, it seems (P. Morris

1975), 'quickly pick up where they left off' and their fears of being stigmatized by friends and neighbours are not usually realized. However, a sizeable minority of prisoners do not have a home and relations to go to, and have the much more difficult task of starting life outside from a lodging house or a hostel; often they will be without money or a job to cushion them and with no close relationships to help them in becoming part of a group who share what Irwin describes as a world of meaning. Irwin (1970) is describing prisoners released from long sentences in a prison in the United States but his description is useful in understanding the situation of British prisoners. He gives a graphic account of 'the disorganizing impact on the personality of moving from one meaning world to another, the desperation that emerges when faced with the untold demands for which he is ill-prepared and the extreme loneliness he is likely to feel. . . .' He moves from 'a state of incarceration where the pace is slow and routinized, the events are monotonous but familiar, into a chaotic and foreign world outside. The cars, buses, people, buildings, roads, stores, lights, noises and animals are all things he hasn't experienced at first hand for quite some time'. To make this change, former prisoners need help which after-care may provide and thus not only ease the pains of re-entry but prevent the ex-offender becoming involved in criminal behaviour as a means of dealing with the tension and anxiety his new world provokes in him.

After-care as a means of easing the pains of re-entry and countering the damaging effects on the personality of in-stitutionalization shades over into after-care as special help for members of a socially, emotionally and educationally disadvantaged group. In this view, prisoners are regarded as damaged, not so much by prison, as by their life experiences before imprisonment. Those experiences, it is alleged, led to the original prison sentence and are likely to lead to further such sentences unless something can be done by the supervisor to help the former prisoner to establish a new and more productive relationship with society. An example of this attitude towards prisoners, and hence to a particular interpretation of the meaning of after-care, is provided by Taggart (1972) who, in a manpower approach to prisoners, points out that they tend to be one of the most disadvantaged groups in American society with regard to employability. He points out that,

> the price of removing an individual from the community is not only the direct costs of shelter and supervision but also the indirect costs of underutilization and depreciation of human potential. In the case

of offenders these tend to be underutilized and underdeveloped to begin with. We must therefore run to stay in place if we are to return individuals to society who are not worse off and more dangerous than they were when they first entered the system.

Another frequently stated aim of after-care is to prevent further offences both for the sake of society and for the sake of the offender. It is difficult to assess whether supervision actually achieves this aim. There is some evidence to suggest that prisoners on parole offend less frequently than might be expected during the parole period but even if this is so it certainly cannot be taken to mean that it is the supervision which produces this effect (Davies 1972).

Protection of the public is another aim and has been emphasized particularly in relation to parole. It is in fact very difficult to see how supervision, as it is usually exercised, can actually provide much protection for the public except that the fact of being under supervision may help a man to control his own behaviour. The actual check which a social worker would either be able or willing to keep on an ex-prisoner is minimal. Contact takes place most often in the worker's office and, less frequently, in the ex-prisoner's place of residence. Even in the unlikely event of supervisor and ex-offender spending an hour together more frequently than once a week, the social worker usually does not know how the parolee spends the rest of his time, unless the parolee wishes to tell him. One of the results of having after-care undertaken by social workers is that they are unwilling, nor have they ever been trained, to make the kind of enquiries about a client's life which, for example, the police might be prepared to undertake. Almost everything social workers know about their clients comes from the clients themselves. The claim that supervision provides protection for the public may be useful to politicians who wish to carry the public with them in liberalizing penal policy. Its meaning, however, needs to be explored. Supervision may protect the public because an ex-offender may be helped to avoid further trouble by the knowledge that he is under supervision. It may also protect the public because a relationship can develop between some offenders and their supervising officers which will enable the ex-offender to change himself and his environment.

The aims of after-care are not restricted to serving either the individual ex-prisoner or society in the form of future victims. The Scottish Parole Board (HMSO 1973) points out the importance of after-care for the wives, husbands, parents and children of former prisoners. Their future happiness and development may depend upon the prisoner's ability to perform the roles of spouse, child or parent, and this he may be helped to do by a supervising officer.

So after-care may be an apology for vengeance, a means of countering institutionalization, a special service for the socially disadvantaged, a means of reducing further offences or a protection for the public. It can be any of those things but is most likely to involve the idea of at least some care for the offender and some control by society over his behaviour.

What is parole?

The need to balance the sometimes conflicting aims of care and control have always been apparent, but the addition of parole as another means of release on licence has meant that more attention is being paid to the purposes and aims of after-care and particularly of parole.

Parole was hailed as a way of ensuring that no one stayed in prison longer than was necessary for the protection of the public and it would be wrong to suggest that this is not one of its aims. It has resulted in some prisoners being in prison for a shorter time than they would have been had no parole system been introduced. However, parole may serve other purposes. Some suggest it was designed to reduce the prison population, although if this were an aim it has certainly failed. Another suggestion is that it provides a means of controlling prisoners by holding out a carrot, in the form of early release, to those who behave well. Such methods of control, it is suggested, are necessary since society will no longer tolerate the older physical forms of control. Certainly some prisoners in English gaols maintain that parole is a con trick by the establishment and some 'self-rejects' are said to be opting out of what they consider to be a corrupt system. This, it is alleged, has not occurred in Scotland where prison staff maintain that the introduction of parole has improved the relationships between prison officers and prisoners.

There is discussion not only about the purpose of parole but about its legal status. It is certainly seen as different from other forms of release on licence because it involves release during the period of the sentence, whereas whatever the courts may say, other forms of licence are seen as release after the completion of the sentence. Thus one view of parole is that it means serving a prison sentence 'outside the walls'. This explanation makes more sense in the United States. There the decision to grant parole is often made by a full-time board, composed of members of the Department of Corrections, which also administers the prisons and where parole officers are part of the same Department. There parole may be seen as an administrative arrangement in the same way as is, for example, transfer from a closed to an open prison. However, in Britain, where special Boards, whose members are unconnected with the penal system, make the recommendation for parole, and where supervision is carried out by a separate service, this explanation seems less tenable. Another explanation of parole is that it is a contact between the paroling authority, the prison authority and the prisoner, whereby, in return for release, the prisoner agrees to accept supervision and to abide by the terms of the parole licence. Yet another explanation is that parole is an act of grace on the part of the administration and is thus comparable to a pardon. Discussion of what parole is has become of vital importance in the United States because of the development of concern about the rights of parolees, particularly in relation to recall. This movement is largely in the hands of lawyers and from their point of view the question of entitlement to rights depends considerably upon the legal status of parole. Those who oppose the extension of due process rights to parolees tend to define parole as a sentence outside the walls or an act of grace. Those who wish to extend rights see more scope in a contract definition or perhaps in a definition of parole as a second sentencing. Arguments such as these are little heard in Britain presumably because equally little is heard on the subject of the rights of those subject to after-care.

In the United States the focus of the rights issue is recall. In Britain the two distinctive features of after-care are supervision and recall. Any ex-prisoner who is released on any form of after-care is liable to recall to a penal institution if he breaks the conditions of his licence. The decision to recall is never made by the supervising officer although it is his responsibility to report any suspected breaches to the prison administration. Recall can follow either the commission of further offences or breaches of the conditions of the licence, which require the ex-prisoner to keep in touch with the supervising officer, attempt to get and keep a job, and to be of good behaviour, etc. The prison administration in the Home Office and the Scottish Office send the information which they receive from social workers to the relevant Board. If the Board recommend recall the person subject to licence is arrested and taken to a penal establishment. Parolees and Scottish young offenders are then allowed to prepare a representation to the Parole Board against recall and at a subsequent meeting the Board decides whether or not to confirm their recall order.

After-care and justice

What discussion there is about rights in relation to after-care in Britain is focused upon parole and in particular upon the question of giving prisoners reasons for being rejected for parole and upon the procedure of recall.

Legally parole is granted by the Home Secretary or the Secretary of State for Scotland, but the Ministers cannot parole a prisoner unless they have a recommendation to that effect from their respective Parole Boards. They can, however, refuse to grant parole to prisoners who are recommended for parole by the Board although in Scotland this does not occur because the Secretary of State submits to the Board for consideration only those prisoners whom he would, in principle, be prepared to parole. There has been a great deal of discussion on the English Parole Board about whether prisoners should be given reasons when they are not granted parole. Those who support giving reasons argue that if a prisoner does not know why he is turned down he is in no position to improve himself or his situation before his next consideration. They also argue that it is unjust to refuse reasons and to treat prisoners as if they were children rather than adults. Those who oppose giving reasons say that many times the reasons do not relate to anything a prisoner can change, and, for example, to tell him he is not getting parole because of his previous criminal history or the nature of his offence is at best discouraging and at worst may make him desperate and therefore a difficult or dangerous prisoner. It is also suggested that some reasons might implicate the prison staff and they might then be at risk of retaliation from the prisoner. The English Board has conducted 'a reasons experiment' in which the Board formulated their reasons in certain cases and these were then sent to the governor of the relevant prison. The governor commented on what the effect on the prisoner might have been had the reasons been disclosed to him (which they were not). The results of this rather curious and certainly cautious experiment were questioned on, amongst other grounds, the possible bias of the governors, and another experiment is now planned. In Scotland no such experiments have taken place and while the subject is frequently discussed by the

Board there is no apparent impetus for change. This may be because what actually happens in Scotland is that the secretary to the Board sets down the reasons against parole expressed by members during discussion. These are recorded in minutes which, after approval by the Board, are sent to the Governors concerned, who in turn present them to the Local Review Committee. The Governor may at his discretion use this information in subsequent discussions with the prisoner.

There are two other points in the parole system where it seems there should be more concern about rights, and social workers are involved at each of these points. The first is that part of the process leading to the LRC discussion. The statute says that each prisoner who wishes to be considered for parole shall be interviewed by a member of the LRC who is not the member from the prison staff. The purpose of this interview is to allow prisoners who may have difficulty in expressing themselves on paper an opportunity to make a case for parole. Here the LRC member is clearly expected to help the prisoner make as good a case as possible and then to convey this case in writing and perhaps also verbally to the LRC. The LRC member who interviews the prisoner is not assessing him for parole, although when the same member sits on the LRC he does have that responsibility alongside his responsibility to put the prisoner's case. Even when the system works well and the LRC member understands his role he is in a conflict of interest situation. Often however, at least in Scotland, it seems the LRC members do not understand their role and use their interview to assess the prisoner's suitability for parole and their report to the LRC as a means of communicating a recommendation. Probation officers in England and social workers in Scotland serve as members of the LRCs together with lay people, prison governors and, in England, magistrates. Even those social workers, who might be expected to have some understanding of prisoners and of interviewing, have *not* protested about the conflict of interest in their role which requires them to be advocate for, and judge of, the same prisoner.

They have shown a similar lack of concern at the equally problematic situation about recall. Recall can be recommended either because of a further conviction or some other alleged breach of licence conditions. From the point of view of rights the more important distinction is perhaps between those breaches where there is a clear factual situation such as a further offence or a failure to keep in touch and those which depend more upon the social worker's judgment, such as failure to try to get work or failure to cooperate with the supervising officer. The probation officer or social worker who submits reasons such as these as grounds for recall may not have to give any facts to support them. Recall can result from a letter containing opinions. This could never be sufficient to give a court power to sentence a person and yet it is enough for Boards to order recall and so deprive someone of his freedom. There is no hearing of any kind and the licensee has no form of representation. After recall the prisoner may make written representations (and may request an interview with an LRC member) but his ability to do so may be limited, not only by having no legal assistance, but because being in custody he cannot collect evidence to support his case. It should not be assumed that social workers frequently abuse their position or give inaccurate accounts of a parolee's behaviour. In fact the great majority of recalls result from further offences or from the disappearance of the licensee. However, when a situation exists where people can lose their freedom for long periods, questions about rights to procedural fairness at least need to be raised.

Recall also raises the question of equal justice. In theory, supervising officers are required to report any breaches of the conditions of licence. In fact it is well known that they exercise considerable discretion. There is obviously most room for discretion where recall may arise not because of a new offence but from a breach of the licence conditions. For example, how long must a parolee be out of contact before he can be said to have 'failed to keep in touch' with his supervising officer, and what efforts should that officer make to find him before reporting him for a breach? Even with new offences there seems room for some discretion, at least in Scotland, where it is not unusual to discover when reading a final report at the end of a parole period that the parolee has been convicted of a minor offence during the parole period of which the Board knew nothing.

Supervision in after-care

What little we know about the attitudes and expectations of probation officers and ex-offenders towards supervision and what it actually involves comes largely from recent research into the operation of parole in England. It seems that politicians, administrators and prisoners themselves all expected that supervision for parolees would be different in some way, both from that exercised over probationers and from other forms of after-care supervision. It was going to be stricter in order to provide more protection for the public. Many prisoners expected that 'they would have to report regularly to the police, that they would not be permitted even the odd alcoholic drink, that they would have to be home by 11 pm and that the probation officer would be constantly on their tail' (P. Morris 1975). In fact neither Martin Davies (1972) nor Pauline Morris (1975) found this to be the case. Supervision of parolees seems to be very much like any other kind of supervision so far as a majority of the probation officers is concerned. The typical pattern of contact is a weekly office interview of fifteen to thirty minutes, with occasional home visits and with a reduction in the frequency of contact over the parole period. This typical pattern raises many questions but only three will be considered here: the question of combining care and control, the individual focus of after-care supervision and the need for classification.

Combining care and control is nothing new for social work although historically it has been regarded as a special feature of the probation service. Since the reorganization of the social services the authority inherent in other types of social work has been recognized. To work comfortably and helpfully in such situations requires clarity and confidence in the social worker which is apparently lacking at times. There is no doubt that for some people the fact that they are obliged to see a social worker or probation officer and that the officer is obliged to see them means that a relationship may develop between two people who would never have sought each other out. On the other hand the fact that supervising officers have the power to instigate recall and are associated with the courts and the penal system makes it impossible for some offenders and difficult for many others to see them as helpful or trustworthy people. This situation is made even more problematic by the lack of agreement as to the meaning or purpose of after-care. Thus although care and control are not necessarily incompatible they may be so for some clients with some social workers as chapter 8 demonstrated.

One way of improving this confused situation might be a wider use of contracts. Morris (1975) has suggested that at present probation officers and parolees seldom share their expectations of supervision, and contracts would necessarily involve such sharing. 'Contracts' in social work were developed in the United States and their best-known advocates are Reid and Shyne (1969). Contracts have now spread to Britain although their use has been largely restricted to voluntary clients who themselves come to the agency seeking help. However it is possible to adapt the idea to 'compulsory' clients and to work out with a person subject to after-care what supervision is to mean for both those involved.

The Scottish Parole Board is at present trying to engage social workers to draw up with parolees a statement about what supervision is to mean. Social workers will spell out the frequency of contact and whether or not they will meet the parolee alone, with his family or in some form of non-family group. They will decide whether there are any specific problems facing the parolee such as housing or employment, problems with relations or peers, or problems of physical and mental health, and consider how, if at all, and by whom, these problems are to be managed. The hope is that such contracts or plans should be sent to the Parole Board at the start of parole, for two reasons. The Board would then share the responsibility in cases where the social worker and parolee decided the need was for minimal supervision. The Board would also have a statement to which to refer in the case of possible recall and could assess the part played by the social worker as well as that of the parolee.

The idea that after-care means social casework which permeated the ACTO Report in 1963 still lingers powerfully over after-care in 1977. However there have been recent developments in work with offenders such as Community Service Orders and day centres, which give hope that those who are subject to after-care supervision may in the future be offered a wider range of provisions and services. Perhaps the ideas which have inspired intermediate treatment could be used to open up a similar range of possibilities for former prisoners. It would be a major step forward if office reporting were to become but one of a choice of ways of working instead of the method not so much of choice as of routine.

This essay has referred to people who are subject to after-care as if they formed some kind of group. They do only in so far as they share an experience of custody, a liability to supervision for a period on release, and to recall. These features might be sufficient if the purpose of after-care were only checking up and control. As the basis for social work – which is the other component of after-care – they are totally inadequate. The fact that a person is subject to after-care tells the social worker nothing about his or her needs. At present there are no developed criteria for grouping former prisoners according to their needs although some of the classifications of prisoners used by researchers might be usefully adapted. Pauline Morris uses five categories whose names suggest they are separated by their offence behaviour, but they are also distinguished by certain social factors such as their family relationships and employment and leisure patterns. They are:

Crime-interrupted non-criminal offenders
Impulsive offenders
Non-systematic habitual offenders
Professional offenders
Petty persistent offenders

It might be possible to classify ex-offenders on a similar basis to suggest their needs during the period of supervision. The areas which need to be considered in planning supervision are familiar to probation officers and social workers not least because they form the headings for social inquiry reports to the courts. They are equally appropriate however for planning with an after-care client the nature and content of supervision. Perhaps some social workers and probation officers engaged in after-care could undertake to develop such a classification and so end the myth that being subject to after-care is a description of a person and his needs.

Recommended reading

DAVIES, M. 1975: *Prisoners of Society*. London: Routledge & Kegan Paul.
HMSO 1967: *The Organization of After-Care*. London: ACTO Report.
MORRIS, P. 1975: *On Licence*. New York: J. Wiley.

Chapter 10

Social Work in the Courts in Northern Ireland

Greg Kelly

The purpose of this chapter is to highlight and offer some explanations for the more important respects in which social work in the courts in Northern Ireland differs from that in the rest of the United Kingdom. There are a number of important historical and political reasons for these differences and three central themes which have a special relevance will be outlined:

1 The nature of politics in Northern Ireland.
2 The 'step-by-step' policy designed to keep the Welfare State in Northern Ireland parallel to that in the United Kingdom.
3 The professional magistracy in the province, where all the lower and juvenile courts are chaired by a professional Resident Magistrate.

The nature of politics in Northern Ireland

The state of Northern Ireland was created by the Government of Ireland Act 1920 which was the result of the resistance by the Ulster Protestants to the struggle for Irish independence. The existence of the state has been opposed politically ever since by the great majority of the minority Catholic population in the 'six counties' and regarded with varying degrees of hostility for most of the time by the Government and people of the Irish Republic. Politics in Northern Ireland, then, have centred on whether or not the state should exist, and not on the issues of economics and social welfare that have dominated political debate in most western democracies since World War I. The political parties, with the recent exception of the Alliance Party and occasional ·flurries by the Northern Ireland Labour Party, draw the bulk of their support from all classes on their side of the religious divide. There has never been a major working-class movement which· has crossed the sectarian divide. One commentator (Mansergh 1936) wrote: 'The main criticism, therefore, that one would direct against the operation of the party system in Northern Ireland is . . . that it subordinates every vital issue, whether social or economic, to the dead hand of sectarian strife.'

Not only has the working class never made its voice heard as a united political force, but there has never been a strong party of reform. This can be accounted for not only by the sectarian divide but also by the Northern Irish people's political conservatism. They adhere to particularly conservative brands of their respective religions, and outside Belfast live mainly on the land or in small towns. Northern Ireland politics, then, has lacked the 'centre' and the 'left of centre' groupings which in Britain have done so much to foster and debate developments in penal reform and the social services.

As long as the constitutional position of the country remained the overriding political issue then the power base of parties who relied on the loyalist/nationalist split remained secure almost irrespective of the social conditions they presided over. Housing is an example of the most spectacular neglect under the Unionist government. Two recent publications (Weiner 1975; Exason 1976) emphasize the massive deprivation suffered by the working classes of both sides of the community as a result of the failure of government to develop a meaningful housing policy: in 1974 '19·6 per cent of the housing stock was classified as unfit for habitation . . . the comparable figure in Britain was 7·3 per cent' (Exason 1976).

These conditions developed despite the existence of the 'step-by-step' policy for the development of the social services discussed below, and they have been a major factor in the growth of community groups and tenants' associations which have in many instances 'lost faith in the government institutions being able to help them' (Weiner 1975).

The 'step-by-step' policy

Historically, the relationship between the parliaments of Northern Ireland and Westminster is a complicated one, but it was simplified by the declaration in 1938 by the then Chancellor of the Exchequer, Sir John Simon, that Northern Ireland should enjoy the same social services and have the same standards as Great Britain: 'that parity of services and taxation between Great Britain and Northern Ireland will be the guiding principle' (Barritt and Carter 1962).

The principle, simple though it sounds, is confusing or has become confused in its implementation. In the income maintenance services it has been followed more or less rigidly until recent times. Thus, the scale rates of payment of National Insurance, Supplementary Benefit, family allowance, etc., are identical with those in the rest of the United Kingdom. The one major legislative difference in these services is the Payment for Debt Act 1971 which enables the Government to deduct money at source, without their permission, from the benefits of anyone who is in debt to the Government or to a government agency. This legislation arose as an attempt to combat politically motivated rent and rates strikers, but from March 1976 has been used to collect rent arrears irrespective of the reason for their accumulation (O'Hara 1977).

The situation in relation to social services other than income maintenance is more complicated, for, although there was provision 'to make up leeway in those services which had lower standards than in Great Britain' (Wallace 1971), the Northern Ireland government was in a position, under powers devolved to it, to choose which of the services under its control to develop and which not to. For reasons which we shall consider later, that government appears to have chosen not to develop the probation service or social services in the court setting to anything approaching standards in the rest of the United Kingdom. The Westminster government always had the power to intervene in the exercise of the powers it had devolved to the Northern Ireland government but it chose not to do so, whether in a major area of expenditure like housing or in a relatively minor one like the Probation Service. 'The Imperial Government has displayed no little anxiety lest any public discussion on any aspect of the relationship between Great Britain and Northern Ireland should reopen the Irish question as a whole. This anxiety is shared by the Government of Northern Ireland' (Mansergh 1936).

The argument about how devolved powers are used is not unlike the discussion in the rest of the United Kingdom between those who would have autonomous local authorities and those who would give central government strict inspectorial powers to ensure an even distribution of services across the country. The solution is to achieve a balance so that local authorities can take account of local need but to leave central government powers of coercion where a particular client group or service appears to be unreasonably discriminated against. BASW has recently been arguing that the balance is not yet right in Britain (Bamford 1977).

With devolution in the offing for Scotland and Wales and the consistent pressure for another attempt at devolution in Northern Ireland, this continues to be an issue of wide importance. The Probation Service in Northern Ireland illustrates the enormous variation that can develop in the services offered to some client groups when devolved powers are not supervised.

With the prorogation of the Northern Ireland parliament and the commencement of direct rule from Westminster, the step-by-step policy has taken on a new meaning, and the Secretary of State and his ministers, with a much keener sense of the discrepancies in social legislation between Northern Ireland and the rest of the United Kingdom, have been discussing a whole host of proposed measures of reform: divorce law, comprehensive education and, most importantly for our purposes, in legislation for children and young persons (Black Committee 1977).

The professional magistracy

Because of the centuries of political and social upheaval in Ireland, the courts and law enforcement policies have often been at the very centre of the political stage. The current controversy about 'no jury' trials in both Northern Ireland and the Irish Republic is the latest in a long series of conflicts arising from the civil insurrections that have peppered Irish history. The fundamental problem for the various British and Irish administrations has been: to what extent can politically motivated offenders, often operating in a time of widespread civil disturbance, be dealt with by the normal judicial processes?

An early attempt to come to terms with this problem and the overall one of confidence in the administration of justice involved the professionalization of the administration of justice. This required, among other things, 'the replacement of the local Justices of the Peace, the voluntary magistracy, by a system of legally-trained stipendiaries under government control' (Boyle, Hadden and Hillyard 1975). The full effects of this system were not felt in Northern Ireland until after partition, but the situation is now that all Petty Sessions Courts (which have similar powers to the Magistrates' Courts in England and Wales), including the Juvenile Courts, are chaired by a Resident Magistrate who is a qualified solicitor or barrister of six years standing.

The development of legislation in relation to social work in the courts in Northern Ireland

I have indicated above that through the step-by-step policy the Northern Ireland government was guaranteed the resources to mirror Westminster legislation and services in the social services field, and through powers devolved to it under the Government of Ireland Act 1920, also had the power to decide when it would follow its own independent line. Many of the Northern Ireland Statutes are slavish repetitions of Westminster legislation, and ministerial pronouncements are dotted with statements like that of the then Minister of Home Affairs on the introduction of the Adoption Bill 1967: 'Its effect will be to bring adoption law and practice in Northern Ireland more closely in line with that which has been operating in Great Britain since the Adoption Act 1958.'[1]

Where the current legislation is different in Northern Ireland it is usually for one of two reasons. First, the Northern Ireland legislation has not caught up with that in Great Britain. Secondly, the Northern Ireland Government has enacted different or partly differing legislation to cope with the province's needs as it saw them. Thus, those familiar with the current legislation and the development of that legislation as it affects the various areas of social work practice in England and Wales will have a good basis for understanding the legislative provisions in Northern Ireland. Perhaps the most fundamental difference, which is beyond the brief of this chapter, is the organization of the personal social services. These were amalgamated with the various branches of the National Health Service into Area Health and Social Services Boards, and taken out of the control of local government. The Probation Service has remained a distinct service separate from the other personal social services.

The legislation dealing with juvenile offenders and children in need of care, then, has tended to follow the Westminster legislation with varying time lags. The 1950 Children and Young Persons Bill was described by one MP as 'really only a conglomeration of the 1933 and 1948 (Westminster) Acts'.[2] The common pattern has been for the Northern Ireland government to appoint a committee to look at how the new Westminster legislation was working and recommend what form the legislation should take in Northern Ireland.

One of the first of these committees (Lynn Committee 1938) said of the child care services in London: 'It would hardly be an exaggeration to say that the right kind of training is now available for almost every type of child or neglected delinquent.' . . . and that was in 1938! Official reaction to developments at Westminster have not always been so favourable. When there was much discussion about the role of the juvenile courts in the late 1960s, Mr William Craig, the then Minister of Home Affairs, said: 'Until there is convincing evidence to the contrary, I believe that our juvenile courts are still the most satisfactory way of dealing with juvenile offenders.'[3] There was indeed a suspicion in his speech that the Government was hurrying through the Children and Young Persons Act 1968 before they would have to consider implementing the more radical changes contained in the Children and Young Persons Act 1969. The Children and Young Persons Act (NI) 1968 enacted the power to do preventive social work contained in the Westminster Children and Young Persons Act 1963 and re-enacted the Children and Young Persons Act (NI) passed in 1950. It left all the provisions for dealing with juvenile delinquency untouched. The result is that for someone with a long experience in England, the juvenile courts in Northern Ireland are like taking a trip down memory lane. In criminal proceedings, the probation service prepare the social enquiry reports (except in some country districts where they have not the manpower and there they are done by social workers from the area boards). Magistrates can make Training School Orders which are in all but name the same as the old Approved School Orders. Their effect is that the child has to go to a training school and social workers or probation officers have no discretion to send children 'home on trial' as they have under the Westminster 1969 Act. Young people between fourteen and seventeen are still placed on probation although those under fourteen can be placed on supervision.

In care proceedings there are fewer fundamental differences, the conditions that apply to bringing a child before the court as in need of 'care, protection or control' are in most respects the same as those under the 1969 Act but again the Northern Ireland Act has maintained the power of the court. It can make a Fit Person Order committing the child to the care of the Health and Social Services Board, or a Training School Order. A child, the subject of a Fit Person Order, cannot be transferred to a training school unless the area board return to the court and apply for the revocation of the Fit Person Order (Section 142 (6) Children and Young Persons Act (NI) 1968). The power of the court is further reinforced by the provision (Section 103) that to obtain a parental rights order on a child in care the Board must apply to the juvenile court for that order instead of as in England and Wales where local authorities are able to assume these rights under Section 2 of the Children Act 1948 with the question only coming before a court if the parents appeal against the decision.

In a number of important areas, then, the decision-making of social workers in Northern Ireland is much more subject to the control of the courts than is that of their colleagues in the rest of the United Kingdom. There has been much questioning recently of the 'welfare' approach to juvenile delinquency in particular (Giller and Morris 1977) and in a country beset with law and order problems of the most intractable kind, which have led to numbers of juveniles committing, and being associated with organizations who have committed, killings and bombings, social workers have shown little enthusiasm for the wide powers bestowed on their colleagues in England and Wales under the 1969 Children and Young Persons Act or the discretion inherent in the role of the Reporter in the Scottish panel system.

In the wider child care field, Northern Ireland has had no tragedies of the magnitude of those of Maria Colwell or Stephen Meurs, nor have there been any 'tug-of-love' cases which have gained widespread publicity, so the debate surrounding the Children Act 1975 has largely passed it by, although the Black Committee in its consultative document has raised all the pertinent issues.

Most of the concern in recent years has focused on the standard of service that the social work profession has been able to offer children in trouble or children in care. There has been criticism from within the profession of both the Probation Service and the Area Boards for their failure to provide an adequate service particularly in large areas of Belfast. It is difficult to gauge the effects of the civil unrest on the service provided but the area of Belfast which has attracted much of the criticism contains almost all the city's 'troubled' and socially deprived areas. The situation is delicately summarized in one Government report dealing with the city's 'Areas of Special Social Need': 'In respect of the personal social services, the problem raised most frequently was a perceived lack of balance between field staff and resources on the one hand and numbers in need on the other.'[4] In 1976 a principal social worker for one of the areas wrote that staffing levels were 'about 60 per cent *below* full strength' (Park 1976).

The struggle in many of these areas has been to offer any social work service at all, and the improving of this service rather than legislative changes appears to be the principal challenge for the social work profession and its masters in the immediate future.

The growth in community work

The failure of the statutory social services to provide adequately, especially for the province's troubled areas, has been one of the factors in the rapid growth of community groups, tenants' associations, advice centres and welfare organizations of various kinds. By 1973 there were 'some 300 operational (community) groups' (Weiner 1976) in Belfast. A study in 1975 put the number in the city at 450 and a total of 828 in the whole of Northern Ireland (Duffy and Percival 1975). Other factors in this growth have been: the violence which has created problems such as intimidation and mass movements of population which government services have not been able to cope with; the steady worsening of the housing situation; the transportation and general redevelopment plans in Belfast (Weiner 1976). As well as being active in all these fields, a number of community groups have been active in the welfare rights field and involved in opposition to the Payment for Debt Act. Their abilities in this direction have been strengthened by the opening in 1977 of the Belfast Law Centre which is to service local advice centres, citizens' advice bureaux and community groups.

The role of the Probation Service

As I have indicated above, the Probation Service in Northern Ireland is heavily committed to work with juvenile offenders and indeed throughout its history this has formed the bulk of the Service's work. Most of the developments that have occurred in the Service in England and Wales as a result of the 1969 Children and Young Persons Act and the 1972 Criminal Justice Act have largely passed it by; so there has been no major shift to working with adult offenders or into the after-care field. The recommendations of the Streatfeild Committee (1961) that social enquiry reports should be provided on certain categories of defendants have not been implemented, nor has provision in the Criminal Justice Act 1972 which instructs the courts to 'obtain and consider information about the circumstances' of a person before sending them to prison for the first time, the effect of which was to increase the demand for social enquiry reports on a key group of people.

Because the range of duties of the Probation Service in Northern Ireland is so different from its counterpart in England and Wales and because no two areas are ever exactly comparable, it is difficult to make comparisons as to the relative strength of the service. It could be argued, however, that the relative strength of the service determines the range of duties it can carry out; the difficulty in developing community service orders mentioned below is just one example where the shortage of manpower has hampered development of the Northern Ireland Service; so a comparison can be useful.

Table 10 : 1 compares the service in Northern Ireland (Beresford 1976) with that of the Metropolitan County of Merseyside.[5] I have chosen Merseyside because it has approximately the same population ($1\frac{1}{2}$ million) as Northern Ireland.

Table 10:1   Staff levels in the Merseyside probation and after-care service for March 1977 and staff levels in the Northern Ireland probation service at 1 December 1976

	Merseyside	Northern Ireland
Chief Probation Officer	1	1
Deputy Chief Probation Officer	2	—
Assistant Chief Probation Officer	8	1
Senior Probation Officer	39	10
Probation Officers	192	45
Trainee Probation Officers	6	23
Ancillaries	24	7
TOTAL	272	87

These figures occur after the period of greatest expansion in the history of the Northern Ireland Service from '23 in 1966 . . . (to) 87 in 1976' (Beresford 1976). One other interesting point about the Northern Ireland figures is the very high proportion of trainees. It is only since 1970 that the government have committed themselves to a trained probation service, but the policy is now bearing fruit – of the staff (excluding trainees and ancillaries) in post in December 1977, 80 per cent are Certificate of Qualification in Social Work (CQSW) holders.

Why then, over the years, has the Probation Service been neglected and failed to develop in Northern Ireland? I consider possible explanations under three headings:

The low crime rate

It is generally accepted that before 'the troubles' the crime rate was considerably lower than that prevailing in the rest of the United Kingdom.

Mr William Craig said on introducing the 1968 Children and Young Persons Act: 'The latest available statistics show that . . . 9·5 per 1,000 of the juvenile population are guilty of offences in England and Wales as compared with 4·8 here in Northern Ireland.'[6] However, one recent work on the subject warns of the danger of placing too much reliance on criminal statistics in Northern Ireland.

> The official criminal statistics provide some evidence of patterns of crime, but there are many problems in interpreting such evidence: in particular, before the troubles the criminal statistics were not properly collected in Northern Ireland, while after the outbreak of the troubles the apparent pattern and levels of crime revealed in official statistics may well, to a large (but undetermined) extent, simply reflect variations in police activity. (Taylor and Nelson 1977)

Nonetheless, one may accept that the lower crime rate in Northern Ireland may go part of the way towards explaining the smaller staffing in the Probation Service. It does not explain, however, why the Service was not even allowed to grow to a point where it could cope with what was its main remit: juvenile crime. Nor does it explain why it has not expanded into the adult courts, the higher courts and after-care.

The failure of penal reform

I have dealt briefly above with the nature of politics in Northern Ireland and how this has worked against any reform movements. A recent essay explores this problem more fully in relation to the ill-fated Community Relations Commission (Ralston 1977).

One of the forces for expansion of the Probation Service in the rest of the United Kingdom has been its use by government to advise courts on new methods of dealing with offenders. The nature of politics and its associated attitude of repression towards crime ensured that there were few new ideas in the penological field which gained widespread acceptance amongst the public or the policy-makers. So with few alternatives available to the courts this incentive to develop a social work service in the courts has been absent.

> With a consistently lower deliquency rate than elsewhere in the United Kingdom, Northern Ireland has a substantially higher level of expensive residential provision for young offenders. An obvious

explanation for this anomaly has been a lack of adequate alternative provision. (Manning 1977)

Two recent examples of penal reform illustrate the problems that can arise when the Government does try to implement new policies, problems that derive in part from the failure to develop the probation service. There has been extensive lobbying for the introduction of community service orders by small but well-organized pressure groups who hope the scheme will capitalize on the growth of voluntary and community activity in the province.[7] The scheme was given the go-ahead by an Order in Council in 1976 but there have been considerable problems in making it operational because of the shortage of staff in the Probation Service and because it is not involved to a sufficient extent in the adult courts where the orders would be made.

The same Order in Council introduced a parole scheme which is now operational. Its effect will be that *all* prisoners serving determinate sentences of twelve months or longer will be conditionally released after serving half their sentences, the essential condition being that they do not offend again during the period of their parole. Thus, prisoners do not have to apply for parole. There is no Parole Board and there is no supervision by probation officers of parolees. The scheme seems to be the Government's main weapon in its attempt to control the burgeoning prison population. As well as its lack of manpower, there are other reasons (see below) why the Probation Service might not have welcomed participation in a scheme involving compulsory supervision of large numbers of terrorist offenders. Nonetheless, it is a strange anomaly of the administration of justice in the United Kingdom that in England, Scotland and Wales there is a large bureaucratic organization agonizing over the release of prisoners on parole while in Northern Ireland prisoners convicted of the same or worse crimes, some terrorist, some not, are released as a matter of course and subject to no supervision in the community.

The administration of the Probation Service

Probation officers in Northern Ireland are civil servants, they are hired and, since direct rule, their conditions of service are governed by the Northern Ireland Office – previously by the Ministry of Home Affairs. This is another fundamental difference between the Service here and the Service in England and Wales, where it is administered by committees of local magistrates albeit with money provided by the Home Office. The Morison Report (1962) made much of the advantages of the involvement of magistrates in the administration of the service: '. . . for we have no doubt that this relationship has been of prime importance in the growth of the probation system. It has fostered the courts' interest in probation and it has encouraged probation officers in their work by the assurance that their employers are people who are in daily touch with their practical problems.'

The same report went on to recommend the reorganization of the London Probation Service, which was administered directly by the Home Office, and noted the kind of criticism of the Civil Service often heard amongst probation officers in Northern Ireland: 'The Home Office was seen as essentially remote from the problems and interests of the probation officers, and its administration as, consequently, inefficient.'

The Northern Ireland Office (and before it, the Ministry of Home Affairs), which is responsible for the Probation Service, is also responsible for the police, the prisons and security policy in general. This, in a state which, not infrequently during its life, has seen its existence threatened by armed struggle. It is not the kind of environment one would expect such a delicate flower as a social service to the courts to thrive in!

It is difficult to assess whether or not the system of Resident Magistrates rather than a lay panel has affected the development of the Service in Northern Ireland. In the very early days of the Service when it was operated on a part-time basis, one Minister of Home Affairs blamed the magistrates for the Service not developing. On the other hand, in another report, the Resident Magistrates speak highly of the contribution of probation officers. There is, however, no evidence of the magistrates as a body pressing for the development and extension of social work services into the adult courts or of their acting as a force for the growth of the Service in the way the predominantly lay magistrates have done in England and Wales. Not only has the Northern Ireland Service suffered the disadvantages associated with its officers being civil servants, it has failed to reap the benefits that accrued in England and Wales where the Service is the responsibility of influential local people, significant numbers of whom are committed to its development.

The problem of political offenders

There has been a plethora of discussion in British social work circles of the relationship between social work and the political structure, e.g. Bailey and Brake (1975). An abiding source of conflict within and between BASW, Case Con and the unions representing social workers, has been what social workers' attitudes should be to social problems like poverty, housing, unemployment, and indeed to the whole capitalist state, which are variously credited with responsibility for the ever lengthening ranks of social work clients.

A fundamental difficulty which many social workers face when confronted with a client in need is to make the connection between this person 'warts and all' and the wider political process. The weight put on the various causative factors in a client's problem is often a matter for argument and it certainly leads to a more comfortable existence within the state bureaucracy to attribute at least some of the problem to the individual client's shortcomings. This process is aided by the fact that very few of our clients perceive their problems or actions in explicitly political terms.

This ambivalence within the profession, individual social workers and clients, about the aetiology of client problems, means that social workers rarely have to deal with clients whose motivation is and can be perceived as unequivocally political.

The Probation Service in Northern Ireland has been faced with the problem of what its attitude should be to those whose crimes have an explicit political motivation. Even in Northern Ireland political motivation has not always been easy to isolate but its definition has been made considerably easier by the passing of the Northern Ireland (Emergency Provisions) Bill in 1973 which created 'a new category of scheduled offences covering broadly all those crimes regularly committed by terrorists and their supporters' (Boyle, Hadden and Hillyard 1975). Under this legislation the courts still have the power to ask for social enquiry reports on scheduled offenders and to place them on probation. In 1975 at the annual general meeting of the National Association of Probation Officers, a resolution sponsored by the Northern Ireland branch was passed to the effect that association members would not prepare social enquiry reports on scheduled offenders or accept them on statutory supervision. The resolution said nothing that would prevent probation officers from offering their help on a voluntary basis to politically motivated offenders and, most notably in the prisons, this work has carried on throughout the present emergency.

In relation to social enquiry reports, the main argument for this stance has been that as these offenders are politically motivated and as probation officers are not trained to assess or work with political motivation, they cannot fulfil the aims of the social enquiry as laid down by the Streatfeild Report (1961) to provide:

1   information about the social and domestic background of the offender which is relevant to the court's assessment of his culpability;
2   information about the offender and his surroundings which is relevant to the court's consideration of how his criminal career might be checked;
3   an opinion as to the likely effect on the offender's criminal career of probation or some other specified form of sentence.

The same argument is applied to working with individuals on probation or statutory after-care with the added difficulty of how a probation officer would enforce the conditions of a probation order or an after-care licence on a political offender without being in considerable personal danger himself and without him and his colleagues being bracketed as persona non grata in whole areas of the province.

Although this stance has been widely supported within the Service, there have been arguments against it. These have accepted that it is not a probation officer's role to alter a person's political beliefs, but that it is his role to try to prevent the expression of these beliefs in a criminal or a violent way, and that the degree of political motivation of many 'scheduled' offenders is open to question; often they may be the young and the misguided who could benefit from social work help. The small amount of evidence there is gives little support to this thesis. Boyle (1976) found on looking at the backgrounds of 467 defendants on terrorist charges that they were 'broadly representative of the communities – both Catholic and Protestant – from which they have come. Their violence is one manifestation of the complex conflict which is being pursued on another level through institutionalized political channels.'

It seems unlikely that the service will become involved to any great extent in statutory work with political offenders in the community, but compromise seems likely in the preparation of reports where courts specifically request them, and this is most likely to be in situations where the degree of political motivation is in doubt.

Conclusion

A social work service to the courts, other than the juvenile court, has failed to develop in Northern Ireland, and even in the juvenile court the social worker has considerably less power than his colleagues in the rest of the United Kingdom. It has been the main contention of this chapter that this failure is a reflection of the prevalent value system in the province and of the political instability, which have favoured a legalistic and punitive attitude towards criminals. The situation has been exacerbated by the nature of the relationship between the Northern Ireland and the Westminster governments. Thus, the kinds of administrative machinery that would enable a court-based service to develop have not been created, and the kind of legislation which would give that service power and influence in the court has not got on to the statute book. It should be added that social workers, being very much a part of the province, its value system, and its political structure, have largely accepted their assigned role. The main thrust of their effort has been to establish themselves as a viable professional grouping within the existing structures.

The experience of the last eight years has posed the question of the role of a court and prison social service in a situation where a high proportion of the offending has an explicit political motivation and in such circumstances it is difficult to see how such a service could survive if it eschewed such work completely. It is equally difficult to see how it could retain its traditions as a social work service if it became a significant element in the statutory provision for politically-motivated offenders.

The future of court-based social work in Northern Ireland hangs very much in the balance. At the time of writing (spring 1978) there is a deal of activity in this field. There appears to be a shift of resources away from institutional care and towards intermediate treatment for the young (Manning 1977). There is the Community Service Order scheme, and an investment of funds in Belfast's areas of social need, being proposed. Added to these we have the Black Committee's review of the child-care legislation and services, which is giving rise to considerable discussion in the social work profession about the future direction of social work with offenders. There is a substantial lobby who are not anxious for social work to be given the kind of overall responsibility for young offenders they have under Westminster legislation. There is, too, an apparent determination on the part of the Government to strengthen the Probation Service (N. Ireland Probation and After-Care Service, 1978), but it is by no means clear what balance is to be struck between the Service's court and prison base and its aspirations to become more extensively involved in community-based remedies for delinquency. Finally, how such innovations as come about will be accepted by the community in the long term and how they will fare under any new local political forum are very much open questions.

Notes

1 Official Report of Debates, Parliament of Northern Ireland, Vol. 64, col. 1003.
2 Official Report of Debates, Parliament of Northern Ireland, Commons, Vol. XXXIII, col. 1899.
3 Official Report of Debates, Parliament of Northern Ireland, Commons, Vol. 68, col. 57.
4 *Belfast Areas of Special Social Need.* Report by Project Team 1976. HMSO.
5 Annual Report of the Chief Probation Officer to the Merseyside Probation and After-Care Committee for 1976.
6 Official Report of Debates, Parliament of Northern Ireland, Commons, Vol. 70, col. 1093.
7 An alternative to Prison: Community Service Orders in Northern Ireland, Extern 1976.
8 Official Report of Debates, Parliament of Northern Ireland, Commons, Vol. 10, col. 1044.
9 Moles Report. Cmnd (NI) 14. Belfast: HMSO.
10 The full text of the original NAPO resolution was: 'This Association deplores the involvement of its members on a statutory basis with those offenders whose actions are determined by motives of a patently political nature.

    Consequently we call upon the NEC to issue instructions to all members of the Association to refuse to conduct any Social Inquiry Report on any person charged under the conspiracy laws, or in Northern Ireland, those dealt with under the Schedules of the Emergency Provisions Act 1974, and further to refuse to carry out statutory supervision of any person convicted in similar circumstances.'

Chapter 11

Representation and Advocacy in Tribunals: A Social Work Role?

Paul Burgess

Apart from the court room, there exists another arena which many social workers appear to view with considerable trepidation – the appeal tribunal. There are various reasons for this, of course, as always, and not the least important of these is ignorance of the nature of tribunal procedures and practice. However, the last ten years have seen a large expansion in the use of tribunals as a means of recourse against administrative decisions, and there can be little doubt it is time that social workers got to grips with them in a far more serious way than hitherto. This is so especially when we realize that social workers' clients will almost certainly have a much higher probability of being affected by some aspect of the welfare state bureaucracy than the average citizen. Consider, for example, the chronically sick and disabled. In the last five years a number of new benefits have been introduced which are directed at meeting many of their special needs; for instance, attendance allowance, mobility allowance and non-contributory invalidity pension (extended to disabled housewives in November 1977); and all of them, while unequivocally to be welcomed, especially as they are non-means-tested, extend the possibility of conflict with bureaucracy. It is not at all uncommon to find disabled people reasonably applying for all of these benefits *and* supplementary benefit as well, thus effectively quadrupling the opportunities for bureaucratic impingements upon their lives.

Until we have an answer to the problem of the citizen versus an increasingly pervasive modern bureaucracy, described by Inglis (1977) as the 'central and lethal tension in all advanced societies', things are in this respect paradoxically going to get worse the more benefits are introduced. And as things do get worse, whether for technical reasons to do with the unmanageable volume of information, or because of the failure through overload of an already inefficient and ramshackle system, weakened by cuts in staffing and resources, or for both of these reasons, the machinery for appealing will become increasingly used by those hoping to find openness, fairness and impartiality elsewhere than in the offending bureaucracy. How many will meet these principles in application on exercising appeal rights is, unfortunately, another question. Franks (1957), however, considered them 'essential characteristics of appeal tribunals'.

In one repect the fears of social workers in relation to tribunals are rather puzzling. On the figures available for supplementary benefit appeal tribunals, which are the most controversial of the tribunals we shall be looking at, social workers' efforts on behalf of clients appear to produce better results than any other kind of representative. One would have thought this evidence would have encouraged more to take an interest, but this does not appear to have been the case. One factor going some way to explain the apparent effectiveness of social workers as representatives is the emphasis SBAT's place upon reliable, sympathetic, corroborative evidence (sadly to the neglect of often much clearer legal points) of the kind a caseworker is able to furnish. It could also be true, as DHSS officials often say of representatives in general, that social workers only make their way to tribunals when their client is clearly on a winner – an issue we shall return to later.

Not all social workers, though, feel able to act as representatives because of the discouragement against such activity by their Social Services Department, as Lawrence (1977, 19) observes. Indeed in my experience every class of social work students addressed on this topic has produced examples of either unambiguous departmental embargoes or fairly obvious discouragement on the part of senior staff against involvement by social workers in appeal tribunals.

Even more inhibiting in the long run is the view that social work should not really be caught up in 'welfare rights' at all. The advent of welfare rights officers whose function in many instances is, regrettably, solely to advise social workers' clients, is probably in part an expression of this view.

To the non-social worker it is rather difficult to appreciate how a distinction can be drawn between say, counselling a client undergoing severe mental stress associated with debts and managing with several children on a low income, and helping that person secure cash benefits to which he or she is entitled by statute or by virtue of discretion exercised in response to the problems confronting the family. Of course, there are difficulties and it would be unrealistic, not to say unfair, to ignore them. The most important is the sheer inadequacy of the average social worker's grasp of the information concerning the wide range of welfare benefits. A recent study by Melotte (1976) which included 71 per cent of Kirklees Social Services Department's social work staff found that for many the problem was finding and maintaining a reliable source of information, given that they themselves lacked the time, the energy, and sometimes the motivation, to ferret out the details. Clients, of course, very often detect that their social worker is weak on hardcore advice and help in the face of their adversities with the welfare state bureaucracy, and the 'casework' then continues on a superficial basis as a result. But it is unjust to lay the responsibility for such circumstances wholly at the feet of individual social workers; the fact is, the modern welfare state is becoming an immensely complex and disjointed system, and there are very many signs that it is suffering overload, not the least significant being the increasing incidence of officials giving out wrong information – a phenomenon also noted by the Liverpool-based Check! Rights Centre (1977, 28).

Another difficulty stems from seeing welfare rights problems of clients from a casework perspective. As an illustration, a claimant who had been over a period of months subject to some pretty gross administrative incompetence by his local social security office went to the office to extract an explanation, was given the usual stonewall treatment, lost his temper, and left the office even more aggrieved than when he went in. A welfare rights officer wrote to the manager on the claimant's behalf and listed point by point the man's grievances. With the worst form of bureaucratic disdain the reply made only the slightest acknowledgment of the claimant's legitimate grievances: instead it was pointed out that a visiting officer had called to see him and, in his absence, his wife had apologized to the officer for her husband losing his temper. The welfare rights issues which were quite straightforward merited pursuing further through official channels, but the senior social-work staff who were consulted disagreed and, instead, suggested with unconscious irony that the claimant's wife should be interviewed. (The poor man had, in fact, been getting it in the neck from his wife each time the DHSS mistakes delayed his benefit payment!).

It is a conclusion reached with some reluctance therefore that welfare rights specialists are needed, not necessarily inside social services departments, to provide at the very least an alternative information source to that of the official bureaucracies. But what of tribunals? Can social workers risk taking on the role of representative or even advocate when their knowledge may be quite shaky? My answer has to be yes, since legal aid is not available for clients to engage solicitors (except for preliminary advice beforehand) and they are otherwise going to find it difficult to get help elsewhere. So what is involved in representation?

The effectiveness of representation and advocacy

Until fairly recently the Citizens' Advice Bureaux declined to become involved in tribunals, choosing instead to adopt a position of 'impartiality'. But, at least since 1974, the CAB, having decided that the odds were heavily stacked against unrepresented clients, have pioneered some of the most interesting and valuable projects concerned with representation at tribunals.

One of the first to attract attention was the Newcastle-upon-Tyne CAB tribunal assistance scheme following the report by Galbraith and Taylor (1976). The aim of the service was that it should provide comprehensive help to its clients rather than 'mere representation' at tribunals.

This meant being prepared to take matters up on behalf of clients at the early stages when adverse decisions were first issued; to draft letters of appeal, prepare the arguments, and eventually represent at the tribunal hearing in appropriate cases. In their first year the two part-time project workers dealt with just over 400 cases, of which 41 per cent were to do with employment problems, 36 per cent with national insurance problems, and 23 per cent with supplementary benefit, reflecting the very wide cross-section of people ready to use their service. The relatively low proportion of supplementary benefit cases, at a little under a quarter, was contrary to the project workers' expectations. But their experience of SBATs led them to suggest the idea of a 'duty representative' in the waiting-room to help and advise those about to go into the tribunal unrepresented and often ill-prepared. The inclination to offer help to other appellants in the waiting-room is one shared by many who frequently represent at SBATs, simply because any help at all can make a lot of difference to the outcome; regrettably there are no guarantees that the tribunal or the officials involved would otherwise respond to the individual's needs. In fact, supplementary benefit cases did produce their highest proportion (38.5 per cent) of cases going to tribunal hearings. Out of eighty-three cases going to a hearing the project workers (one of whom described herself as an absolute novice before the scheme began) represented at seventy. A further forty cases were settled without the need for a tribunal hearing, but unfortunately the report does not say what happened to the rest of the 402 cases seeking their help. It would have helped also had the project workers not declined to count those tribunals which were won or lost following their help, on the grounds that 'support was as important as winning'. The report considers their shifting attitude towards those seeking help with appeals, from the help to all comers offered initially to the more discriminating position adopted as the project progressed. They rightly recognized this as a tricky issue, involving judgments on their part in cases that perhaps were more properly left to their fate in the appeals systems. Wisely, the project workers recognized that supplementary benefit cases, and national insurance cases turning on medical points, were best treated in this way with the workers' role being to present the appellant's case in the best manner possible. Experience brought them to conclude in other types of case however 'that a client could not succeed, and we advised him accordingly'. It is worth stressing that experience is the only qualification allowing discrimination of this kind.

A similar tribunal assistance unit was established in Leeds in August 1976 and reported on by Storey (1977). At the time the report was published, twenty-seven of their 126 cases had not yet been resolved. The unit advised abandonment in only five cases because they considered them hopeless, and generally had a policy of 'being prepared to contest all but the *very* hopeless cases'.

It may be helpful to make a distinction between simple *representation* and *advocacy*, although often in practice the two merge imperceptibly. Representation may involve no more than being there with the client and putting the details of the client's circumstances to the tribunal. Advocacy, on the other hand, as Napley (1975) explains, presumes a much more active role, an attempt to influence and persuade the tribunal of the fairness and justice of your client's claim. Some legal voices have expressed the view that social workers 'by training and temperament' would not make suitable advocates, arguing that advocacy done badly is better not done at all – and indeed could even lead to an action by the client on grounds of the social worker's incompetence! To caution against excessively zealous advocacy, certainly against going further than one's client would have wished, should not of course perturb those disposed simply to represent clients. At the very least, accompanying a client gives him moral support.

So far tribunals have been discussed in a fairly general manner. In reality there are important differences between them. Of prime concern to social workers must be Supplementary Benefit Appeal Tribunals and National Insurance Local Tribunals, but recent developments in the provision for the sick and disabled, in particular the new mobility allowance, make a knowledge of Medical Appeal Tribunals more important than before. What follows is an attempt to familiarize readers with these tribunals, the way they operate, and the kind of problems associated with them. For tribunals concerned with housing matters – rent tribunals for example – it is advisable to seek advice from a housing aid agency. On the other hand, since ombudsmen provide valuable opportunities for obtaining redress against unjust treatment by bureaucracy we must find space to deal with them.

Supplementary Benefit Appeal Tribunals

In 1976 there were about one and a half times as many appeals heard against supplementary benefit decisions as there were of the rest of Social Security benefit decisions put together. Many more were lodged but for one reason or another did not proceed to appeal. SBATs have been described as the 'misery end of the tribunal system' being concerned with the poorest and predominantly with discretionary decisions about their rights to grants for clothing, shoes, bedding, etc. The supplementary benefit scheme is often described as the safety net of the income maintenance framework of the welfare state. Its purpose is to ensure no individual suffers poverty of an unacceptable degree as defined by Parliament. Responsibility for the scheme rests with the Supplementary Benefits Commission, a body of eight people appointed by the Secretary of State for Social Services, although the day-to-day administration is conducted by the DHSS through whose offices the policies of the SBC are implemented.

Although presented as part of the package of reform from National Assistance to Supplementary Benefit in 1966, SBATs have direct antecedents in the National Assistance Appeal Tribunals which functioned between 1948 and 1966, and before that in the Unemployment Assistance Tribunals dating from the Unemployment Assistance Act 1934. The principal current legislation is the Supplementary Benefits Act 1976, and the right of appeal is contained in Section 15 of that Act. People claiming or receiving supplementary benefit can appeal against:

1 The amount of an award, the refusal of benefit, and the withdrawal of benefit;
2 refusal to review an existing award;
3 payment of benefit to a person other than the claimant;
4 payment of the whole or part of benefit in goods or services;
5 recovery of the whole or part of any benefit paid on an urgent basis to a person in employment;
6 recovery of supplementary benefit from arrears of national insurance benefits and family allowances;
7 a requirement to register for employment as a condition of receipt of benefit.

> Appeal tribunals can also consider (under Sections 10 and 20 (2) of the Act respectively)

8 a report by the Commission seeking a direction that supplementary benefit should be paid subject to a condition that the person concerned attends a re-establishment or other training course;
9 whether, as a result of misrepresentation or failure to disclose a material fact, benefit has been overpaid and, if so, the amount that is recoverable.

The number of appeals made has been rising steadily in the last few years although 1976 saw a really dramatic increase of 44·6 per cent over the previous year. Table 11 : 1 provides the details for 1972 to 1976.

The table shows (column 3) that a large proportion of decisions are revised by local social security offices on receiving the Notice of Appeal (which must be in writing and normally within twenty-one days of the decision) from the claimant. This follows from an 'urgent re-examination' of such decisions which can be changed

Table 11 : 1   Supplementary benefit appeals analysis of results 1972–6

Year	1 Total appeals lodged	2 % Withdrawn or not admitted	3 % Revised by local offices	4 % Revised by SBAT	5 Overall % of decisions revised
1972	5,9136	14·65	28·29	8·77	37·06
1973	5,0752	17·11	34·63	9·51	44·14
1974	5,5743	16·66	37·39	8·02	45·41
1975	6,8975	17·43	35·06	9·48	44·54
1976	10,1112	21·88	23·59	10·30	33·9

Source: SBC Annual Report for 1976.

under powers contained in Regulation 5 of the Supplementary Benefit (General) Regulations 1966. The remarkable fact is that when, as in column 5, the proportion of decisions changed by the local offices is combined with the proportion revised by the Appeal Tribunal in the appellant's favour, for 1973–5 nearly a *half* of appeals made resulted in a *revised decision* for the claimants concerned.

The proportion of decisions reportedly superseded by local DHSS offices fell quite dramatically in 1976, partly due to a policy change, although tribunals maintained an average success rate for appeals heard by them of approximately 19 per cent overall. Appealing is not, therefore, on the face of it a waste of time. Of course, the statistics do not reveal how close the revised decisions came to giving the claimants what they wanted – and experience suggests that token offers are often made, and accepted, which fall short of the original request. Colman (1971) analyses this process in detail. Although the results of SBATs have been fairly stable, at least over the last four years, the variations between the twelve DHSS Regions have been large. Since 1973, however, a welcome but nonetheless mysterious levelling out of these variations has occurred, without significantly affecting the average success rate.

What part does representation play in all this? Representation is specifically provided for in the Supplementary Benefit (Appeal Tribunal) Rules 1971, Section 11, which we can usefully quote in part:

Hearings before the Appeal Tribunal
    11.—(1) The clerk shall be present at all sittings of the Appeal Tribunal.
    (2) An interested person shall be entitled to be present during an oral hearing, to be heard, to call persons to give evidence and to put questions directly to any other interested person who is present and to any person who gives evidence.
    (3) An interested person who attends an oral hearing shall be entitled to be accompanied by not more than two persons either or both of whom (whether having professional qualifications or not) may represent that interested person at such hearing and an interested person who does not attend an oral hearing shall be entitled to be represented by not more than two persons (whether having professional qualifications or not) at such hearing, but, except with the consent of the Appeal Tribunal—
        (a) an interested person who attends an oral hearing may be accompanied by no more than two persons (whether attending

as representatives of the interested person they accompany or otherwise); and

(*b*) an interested person who does not attend an oral hearing may be represented by no more than two persons.

(4) A person representing an interested person at an oral hearing shall have all the rights of an interested person referred to in paragraph (2) of this rule.

We should note particularly that the representative 'shall have all the rights of the interested person' (i.e. the appellant) and this provides the basis for a vigorous defence of the appellant's interests. How vigorous this can or should be depends upon some important considerations such as are raised by Rose (1973) and an adequate treatment of the issue requires more space than is available here. Suffice it to say the question involves not only the client's best interests, but also the ethics of advocacy, and possibly an overview of the place of the tribunals in the social security system. A good rule is to discuss with the appellant beforehand any strategy involving conflict, and take one's cue from his feelings about it, always subject of course to such a strategy being proposed for no other reason than its expected efficacy. It can never be right to use the privilege of representing a client to rail against the 'system' at his expense: equally, however, some tribunal chairmen, and members, and presenting officers, can be pompous, overbearing, and rude, and an appellant's anger at this treatment will often be shared by the representative. Moreover, as Burgess (1976) reveals, the DHSS appear not to be slow to attempt to influence such role interpretations by local authority social services employees. Table 11:2 gives the results of a statistical analysis of representation for the years 1973–6. It is indisputably an

Table 11:2   Percentage of favourable decisions by type of representative in Supplementary Benefit Appeal Tribunals 1973–6

| Year | Unrepresented | % of favourable decisions by type of representative | | | |
		Friends or Relatives	Solicitor	Vol. Orgs. and TU	Social or Welfare Worker
1973	14·3 (77·9)	34·1 (14·5)	43·8 (0·7)	45·6 (4·3)	52·8 (2·5)
1974	12·3 (79·2)	32·9 (13·3)	38·2 (0·6)	41·8 (3·8)	49·3 (3·0)
1975	14·4 (77·8)	33·4 (14·1)	27·5 (0·5)	49·3 (3·6)	53·5 (4·0)
1976	13·7 (77·9)	31·1 (14·7)	36·1 (0·4)	44·6 (3·1)	50·0 (3·8)

The figures in brackets give the percentage of the total appeals having the type of representation specified. Unrepresented includes those not attending at all.
Source: Figures derived from SBC Annual Report, 1976.

advantage to have a representative, just as it is equally clear that some representatives are more effective than others.

In Kathleen Bell's impressive study of 235 supplementary benefit appeal tribunal cases, appellants who attended alone obtained a successful result in 31·1 per cent of appeals, whereas those with representatives secured successful results in 42·4 per cent of appeals on average. Bell was sufficiently convinced of the value of advice and representation to claimants as to make this a major plank in her several important recommendations (1975).

Prior to the tribunal hearing the appellant receives the papers and these set out the SBC's observations. Good representation begins with a close reading of these papers and the checking of all the facts and regulations to which they refer. The typical layout of a supplementary benefit appeal tribunal, which is conducted in private, is illustrated in Figure 11 : 1. There are many criticisms made of both members of the tribunal and of officials. One of the most penetrating critics is Lister (1974) who provides a revealing account of how they see themselves and each other.

Figure 11:1   Typical layout of Supplementary Benefit Appeal Tribunal

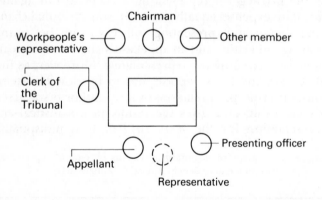

On the latest figures available only 6 per cent of the 287 chairmen, who are the only members paid a fee, are legally qualified, and this deficiency has allowed of much sloppiness passing off as informality in the conduct of proceedings. One of the recommendations of the Bell report was that the chairmen of SBATs should be legally qualified and the Government have in part accepted this. The work-people's representative is selected from a panel nominated by local Trades Councils and the limply titled 'other member' is chosen as a 'person of good standing and sound local knowledge'. If for some reason only one member and the chairman are present the tribunal can only proceed with the appellant's agreement. It is usually better, if the problem is not urgent, to express a preference for the case to the heard by a full tribunal. Again, if the appellant can afford the delay appeals may be adjourned on request, but at the chairman's discretion, if more time is needed to prepare the case.

The role of clerk to the tribunal has come under attack because of doubts about the impartiality of the officials concerned, and these doubts originate because the officials are seconded from the DHSS to the post. The recently published SBAT *Guide to Procedure* (1977) reveals the full extent of the Clerk's possible influence, as well as other interesting information. However, on the positive side, the clerk does an important job in the tribunal waiting-room in receiving the appellants, paying travelling expenses and loss of earnings, and can be generally helpful and informative both on the day and beforehand.

Finally, there is the presenting officer, the official charged with presenting the social security side of the case (in theory they are not advocates for the SBC but in practice nearly always appear so). Bell reported that 'there was no evidence of the overbearing rather intimidating manner and attitude which has been referred to in some publications'. The presenting officer is one of a small team of officials who do this work from the DHSS regional offices. They receive cases from local offices and can often be at a disadvantage because they lack first-hand knowledge, although they will have the appellant's file with them in the tribunal. One of the most important rules for representatives is to clearly isolate SBC policy (which the tribunal can over-rule) from the actual law; presenting officers often cloud this issue, consciously or otherwise. It is usual for the presenting officer to be asked to speak first, and after questions to him by the tribunal the appellant and representative are invited to put their case. When both parties have been heard and the chairman is satisfied with the information obtained, the presenting officer and the appellant and representative retire and the tribunal comes to its decision in the presence of the clerk, whose job it is to record that decision and then notify the appellant. The 1971 Appeal Tribunal Rules allow for not more than two observers to be present by prior arrangement with the clerk. This facility allows social workers, for example, to learn something of the procedures and conduct of the SBAT.

One major defect with SBATs has been the absence of an available remedy when the appellant has felt himself to be the victim of injustice in the hands of the tribunal. Unlike National

Insurance Local Tribunals, they are not regulated by a body of case law emanating from decisions of a higher authority like the National Insurance Commissioners. Although the Bell report recommended, *inter alia*, that a similar second-tier appeal body should be set up for SBATs, the Government has decided instead, without prejudice to further consideration of a second-tier appeal, to make an order, effective from 1 January 1978, granting a right of appeal to the High Court in England and Wales and to the Court of Session in Scotland. Although a form of legal remedy existed formerly it has been far from accessible and then only resulting in a decision being set aside. A right of appeal on the other hand has the advantage of enabling the Court to substitute a decision for the one taken by the tribunal (see de Smith 1973, 357). There is an independent body called the Council on Tribunals which has an interest in the work of the SBATs but it is felt by welfare rights workers to be a virtually inanimate object. Street (1975) and de Smith (1973) offer differing views of the Council's competence and achievements.

National Insurance Local Tribunals

After SBATs the largest volume of appeals is handled by the National Insurance Local Tribunals (NILTs). Generally speaking, NILTs are felt to be more satisfactory tribunals than SBATs and that is probably because, all in all, the results are felt by experienced representatives to be more predictable. In 1975, they dealt with over 30,000 appeals covering a wide range of benefits – mainly unemployment benefit, sickness benefit and industrial injuries, but also including retirement and widows' pensions, maternity benefit, death grant, family allowances (now child benefit) and a tiny number of other benefits.

NILTs history can be traced back through the tribunals established under the 1946 National Insurance and Industrial Injuries Acts to the Unemployment Insurance Appeal Tribunals of 1936 – which were themselves derived from the 'Courts of Referees' provided for under the National Insurance Act 1911. Their present statutory basis is in the Social Security Act 1975, Section 97 and Schedule 10. Amongst a range of other things the Schedule provides, for example, that where the claimant is a woman 'at least one of the members of the Tribunal, if practicable, shall be a woman'. If the claimant is dissatisfied with an insurance officer's decision he may appeal to a local tribunal in writing – a form is provided – within twenty-one days of the decision, or 'within such further time as the Chairman of the local tribunal may for good cause allow', the Notice of Appeal being sent to the claimant's local DHSS office.

The tribunal consists of a chairman, usually legally qualified, and two other members, one from a representative panel of employed persons and the other from a panel similarly representative of employers and others. In contrast with SBATs, the hearings are open to the public unless there is some special reason, agreed between the appellant and the chairman beforehand, about the desirability of a private hearing; and this presents a valuable opportunity for those who intend to represent (or indeed to appear as appellants) to acquaint themselves with the procedure and, often equally important, with the style of the chairman concerned. The important study of NILTs by Kathleen Bell *et al.* (1974 and 1975) concluded that NILTs were 'more various and less confined by law and regulation than is often assumed.' This research took in 272 appeal hearings at 68 tribunal sittings which enabled them to observe at a total of 350 appeals. In the same period (1970) a total of 7,528 appeals was heard in the two areas – Scotland and the Northern Region – on which the study was based. Attendance at NILTs by the appellant in Great Britain as a whole was just 50 per cent and this was seen in the 54 per cent and 50 per cent average attendance rates in the Northern Region and Scotland respectively. However, there is a very wide variation in attendance between the types of benefit appealed; in 1970 in industrial injury cases it was 83 per cent, in family allowance cases 33 per cent. As with SBATs attendance was strongly associated with increased chances of success. The undifferentiated success rate was 38 per cent for industrial injury cases in Great Britain, compared for example with 20 per cent for unemployment benefit and 15 per cent for sickness benefit, contributing to an overall success rate of 21 per cent for NILTs. But whereas, overall, those who attended their hearings had a 35 per cent success rate those who didn't had 8 per cent.

Reflecting a generally held view, one of the chairmen in the study expressed the opinion that 'many appeals which prima facie are hopeless are turned to success by diligent investigation at the hearing'. A point to be noted and recalled whenever faced with an apparently hopeless case! Tribunal decisions need not be unanimous (although 95 per cent were in the study). Dissent in decisions favourable to the appellants was, interestingly, associated with both attendance by appellants and by the chairman being outvoted – suggesting that the other members were *sometimes* more responsive and sympathetic to the appellant who appears in person. An indispensable account of the tribunal machinery from the 'inside' is that of Street (1975) a Professor of Law and NILT chairman. Variation in attendance rates and success rates between the appeals on different benefits is also true of representation and, not surprisingly, evidence in the Bell study suggests a very strong link between all three factors. When attendance was combined with representation a success rate of over 50 per cent was achieved. One surprising fact, which must one hopes now be quite untypical, given the changed attitudes towards welfare rights in social work training, was that of the 1,538 representatives in the study analysis only *two* were social workers. Most were trade union representatives (75 per cent) with relatives (14 per cent) and solicitors (5 per cent) figuring in the statistics.

Representation at NILTs is less exacting than at SBATs, assuming always that the absolutely indispensable preparation beforehand of studying the papers closely and researching any references given (usually the case law procedents) is undertaken. Witnesses can be called and in the absence of the appellant the representative can attend alone. The typical layout of a National Insurance Local Tribunal is similar to an SBAT (see Figure 11 : 1 on p. 198), although often the clerk of the NILT is much more inconspicuously seated. Relatively little criticism has been levelled at the officials involved. The insurance officer who attends is not a Department man in the same way as is the presenting officer in SBATs and much is made of the independence in his decisions. Another difference is that the insurance officer present has actually made the decision and rather than making him more defensive than the presenting officer, it appears to introduce a much greater sense of realism into the proceedings. Even so NILTs have their limitations. In a recently observed case a married couple attended an appeal against a refusal of sickness benefit for the wife. The husband tried to help by describing the effect on his promotion prospects of his wife's illness (whether she was ill or not was in contention); all, predictably, to no avail. What neither of them appreciated was the insurance officer's repetitive use of the term 'functional overlay' and as a result, with the chairman nodding sagely each time it was mentioned, the hearing continued at two entirely different levels without the couple being remotely aware of this, and nobody seeing fit to bring them in on the meaningful level. In the study by Bell *et al.* (1974 and 1975) 40 per cent of appellants had not read or did not understand the appeal papers and 75 per cent had obtained no advice beforehand.

If the insurance officer has a low profile, the clerk to the tribunal, once inside, is literally out of sight unless called on for some reference or other. Beforehand of course, following the making of arrangements in the first place, he has the not unimportant job of receiving people in the waiting-room, paying expenses for travelling and loss of earnings, and ushering people into the hearing. Afterwards he brings the results in writing from the tribunal, (in contrast with SBATs where the decision is posted a few days later) and then sends the full decision and the reasoning by post. If the decision is unfavourable there still remains the opportunity to appeal from the local tribunal to the National Insurance Commissioner (Social Security Act 1975). In 1975 some 900 appeals were made to the Commissioner on unemployment benefit alone, with 25 per cent of these being successful. The appeal should normally be within three months of the NILT decision. If grounds are felt to exist for appealing to the Commissioner it is prudent to obtain advice in the preparation of the appeal. The best way of acquainting oneself with the type of appeals taken, successfully and unsuccessfully, to the Commissioner is to read around the subject area in the Reported Decisions of the National Insurance Commissioners, which can be freely consulted at local social security offices.

Medical Appeal Tribunals

These tribunals have until recently been solely concerned with industrial injuries matters (Social Security Act 1975). Their newly-acquired responsibility to hear appeals on mobility allowance (Mobility Allowance Regs. 1975 SI 1573) will chiefly concern social workers, although a good many of their clients may also require their advice and help with appeals arising out of industrial injury claims – not all of the employed work force are able to benefit from the extensive trade union activity in this field. Here I will consider Medical Appeal Tribunals (MATs) in the light of mobility allowances which are eventually to be received by around 100,000 disabled.

If a client is dissatisfied with a decision, following from the medical examination, not to award a mobility allowance, he has a right of appeal. In the first instance this is to a medical board, consisting of two doctors who will examine the applicant. If the board confirms the original doctor's decision there is a further right of appeal, within three months, to a medical appeal tribunal. This is an independent body which has an experienced lawyer as chairman and two medical consultants. Hearings are in public unless the appellant for a special reason objects and the chairman agrees. The MAT is in a position to arrive at its own conclusions on all matters of medical fact or opinion in the case and is not limited to considering just the points appealed from the medical board's decision. However its decision on medical issues is final and it is therefore very important to ensure that all the medical evidence favourable to the appellant is made known to it. This can mean letters from doctors, or hospital reports, or specialists' reports commissioned by the appellant.

As with all tribunals it is important for the representative to obtain and scrutinize all the relevant documents for the tribunal hearing, in order to be as well prepared as possible. The clerk to the tribunal will send the nominated representative all the tribunal papers in advance. Statistics showing the effectiveness or otherwise of representation in MATs are not available, but since most people are represented, as a result of the trade union interest through the industrial injuries work of the MATs and since the average success rate is around 38 per cent, we may safely assume some effectiveness. Figure 11:2 shows a typical layout of a medical appeal tribunal.

It is usual for the chairman to summarize the issue in contention and then to invite the appellant or his representative to explain his case. Questions may then follow, of both the appellant and the DHSS representative, as may a medical examination if this is

Figure 11:2   Typical layout of Medical Appeal Tribunal

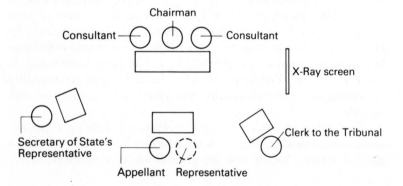

felt to be necessary (obviously this is conducted privately in the appropriate cases). Since the hearings are public, would-be representatives can easily familiarize themselves with the proceedings by visiting the tribunal beforehand. Sometimes the tribunal will communicate its decision at the close of the hearing, but in any case the appellant and representative will receive written notice of the decision a couple of days after the hearing.

There is yet one more right of appeal from the MAT to the National Insurance Commissioner, but only on the ground that their decision is erroneous in a point of law. But leave to appeal, which must be applied for normally within three months of the MAT's decision, must be obtained from the chairman or the Commissioner. In effect, the Commissioner will either accept an appeal or reject it is as not satisfying the criterion. It would be prudent to consult an experienced adviser in the preparation of the submission. Finally, if the case is lost, the client should be advised that a new application should be considered if there is a deterioration in his medical condition; sometimes the disappointment felt by those who are unsuccessful impairs their judgment subsequently.

However, the MAT is strong in all those aspects in which the SBAT is weak: the legally qualified chairman ensures proper attention to rules of evidence and to the pertinence of the proceedings; the other members of the tribunal are specialists and therefore bring expert knowledge to their role in the tribunal; the DHSS representative clearly has no doubts that his job is simply to present the details as objectively as possible to the tribunal, and this often requires, in contrast to the presenting officer in SBATs, no participation at all on his part when the papers are self-explanatory; and finally the clerk of the tribunal appears to experience no temptation to intervene in the proceedings. Doubtless the officials' low profile is related to the status and calibre of the tribunal itself which, again unlike SBATs, puts almost no reliance on the officials for information and none certainly for opinion. There is, further, a body of case law governing MATs as with NILTs.

The use of ombudsmen

In the description of the tribunals, and the role of representation, the importance to be attached to early attempts at resolving the problem was repeatedly emphasized. However, sometimes it appears that the way the case is being handled by officialdom leaves a great deal to be desired. Naturally, when the scale of operations is often so vast – the DHSS alone employs 90,000 staff and handles tens of millions of claims each year (SBC, 1976) – we could expect some mistakes to be made, a degree of inconvenience to be experienced, or a measure of delay. But a point may be reached in the individual case where officialdom is obviously to be reproached for failing to meet standards of administration which one could reasonably expect. In such instances even a favourable tribunal decision may be only partly satisfactory to the aggrieved person, if, indeed, that is the outcome. It may then be that an ombudsman offers the only way of securing anything like an independent scrutiny of the facts and a remedy for the injustice suffered.

As de Smith (1973) recounts, the interest in some form of ombudsman in the UK stemmed from the feeling that where departmental decision making was closed to outside scrutiny, injustices perpetrated had no effective redress. Developments in other countries were observed carefully, and they gave momentum to the movement which led eventually to the Parliamentary Commissioner Act 1967. Six years later the Health Service Ombudsman was established by the National Health Service Reorganization Act 1973, Part III, followed a year later by the establishment of the Local Ombudsman by the Local Government Act 1974 (1975 in Scotland). Thus there now exist three kinds of ombudsman (or 'commissioner') and although they are similar in many respects – indeed the Parliamentary Ombudsman and Health Service Ombudsman are the same person! – it will be helpful to briefly describe the differing access to them. The extent of the matters excluded from their jurisdiction is, however, lengthy and each ombudsman has published a freely available leaflet to help the public understand his role and scope.

The failure to deal with someone properly and fairly, often leading to injustice, is described as maladministration. Delays in dealing with correspondence; providing unhelpful, misleading or evasive replies; failing to fulfil undertakings; failing to acknowledge mistakes or to remedy them; these are some of the things with which ombudsmen are concerned. One problem, however, is that they take a long time to complete their investigations, without real justification in many cases say their critics, for example Street (1975) in relation to the Parliamentary Ombudsman. The English Local Ombudsmen have reported that the average time for investigations undertaken in 1976–7 was 41·4 weeks, and it is a continuing weakness in the ombudsman system.

In one sense, however, those problems which result in formal investigations by an ombudsman are something of a failure for the system, simply because the procedures are designed to give everybody the opportunity to put right what has been wrong. As an inducement to authorities to put their own houses in order, each of the ombudsmen publishes reports on his official investigations, which name the authorities investigated and give the outcome. Unfortunately, publicity of this nature is the only threat the ombudsmen pose and there is some doubt whether it is sufficient. Nevertheless, despite criticisms that they are inordinately slow, that they have 'civil service attitudes', and that their reports are sometimes insufficiently robust on the shortcomings of officialdom, their reports can make refreshing reading for those who, like social workers, are witnesses almost daily to far from satisfactory standards of public administration experienced by clients. Moreover, the outcome of a referral to an ombudsman can result in changes to procedures and practices to prevent similar injustices occurring again, even where no maladministration, strictly interpreted, has been established.

The Parliamentary Commissioner for Administration

The Parliamentary Ombudsman is reached through one's Member of Parliament. He will not usually take cases from the public, although if the individual's MP is uncooperative it is possible to complain directly to the ombudsman. A complaint to an MP should lead the MP to contact the civil service department concerned to try and get the problem resolved; if this is unsuccessful then the MP can refer the case to the ombudsman who may, in the case of an investigation, examine files and documents not available to the MP or his constituent. When his investigation is completed the ombudsman makes his report back to the MP, who should send a copy of the report to his constituent. There is some evidence that the 'filtering' of cases through MPs does prevent many valid complaints from reaching him. Many MPs appear slow to refer cases, mainly, it has been suggested, because of a lack of confidence in the ombudsman's ability to produce the results they require. However, it is equally likely that they simply fail to recognize the ingredients of maladministration in their constituents' complaints, despite, or maybe because of, the observation that their surgeries are 'clearing stations for the walking wounded of the bureaucratic state'.

Social workers can help their clients considerably therefore by preparing with them a clearly written list of complaints – getting it typed should not prove difficult given the resources at the disposal of social workers – and making sure the request that it be referred to the ombudsman is clearly made. A good account of one person's hazardous but eventually successful complaint is reported by the Child Poverty Action Group (1977). In 1976, 815 new complaints were referred by MPs, and 231 cases were carried forward from the previous year. However, 505 were not accepted for investigation (for a variety of reasons) so only 329 completed cases were reported to MPs; of these, maladministration was established in only 139 cases (PCA Annual Report, 1977). The DHSS was the Department against which most complaints were made (169), although 53 per cent were rejected as being outside jurisdiction. Maladministration was established in only 57 of the DHSS cases reported to MPs in 1976.

The Commissioners for Local Administration

Access to one's local ombudsman is via members of the local authority concerned. There are separate ombudsmen for England, Scotland and Wales, with England divided into three areas each the responsibility of an ombudsman of the English Commission. Unfortunately around two thirds of complaints are sent directly to the ombudsmen and have to be sent back to the complainant. Most are not then resubmitted through the correct channels, and the English Commission are researching into what must be considered a serious malfunctioning of the access procedures (CLA Annual Report, 1977). When a local ombudsman receives a complaint through a member of the authority concerned, he makes an informal approach, mainly with the intention of drawing his involvement to the authority's attention. Hopefully things are put right by agreement at this stage. Otherwise a full investigation may result. Table 11.3 shows that the flow of complaints to the Local Ombudsmen in England have been remarkably consistent over the last two years.

The 2,277 complaints in 1976–7 included those (1,449) which the Commission felt it necessary to return, uninvestigated, to the complainant. Consequently only 1,075 complaints were properly referred, according to the Annual Report, of which over 60 per cent were then rejected. Nobody can be happy therefore that around £½ million expenditure resulted in 189 completed investigations for that year. But the accounting on this basis is, arguably, rather unfair because so much more is achieved simply because of the ombudsmen's existence. Their real achievements

Table 11:3 Subjects of complaint to English Commission for Local Administration 1975–6 and 1976–7

Subject of Complaint	1975–6 No.	%	1976–7 No.	%
Planning	691	31	708	31
Housing	488	22	535	24
Education	208	9	192	8
Highways	160	7	138	6
Environmental health	105	5	120	5
Land	113	5	125	5
Social Services	94	4	81	4
Others	390	17	378	17
Total	2,249	100	2,277	100

Source: Annual Report, 1976–7.

are, like icebergs, mainly concealed from view. Whether the long-suffering public will adopt such a measured attitude, however, is surely an open question.

Whatever weaknesses exist, the Local Government Ombudsmen offer some hope of remedies in areas where no proper appeal rights exist, such as is the case in the provision of most local authority benefits and services.

The Health Service Commissioner

Of the three types of ombudsmen the Health Service Commissioner is the most accessible, there being no intermediary involved at all. Complaints can be made directly to him about hospitals and other services, the only proviso being that the authority against which the complaint is made has had an opportunity to deal with the complaint first. His job is to investigate complaints from members of the public that they have 'suffered injustice or hardship' because of a failure in a service, or a failure to provide a service which an authority was in duty bound to provide, or because of maladministration which has affected action taken by or on behalf of a health authority. The Health Service Ombudsman's report which is produced quarterly, makes the most harrowing reading of all the ombudsmen's reports, covering as it does allegations of failures resulting in not merely injustice and hardship but pain and sometimes death.

In his annual report for 1976–7 (HSC Annual Report, 1977) he discusses some of the important areas about which complaints were made. They included delays in admission to hospitals, disputes as to whether consent for treatment had first been obtained, issues arising from compulsory admission into hospitals for the mentally ill, inadequate ambulance services, and the handling of complaints by Health Authorities.

As with the other ombudsmen, however, there are problems in the use made of the Health Service Ombudsman by the public. Of the 582 complaints received in 1976–7, 423 (72 per cent) were rejected without an investigation. The three main reasons were that they related to clinical judgment (which is outside his jurisdiction, although the question is being reviewed), that there was no prior reference to the authorities concerned, and that they were complaints against family practitioners or dentists, for example.

The very high proportion of complaints to all the ombudsmen which are rejected on technical grounds must be a cause for concern. It can only serve to undermine public confidence in their usefulness. Either much better publicity about their limited scope is required, or a modification of their terms of reference, so as to include the areas of main concern to the public.

Help in the courtroom

If we accept the proposition, which here has been the underlying premise, that social workers can be a valuable resource available to disadvantaged clients, one further aspect must be covered. Some clients find themselves involved in legal proceedings which can involve serious consequences for them. Yet a disturbingly high proportion do not seek nor receive any form of legal aid or advice. One issue where this is of the gravest importance is possession hearings in the County Court. A recent study by Leevers *et al.* (1977) embracing eleven separate hearings in two Inner London County Courts, observed that of the 140 cases of this kind coming up only 10 defendants had legal representation, compared with 123 of the plaintiffs. The researchers interviewed 91 of the defendants and of these 74 had not even consulted a solicitor, the main reasons given being 'the expense' or because they 'did not think it worthwhile'. Almost all the hearings, not surprisingly, went against the defendants especially those who neither attended nor were represented, although the researchers, from an experienced housing aid agency, felt that injustice had been done in many cases. Such were the defects in the way the whole process was functioning, the study concluded that a housing tribunal was probably the only answer, introducing an inexpensive and informal setting for both parties to present their case.

This followed Cutting (1976) who also concluded from a sample of sixty-four cases observed in a North London County Court in 1975 that 'reforms are essential if the tenant is to be given a fair chance to present his case'. Cutting noted, additionally, that the most effective representation came from an experienced advice centre worker. We can certainly take it that the reforms suggested are a long way off, and their form is not universally agreed; meanwhile, to whom can confused and anxious tenants turn for advice and representation?

Social workers can help clients in such situations in two ways: first, they can ensure their client recruits the best possible legal aid and advice available, making full use of the legal aid scheme; secondly, if for some reason legally qualified representation is not forthcoming, they can help their client in the courtroom. Under the County Court Act, 1959, Section 89, anybody given the court's permission can represent, and according to Hodge (1977) this opportunity has been used on many occasions by social workers among others. Hodge suggests that the best thing to do is to tell the clerk of the court beforehand of the intention to apply for permission to speak on behalf of the client, and the judge can then be advised. Otherwise, if this is not possible, one can go forward with the client when the case is called and put the request then.

The only other breach of the lawyers' monopoly in the courts is that of the 'McKenzie-man' in the magistrates' court. But he can only sit with the defendant and quietly advise. This is regarded by Hodge as second-best to a well-briefed lawyer.

If social workers were to represent and advocate for their clients in tribunals and courts more justice would certainly result, and for those who see part of the social work task in such terms that should be some encouragement to action.

Recommended reading

BELL, K. 1975: *Research Study on Supplementary Benefit Appeals Tribunals*. London: HMSO.

BELL, K., COLLISON, P., TURNER, S. and WEBBER, S. 1974 and 1975: National Insurance Tribunals: a research study. *Journal of Social Policy*, 3 (IV) and 4 (I).

SMITH, C. and HOATH, D. C. 1975: *Law and the Underprivileged.* London: Routledge & Kegan Paul.

STREET, H. 1975: *Justice in the Welfare State.* London: Stevens.

Bibliography

ANDRY, R. 1960: *Delinquency and Parental Pathology*. London: Methuen.

BAILEY, R. and BRAKE, M. 1975: *Radical Social Work*. London: Edward Arnold.

BALDWIN, J. and McCONVILLE, M. 1977: *Negotiated Justice*. London: Martin Robertson.

BAMFORD, T. 1977: Enforcing Minimum Standards. *Social Work Today* IX, 8.

BARBITT, D. P. and CARTER, C. F. 1962: The Northern Ireland Problem: a study in group relations. London: Oxford University Press.

BEAN, P. 1975: Social inquiry reports – a recommendation for disposal. *Justice of the Peace*, Part I, 11 October, 658–9; Part II, 18 October, 585–7.

BECCARIA, C. 1964: *Of Crimes and Punishments*. Indianapolis; Bobbs-Merrill.

BELL, K. 1975: *Research study on Supplementary Benefit Appeal Tribunals*. London: HMSO.

BELL, K., COLLISON, P., TURNER, S., and WEBBER, S. 1974 and 1975: National insurance tribunals: a research study. *Journal of Social Policy*, 3, IV and 4, I.

BERESFORD, J. 1976: Some Considerations on the Amalgamation or otherwise of the Northern Ireland Probation and After-Care Service into the Personal Social Services System in Northern Ireland (unpublished thesis).

BLACK COMMITTEE, 1977: Legislation and Services for Children and Young Persons in Northern Ireland. N. Ireland: HMSO.

BLUMBERG, A. S. 1967: *Criminal Justice*. Chicago: Quadrangle.

BOCHEL, D. 1976: *Probation and After-Care: Its development in England and Wales*. Edinburgh: Scottish Academic Press.

BOTTOMS, A. E. 1974: On the decriminalisation of the English Juvenile Courts. In Hood, R. G., editor, *Crime, Criminology and Public Policy*. London: Heinemann, 319–45.

BOTTOMS, A. E. and McLEAN, J. D. 1976: *Defendants in the Criminal Process*. London: Routledge & Kegan Paul.

BOW GROUP 1964: *Crime and the Labour Party.* London: Bow Group.

BOWLBY, J. 1946: *Forty-Four Juvenile Thieves: their characters and home life.* London: Baillière, Tindall & Cox.

BOWLBY, J. 1952: *Maternal Care and Mental Health.* Geneva: World Health Organisation.

BOYLE, K. 1976: Who are the Terrorists? *New Society,* 6 May.

BOYLE, K., HADDEN, T. and HILLYARD, P. 1975: *Law and State, the Case of Northern Ireland.* London: Martin Robertson.

BRITISH ASSOCIATION OF SOCIAL WORKERS 1977: *A Policy in Relation to the 1969 Children and Young Persons Act.*

BRITISH ASSOCIATION OF SOCIAL WORKERS 1977a: The Social Work Task. *Social Work Today,* 21 June, 8–12.

BRODY, S. R. 1976: *The Effectiveness of Sentencing.* Home Office Research Study 35. London: HMSO.

BURGESS, P. 1976: Specialist advice services in welfare rights. In Brooke, R., editor, *Advice Services in welfare rights.* Research Series 329. London: Fabian Society.

CARLEN, P. 1976: *Magistrates' Justice.* London: Martin Robertson.

CARR-SAUNDERS, A. M., MANNHEIM, H. and RHODES, E. C. 1942: *Young Offenders.* Cambridge: University Press.

CHECK! RIGHTS CENTRE 1977: *Final report on the project.* London: British Association of Settlements and Social Action Centres.

CHIEF PROBATION OFFICERS' CONFERENCE 1976: Report of Family Law Sub-Committee.

CHILD POVERTY ACTION GROUP, 1977: Welfare rights bulletin 19, London: CPAG.

CHRISTIE, N. 1976: *Conflicts as Property.* Sheffield: University Centre for Criminological Studies.

COHEN, S. 1975: It's All Right For You to Talk: Political and Sociological Manifestos for Social Work Action. In Bailey, R. and Brake, M., editors, *Radical Social Work.* London: Martin Robertson, 76–95.

COLLISON, P. and KENNEDY, J. 1977: The Social Worker, *New Society,* 15 September.

COLMAN, R. J. 1971: *Supplementary benefit and the administrative review of administrative action.* London: Child Poverty Action Group.

COMMISSION FOR LOCAL ADMINISTRATION IN ENGLAND, 1977: *Report for the year ended 31 March 1977.* London.

COMMITTEE ON CHILDREN AND YOUNG PERSONS 1960: *Report* Cmnd 1191. London: HMSO.

COMMITTEE ON CHILDREN AND YOUNG PERSONS SCOTLAND 1964: *Report* Cmnd 2306. Edinburgh: HMSO.

COMMITTEE ON LOCAL AUTHORITY AND APPLIED PERSONAL SOCIAL SERVICES 1968: *Report* Cmnd 3703. London: HMSO.

COMMUNITY CARE 1976: The Youngsters Who'll Be Left in the Cold, 17 November, 12–13.

COMMUNITY CARE 1977: 21 September, 8.

CONSERVATIVE PARLIAMENTARY HOME OFFICE AFFAIRS COMMITTEE 1976: *Study Group on Juvenile Crime.* London: Conservative Political Centre.

CROSLAND, C. A. R. 1963: *The Future of Socialism.* London: Cape.

CURNOCK, K. and HARDIKER, P. 1978: *Towards Practice Theory: Assessments in Social Inquiries.* London: Routledge & Kegan Paul.

CURRAN, J. H. 1977: *The Children's Hearing System: a review of research.* Central Research Unit, Scottish Office, Edinburgh: HMSO.

CUTTING, M. 1976: Tenants in the County Court. *Legal Action Group Bulletin,* May.

DAVIES, M. 1971: Social enquiry for the courts: an examination of the current position in England and Wales (mimeo.). Paper read at the Anglo-Scandinavian Research Seminar in Criminology, Norway.

DAVIES, M. 1972: Parole and the Probation Service. Unpublished report lodged in the library of the Institute of Criminology, Cambridge.

DAVIES, M. 1974: Social inquiry for the courts. *British Journal of Criminology,* 14 (1), 18–33.

DAVIES, M. 1975: *Prisoners of Society.* London: Routledge & Kegan Paul.

DELL, S. 1970: *Silent in Court.* London: Bell.

DEPARTMENTAL COMMITTEE ON THE TREATMENT OF YOUNG OFFENDERS 1927: *Report* Cmd. 2831. London: HMSO.

DITCHFIELD, J. A. 1976: *Police Cautioning in England and Wales.* Home Office Research Study 37. London: HMSO.

DONNINSON, D. V. and STEWART, M. 1958: *The Child and the Social Services,* Research Series 196. London: Fabian Society.

DUFFY, F. and PERCIVAL, R. 1975: Community Actions and Community Perceptions of the Social Services in Northern Ireland. Unpublished paper available from Coleraine New University of Ulster.

EMERSON, R. M. 1969: *Judging Delinquents: Context and process in the juvenile court.* Chicago; Aldine.

ERICSON, R. 1976: *Young Offenders and their Social Work.* Farnborough: Saxon House.

EXASON, E. 1976: *Poverty: The facts in Northern Ireland*. Pamphlet 27. London: Child Poverty Action Group

FAY, B. 1975: *Social Theory and Political Practice*. London: Allen & Unwin.

FEARS, D. 1977: Communication in English Juvenile Courts. *Sociological Review* XXV, 1. 131–45.

FOLKARD, M. S., SMITH, D. E. and D. D. 1976: *Impact,* II, Home Office Research Study 36. London: HMSO.

FORD, P. 1972: *Advising Sentencers: A Study of Recommendations made by Probation Officers to the Courts*. Oxford: Blackwell.

FOREN, R. and BAILEY, R. 1968: *Authority in Social Casework*. Oxford: Pergamon.

FOX, S. J. 1974: *The Scottish Panels: an American viewpoint on children's right to punishment*. Address given to children's panel summer school, Stirling.

FRANKS REPORT 1957: Report of the Committee on Administrative Tribunals and Enquiries, Cmnd 218. London: HMSO.

FREEMAN, M. 1977: Welfare in Adoption. *Adoption and Fostering* LXXXVIII, 2.

FRIEDMAN, M. and R. D. 1962: *Capitalism and Freedom*. Chicago: University of Chicago Press.

FRY, S. M. 1940: *The Ancestral Child*. London: Clarke Hall Fellowship.

GALBRAITH, A. and TAYLOR, M. 1976: Tribunal assistance scheme report 1975–6. Newcastle-Upon-Tyne: Citizens' Advice Bureau.

GEORGE, V. and WILDING, P. 1976: *Ideology and Social Welfare*. London: Routledge & Kegan Paul.

GILLER, H. and MORRIS, A. 1976: Children Who Offend: Care Control or Confusion? *Criminal Law Review,* 656–65.

GILLER, H. and MORRIS, A. 1977: Juvenile Courts or Children's Hearing. *Legal Action Group Bulletin,* October.

GRAHAM, J. 1976: Is social work really on the map? *Community Care.* 17 November, 22–3.

HARDIKER, P. 1977a: Social Inquiry Reports in an Intake Team Research report (unpublished).

HARDIKER, P. 1977b: Social work ideologies in the probation service. *British Journal of Social Work,* 7 (2), 131–54.

HARDIKER, P. and WEBB, D. 1978: Explaining deviant behaviour: the social context of 'action' and 'infraction' accounts in the probation service. *Sociology,* 12 (3)

HEALTH SERVICE COMMISSIONER 1977: Annual Report for 1976–77. House of Commons Paper 322. London: HMSO.

HERBERT, L. and MATHIESON, D. 1975: *Reports for Courts*. Thornton Heath: National Association of Probation Officers.

HIDDLESTON, V. 1976: Reports for Children's Hearings. In Martin, F. M. and Murray, K., editors, *Children's Hearings*. Edinburgh: Scottish Academic Press.

HODGE, H. 1977: Aid and representation in courts. *Social Work Today*, 26 July.

HMSO 1967: *Report of the Advisory Council on the Treatment of Offenders: the organisation of after-care* (ACTO Report). London: HMSO.

HMSO 1972 and 1973: *The Report of the Parole Board for Scotland*. Edinburgh: HMSO.

HOME OFFICE 1960: *Disturbances at the Carlton Approved School*. Report of Inquiry by Mr Victor Durand, QC Cmnd 937. London: HMSO.

HOME OFFICE 1965: *The Child, the Family and the Young Offender*, Cmnd 2742. London: HMSO.

HOME OFFICE 1968: *Children in Trouble*, Cmnd 3601. London: HMSO.

HOME OFFICE 1976: *The Annual Probation and After-care Statistics*. London: HMSO.

HOME OFFICE, WELSH OFFICE, DHSS, DES 1976: *Children and Young Persons Act 1969: Observations on the Eleventh Report from the Expenditure Committee*, Cmnd 6494. London: HMSO.

HOME OFFICE CIRCULAR 194/1974, 25 October 1974.

HOUSE OF COMMONS EXPENDITURE COMMITTEE 1975: *Eleventh Report, Children and Young Persons Act 1969*. I, Report; II, Evidence H.C. 354 i and ii. London.

HOWARD LEAGUE 1977: *'Unruly' children in a human context: types, costs, and effects of security*. London: Howard League.

INGLIS, F. 1977: Them, us and the welfare state. *New Society*, 17 February.

IRWIN, J. 1970: *The Felon*, Englewood Cliffs, NJ: Prentice-Hall.

JACKSON, R. M. 1970: *The Machinery of Justice*. Cambridge: University Press.

JARVIS, F. C. 1974: *Probation Officer's Manual*. London: Butterworth.

LABOUR PARTY STUDY GROUP 1964: *Crime – A Challenge to Us All*. London: Labour Party.

LAND, H. 1975: Detention Centres: The Experiment Which Could Not Fail. In Hall, P., Land, H., Parker, R and Webb, A. *Change, Choice and Conflict in Social Policy*. London: Heinemann Educational.

LAWRENCE, R. 1977: *Welfare advice and advocacy*, National Association of Citizens' Advice Bureaux, Occasional Paper 1. London.

LEEVERS, M., NEE, P. and ROGERS, J. 1977: *A Fair Hearing? – possession hearings in the County Court.* London Housing Aid Centre.

LEONARD, P. 1975: Poverty, Consciousness and Action, The Sheila Kay Memorial Lecture. London: BASW.

LISTER, R. 1974: *Justice for the claimant.* London; Child Poverty Action Group.

LIVERPOOL CITY COUNCIL 1974: *Crime in the City.*

LONGFORD REPORT 1964: Crime – a challenge to us all. Labour Party Study Group. London: Transport House.

LYMAN, S. A. and SCOTT, M. 1970: *A sociology of the Absurd.* New York: Appleton-Century-Crofts.

LYNN COMMITTEE 1938: Cmnd (Northern Ireland) 187. Belfast: HMSO.

MACLEOD, I. 1958: The Political Divide. In Goldman, P., editor, *The Future of the Welfare State.* London: Conservative Political Centre, 11–19.

MAGISTRATES' ASSOCIATION 1977: The Magistrate 33, 49.

MANNING, M. 1977: Reversing the Residential Trend. *Community Care,* 5 October.

MANSERGH, N. 1936: *The Government of Northern Ireland: a study in devolution.* London: Allen & Unwin.

MARTIN, F. M. and MURRAY, K. 1976: *Children's Hearings.* Edinburgh: Scottish Academic Press.

MATHIESON, D. 1975: Probation Officers: sentencers of the future. *Justice of the Peace,* 22 March, XVI, 2–164.

MATHIESON, D. 1976: The Social Inquiry Report. *Justice of the Peace,* 8 May, 246–8.

MATHIESON, D. 1977: Society inquiry reports – time to plot a new course. *Justice of the Peace,* 16 April, 224–6.

MATZA, D. 1964: *Delinquency and Drift.* New York: John Wiley.

MAY, D. 1971: Delinquency Control and the Treatment Model: some implications of recent legislation. *British Journal of Criminology,* XI.

MAY, D. 1977: Rhetoric and Reality: Ambiguity in the Children's Panel System. *British Journal of Criminology,* XVII, 209–27.

MAYER, J. and TIMMS, N. 1970. *The Client Speaks.* London: Routledge & Kegan Paul.

MELOTTE, C. J. 1976: *Social workers' information on welfare benefits.* Kirklees Social Services Department Research Section, Occasional Papers 10.

MILTON, F. 1967: *The English Magistracy.* London: Oxford University Press.

MOLONY REPORT 1927 : Departmental Committee on the Treatment of Young Offenders, Cmnd 2831. London: HMSO.

MORISON REPORT 1962 : Report of the Department Committee on the Probation Service, Cmnd 1650. London: HMSO.

MORRIS, A. 1973 : *A Criminal Law in Practice: the children's hearings in Scotland.* Paper presented to the Fifth National Conference in Teaching and Research in Criminology, Cambridge.

MORRIS, A. and GILLER, H. 1976 : Reaction to an Act, *New Society,* 19 February.

MORRIS, A. and GILLER, H. 1977 : Juvenile Court or Children's Hearing? Listening to Clients (unpublished).

MORRIS, P. 1975 : *On Licence.* New York: John Wiley.

MUNGHAM, G. and BANKOWSKI, Z. 1976 : *Images of Law.* London: Routledge & Kegan Paul.

MURRAY, G. 1976 : Juvenile Justice Reform. In Martin, F. M. and K., editors, *Children's Hearings.* Edinburgh: Scottish Academic Press.

NAPLEY, D. 1975 : *The Techniques of Persuasion* (2nd edition). London; Sweet & Maxwell.

NEWMAN, D. 1966 : *Conviction.* Boston: Little, Brown.

NORTHERN IRELAND PROBATION AND AFTER-CARE SERVICE 1978 : A Development Plan. Belfast: HMSO.

O'HARA, J. 1976 : Some Aspects of the Payment for Debt Act. *Quest: Journal of Social Work and Welfare Law in Ulster* V.

OXFORD CENTRE FOR SOCIO-LEGAL STUDIES 1977 : *Custody after Divorce.*

PACKMAN, J. 1975 : *The Child's Generation.* London: Blackwell/ Robertson.

PAGE, R. and CLARK, G. 1977 : *Who Cares? Young People in Care Speak Out.* London: National Children's Bureau.

PARK, J. 1976 : Delivering a service to the most difficult area in Britain. *Health and Social Services Journal.* Dec. 24/31.

PARKER, H. J. 1974 : *View From The Boys.* Newton Abbot: David & Charles.

PARKINSON, G. 1977 : Probation by Firing Squad. *New Society,* 12 May.

PARLIAMENTARY COMMISSIONER FOR ADMINISTRATION 1977 : *Annual report for 1976.* House of Commons Paper 116.

PARSLOE, P. 1976 : Social Work and the Justice Model. *British Journal of Social Work,* VI, 1.

PEARSON, G. 1975 : *The Deviant Imagination.* London: Macmillan.

PERRY, F. G. 1974 : *Information for the Court — A New Look at the Social Inquiry Reports.* Cambridge: Institute of Criminology.

PINCHBECK, I. and HEWITT, M. 1973: *Children in English Society,* II. London: Routledge & Kegan Paul.

PLATT, A. M. 1969: *The Child Savers: the invention of delinquency.* Chicago: University of Chicago Press.

RALSTON, B. 1977: Reforming the Orange State: Problems of the Northern Ireland Community Relations Commission in Downey, J., editor, *Thames Papers in Social Analysis* series 1, Northern Ireland. Thames Polytechnic.

REES, S. 1974: No more than Contact: An Outcome of Social Work. *British Journal of Social Work,* IV, 3.

REID, W. J. and SHYNE, A. W. 1969: *Brief and Extended Casework.* New York: Columbia University Press.

REITH, D. 1975: 'I wonder if you can help me. . . .?' *Social Work Today,* 1 May, 66–9.

ROSE, H. 1973: Who can delabel the claimant? *Social Work Today,* 20 September.

ROWE, J. and LAMBERT, L. 1973: *Children Who Wait.* London: Association of British Adoption Agencies.

SARTRE, J-P. 1960: *Critique de la Raison Dialectique* (translated by W. Desan). New York: Doubleday (Anchor Books).

SBAT *Guide to Procedure 1977.* HMSO.

SCOTTISH ADVISORY COUNCIL ON CHILD CARE COMMITTEE 1963: *Prevention of Neglect of Children.* Cmnd 1966. Edinburgh: HMSO.

SMITH, C. *et al.* 1972: *The Wincroft Youth Project.* London: Tavistock.

SMITH, G. 1977: Little Kiddies and Criminal Acts: the role of social work in the children's hearings. *British Journal of Social Work,* VII, 4.

DE SMITH, S. A. 1973: *Judicial review of administrative action,* (3rd edition). London: Stephens.

SOCIAL WORK AND THE COMMUNITY 1966 (White Paper). Cmnd 3065. London: HMSO.

SOCIETY OF CONSERVATIVE LAWYERS COMMITTEE 1976: *Apprentices in Crime: The Failure of the Children and Young Persons Act 1969.* London: Conservative Political Centre.

STOREY, H. 1977: *Tribunal Assistance Unit Progress Report,* August 1976–February 1977. (Leeds): Chapletown Citizens' Advice Bureau.

STREATFEILD REPORT, 1961: Report of the Inter-departmental Committee on the Business of the Criminal Courts. Cmnd. 1289. London: HMSO.

STREET, H. 1975: *Justice in the Welfare State,* 2nd edition. London: Stevens.

SUPPLEMENTARY BENEFITS COMMISSION 1977: *Annual Report for 1976*. London: HMSO.

TAGGART, R. 1972: *The Prison of Unemployment*. Baltimore: Johns Hopkins University Press.

TAYLOR, I., WALTON, P. and YOUNG, J. 1973: *The New Criminology*. London: Routledge & Kegan Paul.

TAYLOR, L. and NELSON, S. 1977: Young People and Civil Conflict in Northern Ireland (papers delivered at conference 'Young People and Civil Conflict', Northern Ireland Office, Belfast).

TERRY, J. A. 1975: *A Guide to the Children Act*. London: Sweet & Maxwell.

WALLACE, M. 1971: *Northern Ireland: Fifty years of Self-Government*. Newton Abbot: David & Charles.

WEINER, R. 1975: *The Rape and Plunder of the Shankill*. Belfast: Notaeme Press.

WILLIAMSON, H. 1977: Processing Juveniles – Defence and Mitigation in the Juvenile Court (Unpublished paper).

WILLOCK, I. D. 1972: Report to the Social Work Services Group on an Inquiry into Parental Involvement in the Work of Children's Hearings (Unpublished).

ZANDER, M. 1975: What Happens to Young Offenders in Care. *New Society*, 24 July.

Index